Really managing
health care

2nd edition

Really managing health care

2nd edition

Valerie Iles

Open University Press

Open University Press
McGraw-Hill Education
McGraw-Hill House
Shoppenhangers Road
Maidenhead
Berkshire
England
SL6 2QL

email: enquiries@openup.co.uk
world wide web: www.openup.co.uk

and Two Penn Plaza, New York, NY 10121-2289, USA

First published 2005

A catalogue record of this book is available from the British Library

ISBN-10: 0335 21009 0 (pb)   0335 21010 4 (hb)
ISBN-13: 978 0335 21009 1 (pb)   978 0335 21010 7 (hb)

Library of Congress Cataloging-in-Publication Data
CIP data applied for

Typeset by RefineCatch Limited, Bungay, Suffolk
Printed in the UK by Bell & Bain Ltd, Glasgow

To Eleanor

Contents

Acknowledgements

Many people have contributed concepts that I use in this book, and stimulated my thinking in different directions, and I am very grateful to them all. First among these is Derek Cramp, an indefatigable provider of ideas and debate. Annie Cushing and John Harries have both lent me more books and papers than I have returned, all of them thought-provoking. Julia Vaughan Smith, too, has introduced me to areas of thinking that I may have rejected from a less credible source, and without Gordon Best Chapter 5 would look significantly different and much less useful. Nigel Edwards, too, has been, as he often is, a catalyst for ideas. There are so many others that it is invidious to include some and not all but Jay Bevington, Nancy Craven, Peter Gill, Annabel Scarfe and Linda Smith have all been more influential than I have told them.

However, the person who first prompted my realization that a new model of management in health care is needed was my partner Colin Smith. As a highly effective manager in the private sector who now 'turns around' ailing companies in the manufacturing and service industries, his behaviour and approach to the management task is very different from that which I observe in senior managers in health care organizations. There are reasons for that, some of which are discussed in the introduction, but this proximity to alternative behaviours has undoubtedly influenced my thinking.

If all these have helped to shape the model I propose here, the people who have tested it out, increased its robustness and challenged me to make it as usable and practical as possible are the students and clients I have worked with. In different universities, learning sets, service teams and organizations, I have learned hugely about what will work and what won't. If I single out my years with the Masters in Health Management at City University, one particular cohort of the MSc in Primary Care and my students at the London School of Hygiene and Tropical Medicine, that is only because they reflect the steepness of my learning curve and the exhilaration that always accompanies that. Several have participated in this book, in giving information for case studies, by reading drafts or debating points, and I will thank them personally rather than here.

Without the two Chrises – Heginbotham and Ham – I would never have written this book. Their confidence in my ability to do so was vitally important for the first edition, and they have both encouraged the second. Chris Heginbotham has been generous in his ongoing support, while Chris Ham has been very tolerant of a book that is a policy-free zone!

The person who has had the greatest impact on the way the ideas here are presented (and hence made accessible to the reader) is its managing editor Steve Cranfield. Steve and I have collaborated now on three publications and each time I have found it a highly productive and enjoyable experience. Not only does Steve have years of editing experience, I find it immensely helpful that he tolerates tasks I hate, and that he is a living database of concepts, related ideas and their history. We have also been very fortunate in having a valuable 'critical friend' in Jonathan Richards.

None of these people, however, can be held responsible for my interpretation of the facts or concepts, or guidance they have provided; any criticisms must be directed at me.

Introduction

Not enough people are managing health care. And that is not because there are not excellent people running health care organizations. It is because that is what they are doing, concentrating on running their organizations. As a result there is a lot of measuring and monitoring, a lot of 'performance management' and, ironically, a lot of health care professionals (HCPs)[1] feeling *over*-managed. It's time for the focus to shift to managing health care itself, and this is a book for people who want to improve services, to regain the goodwill of HCPs and to help them deliver the kind of care we can all be proud of.

Why, when health care is such an important issue for so many people, do we not pay enough attention to management at the level that matters? Why do people called managers manage not health care but something else? In part it is because the job we are currently asking them to do is the wrong one, in part it is because they are tempted to concentrate on the wrong things and in part it is because we want to believe in magic. Let's look at these in turn.

First, the wrong job? Instead of defining the role of the health care manager by considering the health care task and what management can add to it, there has been an emphasis on translating the management role from other settings. Modifying it certainly, to take into account some of the differences between health care organizations and others, but *not* going as far as *defining* it using the distinctiveness of the health care task as the starting point. When we do this, when we aim to *add* to the contribution of those providing health care, and see it as essential to try to avoid wasting their time and good will, we see that the role we need is different, and requires particular skills, behaviours and attitudes of the people fulfilling it.

Second, the wrong things? Joe Batten, in his book *Tough Minded Leadership*,[2] draws a distinction between the 'simple hard' and the 'complicated easy'. The former could be something as simple, and as hard, as being trustworthy; the latter, drawing up complicated plans or redesigning organizational structures. Today's health care managers are concentrating on the complicated easy at the expense of the simple hard. This is understandable. The increasing specialization of health care has led to a culture in which there is an unspoken assumption that if we could just find an expert with a definitive answer, we would be able to solve any problem. While this belief may be well founded for many clinical problems where the constituent elements are cells and organs, in management problems those constituent parts are people and the richness of personality ensures that there is no definitive solution, however complicated. Whenever we interact with other people, we cannot succeed unless we heed the simple hard.

Much of the complicated easy is, of course, necessary. Without it, managers do not have the tools with which to manage. However, without the simple hard the complicated easy does not work. Worse, it can actually impede the individuals and organizations it is supposed to be rendering more effective, and be perceived as unnecessary bureaucracy and constraint.

Third, magic? There has been a tendency over the past few years to identify 'leadership' as different from (and rather superior to) 'management'. But, surely, this is a false dichotomy, on both the practical and theoretical levels. The territories now claimed for leadership and management are not dissimilar from those linked previously to management and administration, respectively, and this suggests that in a little while the term 'leadership' too will have become demoted. This is because people are seeking something that can't exist; what they are looking for is the ability to win hearts and minds, to persuade people to do something they don't want to do, to take on groups who are being difficult and persuade them to work together for the greater good. Heroes and heroines who can do all that may exist in fairy tales and undemanding novels but not in real life. At least not in the quantities we seem to require! It is time to reinvigorate the neglected term 'management'.

What I offer here, then, is an argument that seeks to enrich, extend and indeed challenge current understandings of the word 'management'. In this book I outline a style of management I call *real* management. It is a style built up from tools, behaviours and attitudes I have observed that people working in health care find genuinely useful, find can help them to offer better services, find can help them to help others to work more effectively. Real management straddles the divide drawn between management and leadership, it takes account of the special circumstances of the health care task, it errs on the side of the simple hard, but it draws attention, too, to areas where it is important that the complicated easy is undertaken with rigour and discipline. Because it highlights the simple hard it will be dismissed by some, since the aspects that are simple and hard are indeed conceptually simple, so simple that in practice they often fail to receive the attention they warrant. For some people (particularly those whose intellect is only tickled by the complicated easy) it will prove irritating, simplistic and misguided. I very much hope that others will find it useful, practical, challenging and even transforming.

Is it evidence based? Well, it depends on what is meant by evidence, and I have discussed this in some detail elsewhere.[3] It is rooted in reflection, theory, action and experience – my own and that of others. Above all, it has been tested out by generations of HCPs taking on management roles; I have worked with these people on university courses, training programmes and in their own organizations. For all that, it is a subjective and personal account of the kind of management I believe is needed, so it is perhaps necessary that you know a little of where I am coming from.

For the first fifteen years of my working life I worked as a pharmacist, in the bowels of health care organizations of all sorts, experiencing the dynamics of working within a large complex organization of interdependent professions and departments. After completing an MBA at the London Business School, I moved into management roles just at the time when general management was being established and the old district management teams of district medical and nursing officers with district administrator were being disbanded. In 1990 I moved to City University to establish the Health Management Group there and led the masters degree in health management for nearly nine years. And for the past five years I have worked with a number of different universities and NHS organizations, individuals and teams on all levels, exploring different management challenges and ways of addressing them.

All my observations lead me to conclude that it is vital that the people who directly manage front-line services are allowed and encouraged to flourish, and that organizations where that is the case are those offering the best health care, yet this is the tier of management receiving the least support and development. This book is written for them, for those first line managers (most of whom will be clinicians), for the people who manage them and for those who in turn manage them. In other words, this is a book that assumes that the task of senior managers is to support the clinical front line and the people directly managing that. It is also for a group of people I have had the pleasure of working with recently: non-executive directors in health care organizations. These passionate, able people are often inhibited from making a more valuable contribution because of their lack of understanding of the dynamics of health care. I hope this book will give insight that will help them bring fresh energy to the management task. And it is for a group of people who are becoming increasingly important, people in so-called 'hybrid roles': those clinicians who take on formal organizational management roles in addition to their clinical management ones.

It is always difficult to know where to start in a text about management. I have chosen to start with aspects of managing people, because this is where most anxiety is expressed, and most troubles begin. In Chapter 1 we look at how to work through other people, in Chapter 2 at working with other people, and here we look closely at what happens when those other people are members of different professions. In Chapter 3 we consider working for other people, how to work effectively in large organizations and how to decide whether your organization is the right one for you. Chapters 4 and 5 could easily have been presented in reverse order. In Chapter 4 we think about how to make the most of the resources available to a service, while Chapter 5 explores ways of managing change. Chapter 6 is more personal, and is about how to manage yourself, your time and your stress levels. You may be tempted to read this first but I think you will find it more valuable having read some of the others first. Chapter 7 is about managing organizations or, more accurately, about the role of the manager in health care organizations, and while it refers more to large organizations than small the principles are similar. Next, we come to the case studies. In the first edition readers seemed to enjoy these. Their purpose is to explore how some of the principles can be put into practice while also seeing the world from the perspectives of people in different health care settings. One has been updated from the first edition and two new ones have been added. As you will see, they are not prescriptive, but look more at *how* than *what* must or can be done, and they are set in circumstances that I hope feel real to you, although they are compilations of incidents and people rather than an account of an actual scenario. The concluding thoughts are just that, a résumé of what I see as the most important points, and I hope you will want not only to read them but also to let me know your own thoughts. Every end is a beginning, as the saying goes, and I hope you will want to take what's written here as the start of your own role as a real manager. If you do, then I have included a selection of further reading that I think you will find useful.

If you do, or if you don't, I would welcome your views on what has been said here, so do please write or contact me via the Really Learning website at www.reallylearning.com.

Notes

1   I use the term 'health care professional', abbreviated to HCP, throughout the book. It is used to refer to members of all the clinical and clinical support professions.

2   Batten, J. (1991) *Tough Minded Leadership* (New York: Amacom). In this book, Batten contrasts the complex easy with the simple tough and draws a further distinction between tough and hard – the former resilient, the latter brittle. However, for a British audience, the terms 'hard' and 'complicated' more accurately convey the sense he intends.

3   See Iles, V. and Sutherland, K. (2001) *Managing Change in the NHS: Organisational Change* (London: NCC SDO).

1 Really managing people
Working through others

The art of getting things done[1]

This is a book for people who want to get things done, for people who care about health care services and want them to be delivered well. You may not describe yourself as a manager, or you may. You may value managers, or you may not, but you want to get things done. Management often receives a bad press, sometimes justifiably, and the purpose of this book is to enable you to distinguish between good and bad managers, managers in name and *real* managers. It is a book that aims to increase your skills in the art of getting things done, and we start by thinking about how to get things done through other people.

We increasingly, and routinely, depend on many other people to help us achieve our aims and goals, whether in the home or work setting, and as soon as we ask someone else to do something, rather than undertaking it ourselves, we become managers. We rely on someone else to perform that task in the way we would do if we had the time (and the skill, the knowledge and the patience perhaps). Most of us, then, spend much of our time, in many aspects of our lives, managing other people; even though we may not call ourselves or think of ourselves as managers. Equally, some people whom we may not call managers are faced with the challenges of managing us.

Our own effectiveness and our enjoyment of work and home lives are strongly influenced by whether the people we rely on complete tasks to our satisfaction. Yet many of us are poor at managing others. Although highly skilled in the activities that we ourselves undertake, we fail to observe some simple rules about the management process, which, if implemented, would make us, and the people around us, more productive and more satisfied.

To illustrate the need for these rules, let us join the Johnson family, who have just recruited a new cleaner. As you read about them you might like to reflect on what it is that the Johnsons want a cleaner to do for them, and how they try to get her to do it.

Box 1.1 The Johnson family

The Johnson family recently decided to employ a cleaner in their home. They were pleased when Mrs White replied to their advertisement. She had good references from other clients and seemed friendly and likeable. They asked her to start the next day. With both Mr and Mrs Johnson out at work, Mrs White worked on her own without any supervision. At first the Johnsons were delighted to come home to a tidy house, but after a few weeks Mrs Johnson noticed that the kitchen cupboards were rather dirty, that the floor hadn't been swept in the corners and that the fridge needed defrosting. She arranged to leave work early to speak to Mrs White, and told her that she wanted her to be much more thorough in her cleaning.

A few weeks later the Johnsons came home to find a note from Mrs White apologizing for having broken one of their cups. In it she offered to pay for it by having the cost of a new one deducted from her pay that week. But the Johnsons couldn't find a cup missing, even after looking through all the kitchen cupboards, and wondered what she meant. As they looked at the cupboards they realized that Mrs White was still not cleaning all the shelves every week in the way they wanted. 'But I asked her to be more thorough', complained Mrs Johnson. 'How could she leave the cupboards this way?' She noticed too that the fridge again needed defrosting. So things were not getting any better. They felt disappointed and annoyed.

Later that evening Mr Johnson had a look in a display cabinet in which they kept the antique porcelain they collected. He was startled to find that a pretty and particularly valuable cup was missing. On mentioning it to his wife they both suddenly wondered, and went to look in the rubbish bin. Sure enough, there were the pieces of the porcelain cup. 'How could she?' exclaimed Mr Johnson. 'It would take ages to pay for that cup if we took it from her wages. Doesn't she have any idea? She's got to go.' They told Mrs White not to come back.

At a friend's house, soon afterwards, Mrs Johnson was introduced to one of the people who had written a reference for Mrs White. In conversation she was amazed to hear how thorough and careful Mrs White had been with this other client. 'How lucky you are to have her', lamented the other woman. 'I would love to have her with us still, but we have moved out of her area.'

'But she was so careless for us', Mrs Johnston exclaimed. 'She never once defrosted the fridge, or cleaned inside the kitchen cupboards.' 'I don't suppose she did; I do all that myself and would never dream of asking a cleaner to do it', the other woman replied.

This is clearly a situation that proved unsatisfactory, both for the Johnson family and for Mrs White. Let's now look at some fundamental rules that might have enabled the Johnsons to avoid it.

Three basic rules for managing people

When we are trying to get things done through other people we can greatly increase our chances of success by observing three simple rules:

1   Agree with them precisely what it is that you expect them to achieve.
2   Ensure that both you and they are confident that they have the skills and resources to achieve it.
3   Give them feedback on whether they are achieving it.

Let's look at these in more detail.

Rule 1: Agree with the person you are managing precisely what it is that you expect them to achieve

Unless people know what we want of them, they are unlikely to do it. Not all of it anyway. Some may complete the technical task asked of them, but have offended colleagues with their brusqueness along the way. Others may tackle the task so thoroughly and carefully that they miss important deadlines. Yet others may launch themselves with enthusiasm in a direction we know from experience is unlikely to be fruitful.

So we need to agree with others just what it is we expect them to achieve and how. In different circumstances the means by which we all reach agreement will vary. If, like the Johnsons, you engage a cleaner in your home, you probably expect to *tell* her what you want her to do. It's your home, you know exactly what needs doing and how to do it. You may well defer to a cleaner's judgement about specific cleaning materials, but on the whole you will be fairly prescriptive. When it comes to your expectations of someone who possesses many complex skills that you do not, and is working in areas of which you have no direct experience, as is the case when managing many health care professionals (HCPs), you will focus more on outcomes and leave the individual to determine how to reach them.

Rule 1 seems obvious, but the Johnsons did not observe it. They did not say at first that they wanted the fridge defrosted or the cupboards cleaned, and it may be useful to think about *why* they didn't. Probably they held a mental picture of what a cleaner does, and assumed that Mrs White shared it. When they found she didn't they blamed her for not being a 'good' cleaner. It is easy for this to happen in health care too. We rely on the professional or job title the person holds – physiotherapist, consultant, director – and fail to ensure that our mental picture of what this involves tallies with theirs.

You can test this out by thinking of your own career. How many times has anyone sat down with you and spelled out exactly what they are expecting of you? Most people I put this question to when teaching say 'never' or 'a couple of times'. When I ask whether they have sat down with the people they manage, however, the story is different. 'Ah,' they say, 'in our team we have job descriptions that spell all this out, so we are already observing Rule 1.'

But if you are relying on the job description or job plan alone you are not doing enough: you need to observe Rule 1 by having a frank and detailed, face-to-face discussion. Spelling out in writing what a job involves is certainly a necessary basis for this kind of discussion, but the process of meeting face-to-face, sharing views of what is involved, how you both see what is needed by the organization, what is needed by you, by them, is essential. It is largely through this that the 'how' of any job is negotiated. Not only does the job description focus only on the 'what', but this tends to become quickly out-of-date. Consider the following, for example. When did you last look at your own job description? How well does it describe the work you actually do? When was it last reviewed? Does it express what you care about? As you have probably found, job descriptions may form the basis of a legal contract but not a psychological one, and it is the latter that drives us to perform well, to get things done.

Reaching agreement requires both parties to express their views and respond to those of the other. That's what we mean by agreement. Interpreting expression and emphasis is an important part of this exchange and thus talking together is the only way to do it. Reaching agreement involves bringing together what *you* need the other party to do, with what *they* care about doing and achieving. It is difficult to imagine you finding out what they care about unless you do meet and have a frank conversation.

What is more, it will be necessary to have such conversations at regular intervals to check that both parties are *still* in agreement. Every day as we are exposed to different influences our views change slightly, and so will those of the people we are managing, and these changes may well need to be reflected in a changed agreement about our expectations of them.

Already we can see that *really* managing people involves investing both time and thought, and also being prepared to engage with people very directly.

Rule 2: Ensure that both you and the person you are managing are confident they have the skills and resources they need

Once others know what we expect of them, we need to be confident that they can achieve it; in other words that they have the knowledge, skills and resources they will require. We also need to ensure that *they* are confident that they have these skills and resources. This is not as straightforward as just asking them. If asked, some people will make an overconfident assertion about their level of skills and resources. Others, negotiating for more resources, may insist rightly or wrongly that they do not have them. Some may feel unsure of their abilities, although your judgement is that they will be fine. It may also be the case that both you and they have underestimated what is required.

To be able to diagnose which, if any, of these situations applies, you will need to spend time with your staff, observing the skills they use, the reasoning they employ and the way they deploy their time and other resources. When you are unable to assess their skills yourself (because they are clinical or technical skills outside your own area of expertise), you will need to seek specialist advice. This must, of course, be discussed with the staff member involved. This may sound intrusive and often when I suggest the need for this kind of observation, managers object, saying, 'But I have to trust my staff'; some even say 'Management is about learning to trust your staff'. Both statements are absolutely correct, but they support rather than oppose the concept of managers accurately assessing the capabilities of their staff. Without such an assessment, you do not have trust, you have hope. It is a sensitive issue, however, and you will have to make a judgement about how you do it, and this will vary from role to role.

The situations described above will need to be handled in different ways if you are to implement Rule 2 successfully.

When a member of staff has overestimated their knowledge or skills, then together you should review your expectations of them and consider some relevant training. It is important that you decide whether the person concerned exaggerated their abilities to you knowingly, out of insecurity, or unknowingly due to a lack of insight. You will then be able to choose the kind of relationship you need to build with them: one in which they feel more secure and able to admit areas of weakness, or one where you find ways of constructively challenging their view of their performance.

In the contrasting situation, where a member of staff is not as confident of their own abilities as you are, they will need to draw confidence from you. You must find ways of convincing them, reassuring them of your support, reducing the risk for them, perhaps by putting that support in writing. Soon other members of staff whom you have similarly encouraged will be able to give credence to your case.

If it becomes clear as a result of careful observation and analysis of relevant data that your staff are 'shroud waving', you are in for a different kind of negotiation. The imposition of what you deem an appropriate level of resources will simply not work. Only the most mature of individuals or teams would not try to vindicate their position by failing to achieve performance targets you have set.

Personal credibility is the key here. Most shroud waving takes place when there is lack of faith in the motives, the knowledge or the judgement of the resource allocator. There is no short cut: you will have to demonstrate integrity, a concern for your staff and their needs and an understanding of the operational details. You will also have to convince them that your own aims encompass their own. Of course if you do not have integrity, aims that encompass theirs, genuine concern for them and a knowledge of that detail, then perhaps they are right and you are wrong.

In some cases, the skills and resources required only become apparent as the nature of the task is revealed. When this happens and both you and your staff underestimated the requirements, you must sit down together and reach a new agreement on expectations. If you do not match your expectations to the skills and resources held by your team, then you will have only yourself to blame if they fail to perform.

We do not have to look far to see breaches of Rule 2. In many UK health care organizations resources that were initially adequate for the task have been eroded with no concomitant change in expectations. This has arisen in some cases under the heading of 'efficiency savings'. Using resources efficiently is clearly important, and looking at efficiency can be a useful creative challenge in which outcomes are defined, alternative means of reaching them are compared and the best way of using resources can be chosen. We look at this in more detail in Chapter 4. It takes time for a service to work constructively on this, and it requires someone to challenge the status quo. Whereas a discussion with one person about Rule 2 is, as we have seen, sensitive and requires careful handling and observation, a discussion with a service or a team will often also require courage. Courage and time are not always in plentiful supply and hence departments are often not taught how to think about efficiency and a budget reduction is merely imposed. Where this happens without a discussion that *reaches agreement* that, for example, service levels will be unaffected, or that service levels will change and to what extent, any such imposition is a breach of Rule 2.

The example in Box 1.2 illustrates the point that budget discussions, discussions about resources, *must* include discussion about service expectations. Rules 1 and 2 must run together. So again we can see that really managing involves significant personal engagement, face-to-face contact, active and ongoing interest in what people are doing and how they are using their skills and resources.

How well do we think the Johnsons implemented Rule 2?

They didn't! They did not discuss with Mrs White her knowledge of delicate porcelain, of how to clean it, how often their collection needed that attention. When Mrs White then broke a valuable cup the blame should have rested with them, for not observing Rule 2, but that did not prevent them transferring all the blame to her. Whenever we don't observe Rule 2 we are behaving as unreasonably as the Johnsons.

Box 1.2 The importance of Rule 2

Recently a large teaching hospital found[2] that its overall establishment was at least 70 WTE registered nurses and midwives short of providing a minimal staffing level. Furthermore, the human resources, financial and clinical departments all held different views of what the establishment was, with a discrepancy of 140 posts overall. This had come about for a number of reasons, but significantly there had been no regular discussion with staff to agree budgets and the last review had taken place 18 years earlier. Budgets for the year ahead were based on the amount that had been spent by a department the year before, so if a department had had a vacancy this reduced their budget for the following year, while a department that had overspent was rewarded by an increased budget.

Rule 3: Give feedback on whether they are achieving the expectations you agreed

Once people know what is expected of them, and have the skills and resources to achieve it, they need to receive regular feedback on whether they are doing so.[3] This will enable them to increase their effort in one or more areas if this is necessary. After all, once we know they can do something, whether they do it depends on the choices they make about the effort they put in.

The way feedback is given and received will depend on the circumstances. For example, it may be in the form of anonymized data comparing the activities of different members of staff. It may require a face-to-face meeting between you and the member of staff in question. Or both. It may also involve feedback from others. It is helpful to clarify just how such feedback will be communicated when agreeing on expectations.

The importance of feedback cannot be overstated: it is by receiving feedback from others that we improve our skills, develop and grow. We therefore owe it to the people we work with, especially those for whom we are managerially responsible, to give them the feedback that will enable them to progress, and to give it to them regularly and frequently. Criticism, however, may be so wounding that, far from enabling the recipient to change one of their behaviours and grow, it robs them of the confidence to attempt any change, and indeed can exacerbate the problem. The way in which the feedback is given is what makes the difference. Because feedback can have such an adverse impact, we need to prepare carefully before communicating it.

For this reason I will dwell more on Rule 3 than on the first two. Not because it is the most important – they are all equally essential – but in my experience if Rules 1 and 2 are rarely implemented it is not because they are conceptually difficult. They require only thoughtfulness and courage. Rule 3 is different in that many of us do try to give feedback but we often do it less than well. It too requires care and courage but also a certain degree of awareness about how to do it.

Principles and practice of giving feedback

Balance praise and criticism: the 'sandwich approach'

If the behaviour of the individual you are managing (let us call this person P) is to change in the way you would like it to, P must feel able to make this change and must want to do so. If you can keep these two aims in mind throughout any discussion you have with them about their performance you will find it much easier to avoid leaving them resentful or deflated. One way of translating this into practice is to use a 'criticism sandwich' in which you start the discussion with praise about something P is doing that you genuinely think is good. After all, it is unlikely that everything they are doing is wrong, and most often you will be happy with many aspects of P's work, just unhappy about one or two. Only then introduce criticism, and then finish your conversation with further praise.

This sequence has several advantages, not least that you keep the negative aspects of P's work in perspective. Remember the proportions of a sandwich: the filling is usually no thicker than the slices of bread. If you can stick to that ratio in your discussion then both you and P can leave the discussion feeling confident that improvement will take place.

To increase further the likelihood of your feedback being effective, there is a recipe for the sandwich filling, an approach espoused by Joe Batten. He sums it up as 'ask, listen, expect'.[4] Before you tell P what you think of their performance, *ask* them what they think of it. Often they will have a perceptive analysis of just what they are doing wrong, and if they don't then you may be able to prompt this by refining your questions. Now ask them what is causing the problem and what they can do about it. Listen (really *listen*) to what they have to say, supporting them in their thinking if that is needed (often it is not), and then make clear that you *expect* them to be able to resolve the problem and to do so.

Sometimes P does not have the insight (or perhaps the confidence in their standing with you) for this to work, and then you must provide the sandwich filling yourself. We will look below at some guidelines about how to do this.

Many of us hate giving critical feedback and do it badly. We have not learned to practise it effectively, nor to behave well when we are on the receiving end of it. I often work with managers in group situations to help them learn how to do both better. They take turns to play the manager and P roles in the criticism sandwich, and invariably they discover that P does not believe the positive 'bread slice' that the manager starts with. Why? Imagine being on the receiving end of a general statement such as 'It's very good to have you as a member of the team' or 'You've been settling in very well'. Are you waiting for something? Yes, it sounds like a pleasantry, a preamble. And if you then hear the word 'but' your suspicions are confirmed, you know that it was just a way of leading into some criticism that is to follow. There are two aspects that need to be corrected here: giving praise that is too general, and using 'but'.

When you are giving praise you need to be sincere and specific. If you can single out a particular report that was well written, or a patient interaction that was well handled, and say what you liked about it, then P is much more likely to believe that you mean it. If you then move into the critical 'filling' without undermining what you have just said by using the word 'but' (after all it is now not a very appropriate thing to say), then there is every chance P will be able to hear that in a responsive rather than defensive frame of mind. If you find you are so annoyed at P's poor performance that you cannot think of anything worthy of praise, this in itself is an indication that you are not in the right mood to handle the discussion constructively – it will be better to postpone it until you can see P's performance in the round. On the other hand, if you come across behaviour you want to correct instantly, where there is a danger associated with what they are doing, then finding positive aspects to praise will not only be insincere, they will be confusing for P. So here you would give the critical feedback very directly. It is worth reflecting, though, that the criticism you make on an occasion like this will be much better received if you have already made sincere and appreciative observations over a period of time. In other words, you might like to think about the sandwich as an ongoing activity – and the more 'bread slices' you give the more impact your 'fillings' will have.

There are two other occasions when you may decide to be direct and not to use the sandwich. Some people if given praise first will pay so much attention to this that they underestimate the significance of the criticism.[5] These people prefer a very direct style of communication, and will use this themselves. They expect that if there is anything wrong with their performance this will be pointed out to them clearly and straightforwardly. If you know one of your team falls into this category you have two choices. One is to be blunt and not to use the sandwich. The other is to use the sandwich but to summarize key points for action before you close the conversation.

The other occasion is when you are so concerned about P's performance that you have started to think about disciplinary action. At this point you will probably want to take advice from your human resources department, and in your conversations with P you will need to be crystal clear about the problem behaviours and about the action needed to address them. You will also want to document the conversation. Although many of the points that follow are still relevant I am not referring here to feedback that is part of the disciplinary process, but to the ongoing process of managing P by observing Rule 3.

There will often be times when we are irritated with other people and the criticism sandwich can be a useful mental tool whenever this happens. Thinking of the bread slices allows us to keep a balanced view of their behaviours and to interact with them much more effectively than when we remember only the filling. But now we can look at some guidelines for how to give the negative criticism.

Box 1.3 Guidelines for giving negative criticism

1   *Focus on changing people's behaviour, not their personalities*
    You do not have the right or even the ability to change P's personality. You are concerned with their behaviour or performance and changing this. So talk about what you know they do, not what kind of person you think they are: 'You have arrived late three times this week', not 'You are lazy'. Where possible, you will find your feedback conversation is more productive if you limit your descriptions to things that you yourself have seen, heard or measured, and not information you receive second hand. This avoids P's natural temptation to want to know 'Who says so?' and to attribute negative motives to that person. If you are reporting things you have witnessed you avoid all this. It is always tempting in a management position to ascribe the source of unpleasant news of any kind to someone else. If you can avoid doing so you will discover that people are much more open to examining their problem behaviour and to addressing issues you raise.

2   *Don't jump to conclusions*
    People are complex and individual and you cannot always be sure of knowing the reasons why P is behaving the way they are. Restrict your comments to the behaviour and do not jump to conclusions about the causes: 'It is taking you much longer than your colleagues to do *x*', not 'You're far too tired to do your work properly'. That way you reduce the risk of being wrong, and of discouraging P from taking the responsibility for making the link and doing something about it.

3   *Make the change in behaviour seem realistic and achievable*
    People can often change their behaviour if the change is attainable and explained to them as such. After all, in most situations it is not a case of acquiring totally new skills or eradicating unwanted ones. The problem may be that a certain type of behaviour is more or less inappropriate to the situation; the individual may, for instance, be acting more aggressively, less patiently, more acquiescently or less assertively than the situation demands. If that is the case, say so, describing their behaviour in terms of 'Have you considered doing more of this? Less of that?' Focus on matching the desired change to the nature of the task or goal, rather than for the sake of pleasing

you. People can deal with making changes of this kind, whereas they may feel unable to tackle the complete abolition of a behaviour that to them feels instinctive.

4   *Avoid making simple value judgements*
A behaviour that is a problem in one situation may be an advantage in others, so it is best to keep your description neutral. Avoid categorizing an undesirable behaviour in terms of good versus bad or right versus wrong, just describe it in terms of whether or not it is appropriate to the given situation: 'On three occasions during the team meeting you started talking before X had finished, and that may well inhibit her from contributing her views – views we need to hear. Please allow people to finish before you start talking.'

5   *Be specific rather than general*
It is difficult to change our behaviour unless we know precisely what it is we have to change. So the more specific you can be, the better. If possible give exact details of the time and place when an example of the behaviour occurred, preferably while it is still fresh in both your memories. Unless this is a disciplinary interview, however, you do not need to list a long catalogue of 'crimes', and a few carefully chosen examples are likely to be more effective.

6   *Horses for courses*
Different people find different methods helpful when it comes to learning how to change their behaviour. So although you may have found one particular course, technique or book helpful, others may not. If your advice is seen as an instruction it is likely to be resisted, so do give P information, share ideas and discuss different options, but do not give advice. Let P choose; they will usually know how they learn better than you do.

7   *Choose the time and place carefully*
Even good feedback given at the wrong time or in a place where P is uncomfortable will not be effective. It is highly unlikely that P will feel comfortable when anyone else is present, so if you are tempted to talk in front of others it is worth examining your motives. You may be more concerned to be seen to be acting than you are to challenge constructively the problem behaviour. In practice you may need to do both, but they are separate tasks and should not be confused.

8   *Be clear about your purpose*
The purpose of giving feedback is to enable P to change a behaviour and become more skilful. It is not to make *you* feel better. Although P may find it painful, the feedback is for their benefit. Critical feedback is often badly given because we hate doing it, and rush through it, trying to get it over as

quickly as possible. Developing staff is one of the most important responsibilities of a manager and feedback is an essential element. If you can keep in mind the benefit to P, as well as the importance to your service of achieving a change in P's performance, you will be less inclined to avoid it, and more willing to prepare for it, thinking it through carefully and perhaps even roleplaying it with a colleague or friend until you are confident P will understand your concerns and be willing and confident to make the changes you want to see.

9   *Prepare yourself emotionally*
Do not be deflected from your purpose (change in the behaviour of P) by a defensive or hostile response. It is natural to feel irritated (with yourself and/ or with P) but you need to master this irritation. If you are unable to do so further discussion may prove damaging, so try to move on to the second slice of bread (a positive statement) and schedule a further meeting to discuss the 'filling'. Continuing when you are angry will only exacerbate the problem. Being aware of and able to overcome your immediate emotional reactions is one of the benefits of rehearsing the discussion in advance.

If you are thinking that feedback once a year as part of the appraisal process is sufficient, a word of caution. Whenever you interact with P you will be conveying feedback. Silence and body language can be just as expressive as words. Others will infer their own meaning from any silence on your part, as well as from your body language. Moreover, they will attend to comments they overhear you making to others. Sometimes they will gain a fair reflection of your views by this detective work; often they will misinterpret the clues; more often still they will be confused by what appear to be mixed messages. Feedback is one of the many areas of management when 'doing nothing' is just not possible. Since you are conveying feedback anyway, consider how much better it is to make this constructive and effective.

Management by walking about

Clearly, if you are to be in a position to give feedback you must know how someone is performing, and again there is no short cut here. You must spend time with that person, with their staff, with their clients, taking a genuine, constructive interest. There are a number of ways of doing this but it will inevitably involve spending time away from your office among your staff. Tom Peters has called this 'management by walking about' (MBWA)[6] and it is another concept that causes indignation among senior health managers.

'Surely', they say, 'I must only communicate with my staff through the organizational hierarchy; otherwise I am undermining the authority of my team.' This view would be justified if you were to use your time with front-line staff or patients to impart news of decisions you had not told their line managers about; or if you were to gossip with them about individuals not present.

In this, as in so much of management, the results of your actions will depend on your intentions and your integrity. If you set out to snoop, to find evidence with which to confront or to blame, then you will undermine yourself and your team. If your intention is to evaluate performance so that you can praise, offer support where needed and keep in touch with your organization and its clients – and you have the integrity not to get ensnared in the traps that will be set for you – then the results will be generally positive.

Most often, however, you will be fallible. You will fall into some of the traps inevitably waiting for you; what you say and don't say will sometimes be misunderstood; and you may even find that what you say and do is distorted when it is repeated to others. In other words, you may indeed cause some damage when you go walkabout. Should this stop you doing it? I suggest not, but also that you do not do it lightly or without preparation. Before you do it, while you are there and when you think back on it, you will need to *reflect* carefully on why you are doing this, what the benefits are *to others*; whether there is any danger or potential damage; and whether there are ways of reducing this. These may include checking with your team in advance whether there are any issues that are currently causing concern, or grievances held by individuals. While you are there you will need to be aware of the way people are reacting to you, and of how you are responding to them, and try to work towards the benefits you had previously identified. Back in your office afterwards you will want to analyse your interactions, see what you have learned, think about what you will do as a result and whether there is any specific damage limitation needed.

When you are talking with others about people who are not there, and especially about people senior to those you are talking with, then integrity and transparency are important. You may be given information about the behaviour of one of your managers by some of their subordinates, behaviour they deem unhelpful. When this happens you have a number of choices. You can refuse to listen to it, you can hear it but ignore it, you can hear them out and note it or (especially if you think there may be some grounds for their concerns) you can make reference to the criticism sandwich. You might say, for example:

> X is very good at . . . and excellent at . . . and as a team you have benefited from these, nobody is perfect and she is less good at . . . If

> this is a major problem you must take it up with her, but I suggest you find ways of working with it, and remember how well she does . . .

Others will disagree and suggest that you must never say or agree with anything negative. I agree completely that someone's *personality* is not a suitable subject for such a discussion. However, personally, I observe that ruling out any negative comments about *behaviours* allows ongoing disappointment or frustration with some unhelpful behaviours, and drives discussion of them underground. If put in context, then, constructive discussions can take place at a number of different levels and we can play to people's strengths and avoid their weaknesses. Of course, if you subscribe to the theory that people in senior positions must always be seen as infallible then you won't like this approach.

In health care, particularly where it borders on social care, much of the front-line workload is undertaken off-site. In all aspects of health care, it involves autonomous practitioners working alone with clients. How does MBWA apply here? There can be no spontaneous decision to 'drop in and see how things are going' when we are talking about confidential discussions between a patient and a professional, or when dropping in means catching up with a community psychiatric nurse on her rounds. Yet staff in these areas also have the right to feedback that will help them to develop and grow.

Some of the models developed in other arenas may be helpful. Sales people operate entirely off-site and sales managers typically spend a day a month with each individual team member, observing interactions with some clients and discussing others. This is often seen by the sales rep as an opportunity to shine, and also as an opportunity to bring the skills of the manager to bear with a client they have found difficult. In social work, too, there is a well-used system of supervision in which social workers discuss with their team leader their current caseload. Again, this is seen as valuable, often vital, support. Teachers, working alone most of the time, produce detailed lesson plans for their own benefit, but also as a basis for constructive discussion with departmental heads.

Many HCPs reading this may argue that supervision is already embedded in the culture of health care, and you are right that there are often good systems for supervising clinical practice. But we are talking here about managerial supervision. Many clinicians, after all, are managed by non-clinical general managers, and while they will need other means of gaining feedback on their clinical performance, they too have the right to the support a good manager can offer. So it is worth considering what it is that your manager can contribute. Is it help with designing work processes, with bidding for resources, with thinking about how to use resources more effectively, with managing your own team, with identifying priorities and managing your time? Managers come in all shapes and sizes and all will be better at some of these than at others. If you play to your manager's strengths and take responsibility for ensuring they add value to what you do you will not only be achieving more yourself, you will develop your own skills in helping others to do as well as they can, you will be increasing your skills in the art of getting things done. If after making genuine and repeated efforts you reach a dispassionate conclusion that they cannot add value to what you do, then you may need to challenge the design of the organization (but please do read Chapters 6 and 7 first).

To identity one other cause of problems when giving feedback let us return to the Johnson family.

Box 1.4 The Johnsons: what happened next

Discussing the incident with her friend later, Mrs Johnson wondered aloud how she had ever assumed Mrs White would know what they wanted of her. 'I think I felt it would be an insult to her, it would be questioning her competence, a demonstration that we didn't trust her,' she said. Her friend asked why she had not told her once it was clear there was a problem. Mrs Johnson replied, 'I suppose I didn't want to hurt her feelings, I wanted to be nice.'

I wanted to be nice. It is surprising how often this is the reason given for not being straightforward with someone when we are concerned about their performance. Reflecting on what's meant by 'being nice' can be instructive. Can you recall an occasion when you felt like that too? If so, what did you really mean? People usually say, 'I didn't want to hurt the other person's feelings', just as Mrs Johnson said. Yet Mrs Johnson was quite prepared to give Mrs White the sack.[7]

Whose feelings was Mrs Johnson protecting? Mrs White's, or her own? It is likely she did not want the discomfort of facing Mrs White's reaction to criticism: perhaps hostility or disappointment. Feeling nervous about confronting others or giving bad news is only natural, but giving in to fear and shirking the truth is irresponsible if you are in a position where you are managing someone else. Unless we give feedback about poor performance in due time so that others can act on it to consider changing their behaviour we must share the blame for it. So whenever we are inclined to want to be 'nice' it is worth checking exactly what our motives are, and whose interests we are serving.

Rule 3, then, also requires us to engage directly with the people we are working through, and this involves reflecting on how we are feeling, thinking and behaving as we do so.

Helping your manager to help you

There is one other important use for the three rules, and that is as a guide for how you would like others to manage you. If, for instance, you are feeling aggrieved because your line manager is not observing the three rules as far as you are concerned, you may find it useful to think about how you could help him or her to do so. Simply being annoyed is a waste of time, because you lose the opportunity to shape your role as you would like it. In this kind of situation you can think through for yourself a set of expectations to which you can ask your manager to agree. Your manager will probably want to add to them or amend them but almost invariably he or she will sanction them. You can then explore together your skills and resources, and identify the kind of feedback that will be most useful to you.

Because feedback is often given badly, it is likely that at some time or another you will be on the receiving end of criticism that is less than constructive. The pointers given on pages 14–16 therefore have another use: as a guide for you to prompt constructive discussion about your own performance management. For example, if you are given only negative comments you can widen the perspective by asking for feedback about areas that are going well. If comments seem personalized, you can also gracefully steer the conversation away from your personality and on to your behaviour, and gently refuse to accept those judgements that seem to be making assumptions about your motives for behaving in particular ways.

Using the three rules allows you to manage better all the people around you.

Applying the three rules in different settings

The three rules apply whenever we are managing other people, but the ways in which we apply them, in particular the time horizon and the level of technical detail, will differ.

Imagine you have had seconded to you an administrative assistant who will work closely with you to implement a new record system over the next six to nine months. In implementing Rule 1 you will probably set goals that are specific and short term. You will assure yourself of their skills and of the resources needed (Rule 2) by direct observation and discussion. Similarly, you will be directly aware of their performance, and thus able to give on-the-spot feedback.

If you are managing someone who is managing others, and who is not physically located near your office, then the way in which you implement the rules will be different. Imagine you manage a therapy services manager, in charge of 40 staff who are based at a number of different locations, and whose office is in a building half a mile from yours. The expectations you agree are likely to be longer term than in the first example, perhaps encompassing a 12-month period, and they will probably be expressed as outcomes, with much less prescription over how they are to be achieved. Even when you are confident that resources and skills are sufficient, it is unlikely that assessment of how they are performing in the role will be as fully direct and first-hand as it was with your administrative assistant. So how will you assess this second person's skills and performance? Since a key element of this person's role is managing others, you will probably need to ascertain from other staff how well this is being done. Of course, you will not ask them that question outright, but you will have a number of proxy indicators: you can observe how they behave, how they refer to their own objectives, whether they feel confident of their own skills and resources. You will also be able to discuss with their manager the kind of feedback they are getting and what effect this is having.

If managing someone more senior still, if, say, you were a chief executive managing an executive director of a large hospital, the expectations you agree with them will have a wider scope still, and include activities that have very long-term consequences. The observation you undertake to implement Rules 2 and 3 will now encompass not only the people they are managing, but also individuals from partner organizations and other external stakeholders.

Managing teams

The three rules also apply when managing teams, and here it is important that the rules must be applied to the team as a whole. Team members must be clear about what is expected of them collectively, as a team. They must be confident that within the team they have the necessary skills and resources to achieve those expectations. And team members, as a team, must receive feedback on whether they are being successful.

Multidisciplinary teams

In health care we work in many different kinds of teams, many of them multi-disciplinary, with many different management arrangements. There are many teams where managerially the team is accountable to one person but individual members each have professional hierarchies of their own. Here too the three rules need to be observed but, perhaps because of the confusion over accountability, they are all too often not. Indeed, there is often confusion over the most basic parameters, such as the role of the team. In many of the teams I have worked with there are some members who believe the team exists in order to advise the team leader, and others who perceive it as a decision-making group, with all members having an equal say. When these beliefs coexist in the same group, without being made explicit, then unresolved conflict is inevitable, and typically members will complain about each other and spend a lot of time debating whether the team needs work on team building. Even where the role of the team has been agreed, this agreement will need to be revisited from time to time, because teams will naturally evolve and change in focus, as will the concerns and enthusiasms of their members.

Sometimes a discussion of this sort may result in the realization that the group of people involved are not in fact a team. Instead they are a number of individuals all involved with the same client group but who can work perfectly well serially rather than together. When this happens it can free people from some of the time-consuming requirements associated with being a team – meetings, for example – liberating them from having to agree about everything, and allowing more productive communication about issues where it is genuinely important that information is shared.

Let us imagine that you are managing a team that is indeed a team, but you are outside it. In other words, the team is accountable to you but you are not a member. The members of it, however, are from different professions and do not report to you individually. Let's also imagine that you are attempting to reach agreement with the team on roles and expectations or to communicate feedback on their performance, but that you are finding this very hard going because of disagreements between members, or between them and you. You decide to seek out an individual within the team whom you perceive to be influential and sympathetic to your way of thinking, and you discuss matters with them hoping they will sell your view to the rest of the team. This approach, like most short cuts in management, almost always backfires. The likely result is that the individual feels uncomfortable and both they and the rest of the team now see you as cowardly, in addition to the faults they had ascribed to you already. There is seldom any substitute for sitting down with the team as a whole, for as long as it takes to reach agreement.

Rather than managing a team from outside it, you may be the team leader – a member of the team as well as responsible for its overall performance – and you will also need to ensure the three rules are observed. You will want to contribute your own thoughts about the team's purpose, its goals and objectives, and to listen to those of others. As the leader you will make sure everyone has an opportunity to contribute and you will ensure that agreements are recorded and referred back to when necessary.

Many of us now work in several, sometimes overlapping, teams, and it is likely that in many of these there will be no formal leader identified as such. Indeed, many teams are now deemed to be 'self-managing'; that is, they are expected to monitor their own activity and progress without any one member being placed in an explicit team management role. Some have coordinators rather than managers, people who schedule the business of the team but do not manage it. This is the case for many networks or collaboratives where there is the additional complication of members coming from different organizations. This can work well if the group is cohesive around very clearly identified goals and objectives. If, however, you or other team members find you are becoming frustrated at the team's lack of progress in reaching goals and observe an absence of the three rules, you can still prompt their implementation. You may choose to raise this as an explicit topic for discussion, or you may find it more effective to keep them in mind yourself and ask the kinds of questions or make the contributions to debate that will bring them to life. In other words, you may choose to take on the role of team facilitator. Taking on this kind of role informally can make a very valuable contribution to the team, but can leave you without enough support, so if possible it is a good idea to discuss this aspect of your team membership role with your own manager or within your own professional hierarchy.

Boards

One particular example of a team is the board of an organization. Although they are essential if the board is to provide the leadership the organization needs, the three rules are all too often ignored at this level too. In view of the considerable amount of time boards spend together in meetings, away days and team development activities, you might find this observation surprising. My experience of working with boards, however, is that they seldom discuss – *as a board* – what they see as their role, what it is they are trying to achieve or what skills and resources they need. Moreover, the same applies to feedback on their performance as a board.

Instead, what often happens is that boards prioritize discussion of the strategy of the organization as a whole and ignore their own needs. Where performance of individual members is considered this is usually in relation to their substantive role and not as that of board member. And while executive directors will seek to bring their non-executive colleagues up to speed with current issues, they will often induct them into the role of the board *as they see it*. This is not how to go about implementing the three rules *as a board* or to keep board membership flourishing. There are some proprietary approaches that offer means of fulfilling the three rules, and at clarifying the boundary between board and executive team (one of the better known is the Carver Model[8]). However, the calibre of board members is likely to be such that they will be very able to develop their own approach once they realize the need to do so. Chairs who can keep the three rules in mind will be able to draw on this ability. A well-facilitated away day may be all the time that is needed to agree the systems and processes that need to be set up. Even so, ongoing energy and attention will be needed to ensure that the rules become part of the ongoing norms of board life. This is especially important, as people throughout the organization are more likely to sign up to a 'three rules' culture if they see an example of good practice being set at the very top.

Here too people without formal leadership positions can still exercise influence and board members, including the non-executives, can help to set the tone almost as much as the chair.

We can see from these examples that being a *real* manager doesn't require a formal position or authority, just skills in the art of getting things done, starting with the three rules.

Motivation and personality

Even if you are convinced that implementing the three rules will be helpful and that you want to do so, you may still be hesitating. This is not surprising. If you are seriously considering ways in which you can introduce them, then you may well be having misgivings about the responses of your various staff members or colleagues. They may be hostile, defensive, superior or apathetic. This doesn't sound much fun! However, understanding what makes different people respond in the way they do will help you to engender much more favourable reactions. In this section, we look at what makes different people 'tick'.

Differences that cause difficulties

What happens when you call to mind the members of your team? You might like to try doing so now; if so, notice how you feel about them. Consider the maxim 'the greatest gift you can give to anyone is consistently to expect their best': are you able to do that for your team members? Do you feel pleased with them, proud of them, impressed by them? Or do you find that difficult because they disappoint you, irritate you, make you feel angry, frustrated or despairing? In this section, we look at some of the reasons why they succeed in infuriating you.

Because our personalities are so rich and complex, we naturally differ from one another in many ways. This often adds to our enjoyment of each other, but equally often these differences can cause difficulties, misunderstandings, misinterpretations and mistrust. By looking at some of these differences and at the problems they can cause, we can begin to understand how irritations and conflicts arise and thus become better able to avoid or deal with them.

Different motivation profiles

Much research has been undertaken by psychologists and others into what motivates us to expend our energy. Perhaps the most widely known motivation theorist is Abraham Maslow, who suggested in his book *Motivation and Personality*[9] that there is a hierarchy of human needs and that only when the needs on the lowest layer of the hierarchy are met do we seek to meet the needs of the next layer and so on. The needs he identified are shown in Figure 1.1.

Recently, workers in the field have identified sets of needs, goals or drivers that are similar but not identical to those proposed by Maslow, and that do not remain static; instead, they differ between individuals and between cultures, as well as over time. These researchers suggest that each of these drivers is important to us all to some degree, but that we differ in their *relative* importance. In other words, if we are deprived of any one of these drivers, we will be motivated to regain it; however, some are more important than others to each individual. John Hunt identifies eight such goal categories,[10] which overlap with those of Maslow as indicated:

1 *Comfort.* In addition to Maslow's physiological needs of food, drink, shelter and clothing, this category includes pleasant working conditions and sufficient money to provide a comfortable lifestyle. People who have a strong comfort driver will be motivated by performance-related financial reward.

2 *Structure.* These map on to Maslow's safety and security needs, but relate as much to an individual's desire for certainty as to their concern about physical or financial security. People with strong structure goals will thrive in bureaucracies and environments where there are numerous clearly defined roles and their own role is precisely delineated.

3 *Relationships.* Maslow called this category 'social needs'. It reflects the degree to which individuals seek to form lasting relationships and

Figure 1.1 Maslow's hierarchy of needs.

with whom. For many people, this is one of the most important goals. They seek collaborative rather than competitive working relationships and mourn the loss of close colleagues if their organizations are restructured and teams are disbanded.

4   *Recognition and status.* Whereas Maslow proposed one category of 'self-esteem' needs, Hunt divides them into two: (a) recognition and status and (b) power. As recognition and power often come together (the title and the car go with the decision-making job), they can be confused. People with high recognition needs often gravitate towards academic roles and the professions, so we can expect to find many in health care. Managed sensitively, these people can be helped to maintain high levels of motivation, since they respond best to sincere praise from individuals they rate.

5   *Power.* The degree to which someone seeks to influence and control people, events and situations. Most people who make it to the top of organizations are motivated most strongly by power. Again, it is also a strong driver in many of those who choose one of the professions.

6   (7 and 8) *Autonomy, creativity and growth.* These three together form Maslow's self-actualization needs, but describe them more precisely. The three do not necessarily occur together, although they may do so.

The relative importance that we place on these goals or drivers can be thought of as forming a 'motivation profile'. When we try to interact with someone with a different motivation profile, we must expect not to see things in the same way. For example, my two most significant goals may be recognition and self-actualization, whereas yours may be power and structure. If, in addition, structure is (within limits) unimportant to me and self-actualization is unimportant to you, then we may well see each other in a negative light. You may perceive me as being too ready to take risks, as pursuing ill-considered schemes that are not sufficiently thought through, and in pursuit of my own ambition: 'selfish' you might say. I, on the other hand, may see you as averse to risk when you pour scorn on my ideas, and scheming when you exert your influence through other people and do not claim the credit yourself: 'cowardly' I might think. The more you try to remove risk from my projects by building in contingency planning, requiring from me more and more detail, or the more I try to sell you the grandiose upside and how much it will do for your reputation, the more and more we will irritate each other.

You might like to take a moment now to visualize your most difficult member of staff, the one who simply cannot see sense. As dispassionately as you can, identify the drivers that you think are most important to them. Now look at the 'demotivating factors' for those goals in Table 1.1. Are there any that you are invoking? You might find that unwittingly (or not) you have been provoking this individual into their worst behaviour. Adopting some of

Table 1.1 The motivating and demotivating factors associated with different preferences

Goal	Motivating factors	Demotivating factors
Comfort	Pleasant working environment: view, window, fixtures and fittings, temperature Salary sufficient to provide a comfortable lifestyle outside work	Scruffy, dirty, cold, uncomfortable, dull working environment Salary insufficient to provide the comfortable lifestyle that is desired
Security	Told exactly what to do and how to do it Predictable career path Financial rewards reliable Environment physically secure	Vague instructions relating to outcomes Next step uncertain Risk to income Risk of physical harm
Relationships	Opportunities to meet other people, to chat, to get to know other people and work in a team Culture where staff care for each other	Working on own, competing with others Culture where the task is all-important and people's feelings do not matter
Recognition	Sincere praise, credit given where it is due, thanks, public recognition, advice sought, name associated with project/paper/etc., the good opinion of others Personal satisfaction with a job well done. Knowledge that a genuine contribution has been made	Others taking credit for work, downplaying of role, being 'brought down to size', squashing of ideas or enthusiasm Annoyance with self over a job not well done. Egg on face
Power	Decisions to make, reports to write, opportunity to give advice, decisions implemented, advice taken and actioned (even if not acknowledged), things 'shaping up nicely' even if own name not associated with changes being made	No opportunity to influence events
Self-actualization: growth, creativity, autonomy	New projects, new ideas, developing new skills, expectations expressed in outcomes	The same old thing, new patterns of work involve the same old skills, being told exactly what to do and how to do it

the actions listed under 'motivating factors' may transform your difficult staff member into a valuable asset.

The important point to remember is that if you are trying to motivate someone else, you must consider what it is that motivates them and not what would motivate you in similar circumstances. It is such a simple mistake to make: we like someone; we assume they are like us; we are disappointed if they do not respond enthusiastically to what we perceive as an exciting opportunity; we like them a little less; and soon our relationship is into a downward spiral of disappointment and irritation. If we start by thinking about them, and what enthuses them and what irritates them (without making judgements, just recognizing differences), we can avoid this.

Sometimes we encounter the opposite problem: we are motivated by the same thing and find ourselves locked in competition. This is especially likely if we are both seeking recognition; the more you try to grab all the limelight, the more hostile I become and the less inclined I am to give you any credit. If one of us can be honest about our need for recognition or status, then we may be able to devise ways of working together that will allow us both to gain. So ingrained, however, is the notion that 'showing off' is something to be despised, that such honesty will require courage.

It is worth reminding ourselves, in this situation, that there is nothing inherently right or wrong about being driven by any of these goals. A strong autonomy goal is not 'better' than a strong relationships one, high creative needs are not 'better' than a strong driver towards structure and security. Being sensitive to the goals of the individuals around us allows us to be more persuasive. It requires, of course, that we invest time in getting to know them and the ways they respond. Really managing people cannot be done from behind a closed office door, it demands considerable face-to-face contact.

Different personalities

No discussion of personality could afford to ignore the work of C. G. Jung, the influential Swiss psychologist whose book *Psychological Types* was published in 1921.[11] Jung suggested that differences in personality are due to the way in which people prefer to use their minds. He suggested that when the mind is active, it is engaging in one of two occupations: perceiving (receiving information) or judging (organizing that information and forming conclusions). He further suggested that there are two ways in which we can perceive (sensing and intuition) and two in which we can judge (thinking and feeling). He observed that although everyone uses all four of these processes, individuals have a preference for judging or perceiving and for one kind of perceiving and one kind of judging. We apply these processes to both our internal and external worlds, but again we have a preference for one or the other (introversion or extroversion).

Thus there are four scales on which we will have a preference for one end or the other:

Perceiving	Judging
Sensing	Intuition
Thinking	Feeling
Extroversion	Introversion

These four scales give rise to 16 combinations of preferences and hence personality types. Naturally people who are perceivers may misunderstand, misinterpret or misjudge those who are judgers; sensers, those who prefer to intuit; thinkers, feelers; and extroverts, introverts. So some combinations of personality type will be more relaxed and some more stimulating, and some will be very challenging. Clearly, an understanding of why problems arise can help to defuse them.

A number of tools for identifying these 16 personality types have been devised, of which the best known are the Myers–Briggs Type Indicator and the 16PF. Both of these have been extensively researched by their originators and are available through licensed practitioners. Where relationships appear to be intractably problematic or where a team will be working together for some time, detailed diagnostic work of this kind can be helpful.

Differences in the way we prefer to behave in certain circumstances

For day-to-day purposes, it is often not practical to ask people to undergo this kind of test, yet you will need to make some judgements about their personality if you are going to work effectively with them. There are a number of simpler ways of thinking about this that can be helpful.

Differences when working in teams   Imagine you are discussing an idea at your regular departmental meeting and your staff respond as they always do. Liz comes to a decision very quickly and argues her case forcefully. John also forms his views early on and marshals support to oppose Liz. Sarah tries to make sure that everyone has their say and Charles expresses concern when Liz is so abrupt with Ian that she causes offence. Ian wants to know what the deadline is and who will be writing the report, while Alison is picking holes in everyone's arguments and forcing them to think more rigorously.

If this is how your team operates, then you are very lucky (or clever, or both). R. M. Belbin has demonstrated that if a team is to work successfully, nine roles need to be undertaken by the members of the team over its working life.[12] As most teams do not contain nine members, individuals may have to play more than one role; indeed, some people are sufficiently flexible to be able to play any one of several roles according to what is required. Most of us, however, have a preference for one or two roles and rarely take on others, whatever team we are in. The nine roles are:

- *Coordinator*: guides the group, defines priorities, allocates tasks and roles.
- *Shaper*: is task-oriented, pushes the team to achieve the task, pulling together the ideas of members and keeping them focused.
- *Implementer*: concentrates on practicalities, making sure that the outcome of the meeting is a series of manageable, feasible processes.
- *Team worker*: looks after relationships in the group. Their concern is process rather than task, the welfare of individuals rather than of ideas.
- *Plant*: an ideas person who originates ideas and can be devastatingly critical of counter-arguments, but evangelical once convinced.
- *Resource investigator*: is also an ideas person but trades in them rather than generating them. Spots good ideas, hears of relevant information available elsewhere, links ideas together, prompts further thinking by discussing widely.
- *Monitor-evaluator*: is much less easily enthused. Carefully and critically analyses all arguments put forward.
- *Completer-finisher*: makes sure that the group meets deadlines, completes all the tasks and in the right order. In MBA groups at least, this person is exceedingly rare.
- *Specialist*: in many circumstances, expert advice is needed and, without access to a specialist able to provide it, a project will founder.

While the adoption of all these roles by members of your departmental team will make it very productive, it does not guarantee that relationships between individual members will be harmonious. A coordinator/shaper individual can find a monitor-evaluator/completer-finisher infuriating and vice versa, and other combinations can be just as explosive. If you are conscious of your own preferred team role, then you will be able to guard against the irritation that could be caused by another, by reminding yourself of the value of these differences – the checks and balances, the synergy. Awareness of the roles of others will help you to help them value those differences too.

If your team lacks one of those roles then you could consider delegating it. In the same way that tasks are delegated to different members, someone could be asked to adopt a particular role. They may not find it easy, and it would not be wise to leave them adopting it for too long, but it will improve the performance of your team.

Differences when learning   You attend a course that has given you a lot of fascinating information, the skills you need to utilize that information and the enthusiasm to have a go. A colleague on the same course, however, does not see it that way at all. He cannot find anything good to say about it, except for the food! You wonder whether he was really ready for a course pitched at this level. Although you may be right, it is just as likely that it was the particular style of the programme – how its various sections and activities were put together, what blend of theory and practice it offered – that caused your colleague the biggest difficulty. Each of us tends to prefer to learn in different ways and from different types of activities. A course that is exciting and novel to some may appear gimmicky to others. Some may prefer structured situations or being encouraged to watch, think or chew over activities, while others may like 'here and now' activities and being directly involved with others. Psychologists Peter Honey and Alan Mumford have identified four distinct learning styles preferences, which they term 'activist', 'reflector', 'theorist' and 'pragmatist'.[13] Note that these are preferences, they do not describe how people learn all the time, and people are not necessarily stuck with one learning style for life. It is one of Honey and Mumford's arguments that skilled managers can assist others to consider moving into a different learning style if the situation calls for it.

- *Activists* are open-minded enthusiasts who will try anything once. They thrive on new experiences and change, particularly when left to sink or swim, and become bored with repetition and routine. They learn most when involved in games and role-play and when they have a high profile. They also learn from bouncing ideas off other people. Activists learn least on their own, and when they are told exactly what to do and how to do it. They hate lectures, reading and learning *about* things.
- *Theorists* are analytical, objective, logical and rational. They try to fit any new fact into their wider theory. Theorists learn a lot from teaching others. They need to know exactly what they are doing and why. They respond to well-argued ideas (about anything, relevant or not) and love lectures, papers, books and discussions. Theorists learn least when they cannot explore concepts in depth, when they cannot ascertain the methodology employed to arrive at recommendations or when they are forced to act without sufficiently convincing reasons. Theorists tend to dislike methods geared to the needs of activists and vice versa.
- *Reflectors* are thoughtful observers who like to consider all the options, all the implications, before committing themselves. They are good listeners who take the views of others into account. Reflectors learn most from observing and considering, from thinking before being required to act, by reviewing what they have learned from an

exercise or situation and from being given time to reach decisions. Reflectors learn least when forced to take a high profile, when they cannot plan or when they do not have the information to choose a course of action themselves.

- *Pragmatists* are experimenters, practical people who try out new ideas and accept any that work. They like solving problems and looking for relevant new ideas. Pragmatists learn most when concepts are relevant to them, when they yield practical results and when they can be implemented immediately. They love relevant simulations and action plans. Pragmatists learn least from 'ivory tower' theories and when there are no opportunities for implementation.

It does not take a great deal of imagination to see that what is an exciting learning opportunity to an activist can appear alarming or superficial to a reflector. The explanation that satisfies the theorist may well send the pragmatist to sleep. When planning how to develop your staff, offer them developmental opportunities in keeping with their learning style. Better still, identify with them the learning outcomes and let them choose their own learning programme.

Differences when interacting with other individuals   Here I am going to introduce the suggestions of Alessandra and Cathcart.[14] They concentrate on two aspects of interaction: whether we prefer to relate to people or to tasks, and whether we think in a detailed, slow-paced way or in a more holistic, fast-paced one. By placing our preferences on each of two axes, we fall into one of four boxes, each a different relationship style (see Figure 1.2).

- *Socializers* are enthusiastic, persuasive, motivating and creative. They enjoy being in the spotlight, and are very good at starting projects. They also have a short attention span, they take on too much, they

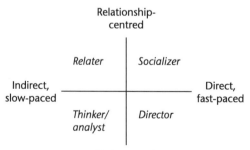

Figure 1.2 Relationship styles.

are impatient and they do not like detail. They hate being bored and working alone.

- *Directors* get things done, take control, make decisions, see what needs doing and make sure it happens. They are also impatient and inflexible, they do not listen, they compete rather than collaborate and they hate people who waste their time.
- *Relaters* are good listeners, are supportive of others, build trust and aim to collaborate not compete. They take time to plan interactions with others and hate friction. They are very sensitive to other people's opinion; they are not assertive and can be bullied.
- *Thinker/analysts* are accurate, independent, organized and take pride in their work. They enjoy detail, are thorough and are pleased to think of themselves as perfectionists. They will insist on a detailed brief. They are surprised that others do not always see perfectionism as a virtue. They cannot be hurried, are critical of mistakes and hate surprises.

Again, it is easy to see how a socializer and a thinker/analyst can rub each other up the wrong way, just as a relater and a director may do. Equally, it should be clear what can be done about it once you are aware of the cause of the tension. If your antagonist is more indirect than you are, then slow down, spell out more of the detail and elaborate on the thinking behind it. Rather than dropping in to see them, make an appointment. If they are less concerned with relationships than you, don't tell them about your family, your feelings or your health, but concentrate on the task. Similarly, if they are more direct than you, try to enthuse about the potential outcomes and check whether you really need all that detail before you can proceed. If they like talking about their family, ask about them, ask how they feel yesterday's meeting went, compliment their choice of office furniture. Remember that together you will come up with ideas, solutions, projects and services that are much better (more secure, more innovative) than either of you could have achieved alone.

This concept is an example of where a pragmatist may be happier than a theorist. The questionnaire that is used to ascertain your own style is, I think, unhelpful. I would be surprised if it were either reliable or valid. Yet the idea is one that people I work with (and I too) find very helpful. It is simple enough to keep in mind in even tense or difficult situations, and the lessons it suggests for modifying one's own behaviour are similarly so. As a pragmatist I encourage you to try it out.

People pollution

These are only a few of the many ways of looking at personalities and there are many others. I find these helpful, you may prefer others. However, the essential point to remember is that there is nothing inherently right or wrong about any of the drivers, behaviours or preferences we have looked at, just differences, and those differences can irritate or they can enrich.

A metaphor drawn from the world of local government comes in handy here. Environmental health officers observe that noise pollution only occurs when two factors are present: (a) noise and (b) hostility to the noise. In other words, we all put up with a lot of decibels when we perceive them to be pleasant. The same is true of people. We get 'people pollution' problems when there are differences *and* when we choose to perceive those differences negatively. Understanding the differences is often the first step to mastering our feelings of irritation. The very fact that such differences exist is likely to cause conflict, but such conflict can be constructive and creative or destructive and damaging. Your role as a manager is to ensure it is the former.

Differences in practice

How can you apply your knowledge of these drivers and preferred behaviours? How will you use this in day-to-day situations? My observation is that people usually find it hard to keep all these concepts in mind on an ongoing basis, and that they tend to work with one. Often the one they find most useful day-to-day is the relationship style, because it is simple and gives a clear indication of how to change their *own* behaviour to get on better with others. And it is worth reminding ourselves of why it is we are interested in 'pigeonholing' people in this way at all: to be able to enthuse, encourage and enable them; to be able to predict their likely response to what we are asking of them; to be able to change what we are doing and saying so that we invite a more constructive or favourable response. Some people see this as manipulative, and indeed it would be if you were to lie or to misrepresent. Most of the time, though, there are many ways of describing opportunities or a situation, and we choose how we do so. An understanding of how other people are likely to respond can simply inform that choice. Sometimes people express concern that we can't be accurate when we mentally allocate someone to one category or another, and of course that is right. In any case these categories are not solid, objectively definable ones, but express tendencies rather than absolutes and will be viewed in different ways by different people. No one is suggesting they are an infallible prescription: 'if you come across someone in this box you must do such and such'. They can be helpful, that is all. If you spot clues in people's behaviours that suggest to you that they prefer behaving one way over another, you can then choose how you interact with them, and you will often be more successful at engaging their interest than you would be if you hadn't.

Concluding thoughts

Three simple rules for managing people. Simple and obvious. But we don't observe them. We don't implement them because to do so takes time, thought, emotional energy and courage. In other words, they are simple but hard. We prefer to spend our time doing things that are more complicated but that demand of us only our intellect, such as writing papers, analysing figures or introducing new systems or structures. We gravitate towards the complicated easy. Yet if we do not observe the simple hard, then we are bound to fail when it comes to the complicated easy.

Unless we implement these three simple rules we are not managing, not *really* managing. Unless we do so we can take no responsibility for the actions of others because we have little influence over those actions. We restrict our role to that of observer, presider, in certain circumstances that of administrator, business or general manager, not that of *real* manager.

You have probably experienced the frustration that results. You have known that you have the energy, the commitment and many of the skills necessary for offering an excellent service. If only it weren't for the other people involved who are getting in the way or not cooperating! Increasingly with clinical networks and new organizational forms and structures management isn't something undertaken by 'managers'. Clinicians of all sorts will be working through many different kinds of others and the three rules will help you to do so.

Max de Pree, in *Leadership is an Art*,[15] suggests that the role of leaders is to 'liberate people to achieve what is required of them in the most humane way possible'. Liberation requires implementation of the three rules in such a way that you take account of all the differences between you and your individual team members, so that you are able to build honest, trusting relationships based on mutual respect.

Another way of thinking about this is in terms of discipline. Implementing the three rules requires discipline on your part, and a willingness to engender the same kind of discipline within your part of the organization. This in turn will help to form a solid cultural bedrock that allows the creativity and commitment of HCPs to flourish. It allows us all to contribute effectively rather than self-indulgently. What is meant by discipline is one of the recurring themes of this book and we will explore it further in the chapters that follow.

Notes

1   This phrase is taken from Harold Koontz (1962), 'Managing is the art of getting things done through and with people in formally organized groups. It is the art

of creating an environment in which people can perform as individuals and yet co-operate towards the attainment of group goals. It is the art of removing blocks to such performance.' From 'Making sense of management theory', *Harvard Business Review*, 40, 4.

2   Osbourne, S. (2003) 'Vacant possession', *Health Services Journal*, 9 January. A report of a review of the nursing workforce at St Mary's Hospital NHS Trust, London.

3   I am referring here to the feedback that is an ongoing part of a manager's or leader's role. The formal feedback that forms part of a disciplinary procedure is different and requires local specialist advice from the personnel department.

4   Batten (1991), see Introduction, note 2.

5   Deborah Tannen describes this in her book *Talking from 9 to 5* (London: Virago Press, 1995).

6   Peters, T. and Austin, N. (1986) *Passion for Excellence* (London: Fontana).

7   If you are thinking that Mrs Johnson is fictional let me reassure you that all these incidents come from real events I have either witnessed or read reliable accounts about.

8   See Carver, J. and Oliver, C. (2002) *Corporate Boards that Create Value: Governing Company Performance from the Boardroom* (San Francisco: Jossey-Bass).

9   Maslow, A. (1954) *Motivation and Personality* (London: Harper and Row).

10   Hunt, J. (1986) *Managing People at Work* (London: McGraw-Hill). This book provides a readable, research-based, wide-ranging discussion of individual motivation, group processes and organizational structures.

11   Jung, C. G. (1990) *Collected Works* (London: Routledge).

12   Belbin, R. M. (1996) *Team Roles at Work* (Oxford: Butterworth Heinemann). The original research is described in Belbin, R. M. (1981) *Management Teams: Why They Succeed or Fail* (Oxford: Butterworth Heinemann). The concepts are now widely disseminated, but it is worth reading about the research on which they are based.

13   Honey, P. and Mumford, A. (1986) *A Manual of Learning Styles* (Maidenhead: Peter Honey). The value of several learning styles inventories has been called into question in recent years as lacking in empirical evidence, especially in educational settings. However, my argument here rests on using Honey and Mumford critically, and as a pragmatic tool.

14   Alessandra, T. and Cathcart, J. (1985) *Relationship Strategies* (Chicago: Nightingale Conant). Available only on audio-cassette.

15   de Pree, M. (1989) *Leadership is an Art* (London: Arrow Business Books). A simple, heart-felt book that deserves to be read carefully and repeatedly.

2 Really managing people
Working with others

To some extent the distinction between working through people and working with people is fuzzy. We saw in Chapter 1 that we don't have to have formal power or authority to encourage use of the three rules in teams of which we are members, or on the part of people who manage us. It isn't a large step to suggest that it might be useful to apply them whenever we are working with anyone on anything.

In Chapter 1 we thought about the ways individuals respond differently according to their particular motivations and preferred behaviours, and an understanding of these is, of course, just as important when working with colleagues we don't manage as with those we do. In health care organizations, however, when we think about working with others outside our department or team, there are other considerations based on the nature and dynamics of professions, which we need to add to our understanding of them as individuals, and this is what we explore in Chapter 2.

At its most basic, working with people involves conveying our own needs and expectations and interpreting and responding to those of others. Yet all too often these interactions are much more problematic than this description suggests. A genuine request from a subordinate for assistance is interpreted as an implied criticism of our management abilities; a friendly offer of advice from outside the team is seen as empire-building; a sensible suggestion for change from one professional is seen by another as an attempt to take over, or to impose a particular model of care. We often fail to appreciate that how we respond to others in health care is affected by our membership of particular groups as well as individual attributes and preferences. Developing insight into these factors can help us not only to communicate and interact more effectively but also to take more responsible and empowered decisions, and to accept charitably the attempts of others to do so, for the benefit of patients. It is worth exploring, then, the factors that affect the quality of relationships between individual professionals and between professional groups.

Professions in health care

First, let's remind ourselves of where professions come from. Nowadays we are all specialists. Few reading this book will grow all their own food, weave the cloth for their clothes and so on. Our history as a species is one of becoming more and more specialized over time, and of the rate of specialization quickening. As a result we all depend on more and more people, as we have become more and more expert in fields that have narrowed and narrowed. One outcome of this has been the development of professions. Another is the formation of large, complex organizations, as the production of goods and services has required the involvement of greater numbers of interdependent specialists.

Specialization has brought great technical advances but also problems of communication, a lack of shared understanding and fragmentation of responsibility. These generic aspects of specialization (professions, large complex organizations and problems of communication and of sharing responsibility) are all very relevant to people working in health care, and we need to understand some of the difficulties these can cause, and the behaviours we can adopt to overcome or minimize them.

One of the features of large complex organizations is that professionals need to work with others from different professions or disciplines. When individual HCPs interact with each other their behaviours will be influenced by all the individual preferences described in Chapter 1. So the nature and quality of their communication will depend on motivational drivers, personality type and the behaviours they prefer to adopt in different settings. But in addition to these, the individuals involved will bring to their relationships the fact that they are members of professional groups with a set of beliefs, expectations and behaviours shaped by that membership.

Just as the purpose of diagnosing the individual factors described in Chapter 1 was to be able to predict responses and dynamics, and thus choose behaviours and frame arguments in ways that enable relationships to be productive, so in this chapter we look at how to predict the dynamics between professionals, to inform and enhance interprofessional working.

Sharing responsibility

Imagine that specialist tasks A, B, C, D and E are all necessary for a successful outcome. Success clearly requires that responsibility for each of these tasks is taken. But by whom? If task C is inadequately completed but this could be remedied by an enlargement of task B or E, then who is responsible for avoiding a poor outcome? In an interdependent situation, who takes responsibility for people taking responsibility? Very often in health care, the answer is 'no one'. If we recognize this, then we will realize that it is not enough for each of us to take our own responsibilities, but that we must also take some responsibility across the boundary into interdependent specialties.

Sharing responsibility is always potentially problematic. If two people share responsibility for a complex task, we could describe their joint responsibilities in the form of a cake (see Figure 2.1a). If each person separately takes half of the responsibility then we run the risk that person A covers half the cake (cross-hatched area) and person B covers a different half (dotted area). This leaves an area (C) for which no-one takes responsibility (Figure 2.1b).

One solution would be for A and B to agree on the responsibility each is taking (see Figure 2.1c). Of course, they will not now be sharing responsibility, unless they agree to keep the whole cake in mind (the complete successful outcome) and to act across the boundary if they perceive it to be necessary. This is what our responsibilities need to be if we are part of an interdependent system. If our responsibility cake has six contributors (see Figure 2.1d), then each must agree the boundaries but each must also be prepared to act sensitively across boundaries if it is thought to be necessary. Just as importantly, each should respond charitably and not defensively when others cross their boundary.

The issue of how to take responsibility across disciplines is a critical one in health care. So many of the problems that arise do so at the boundaries between disciplines and they do so because each profession self-righteously blames the other and vigorously defends its boundaries. It is a feature of the history of mankind that we have always organized into ingroups and outgroups,[1] so perhaps we should not berate both ourselves and others too severely when, as HCPs, we do so. The factors we explore in this chapter help to explain why this occurs, even though the ability and commitment of those entering the professions is very considerable.

First, let's try to clarify some key terms, including what is meant by 'professional', 'health' and 'care' and what happens when these three terms come together in the concept and the person of the 'health care professional'.

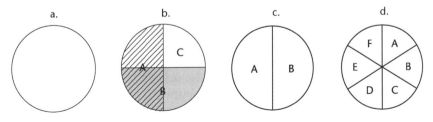

Figure 2.1 The responsibility cake.

What makes a profession a profession?

Let us try to explore what is meant by a profession. You may even want to stop for a moment and reflect on your own idea of what is meant by this word.

Two disciplines have been particularly interested in professions: economists and sociologists.[2] First, here is how an economist might explain the nature of professions:

> Society needs individuals to invest their time and energy in developing a particular knowledge base and skills. In return for this investment society gives them certain rewards, including social status and higher than average wages. As the technical skills are to be found only within each profession, each must be, to some extent, self-regulating, but ultimately they must serve needs valued by society.

We see here that professional status is given to a particular individual by society in return for that individual acquiring and then exercising skills that allow particular needs within a society to be met. The corollary to this is that as society's needs or concerns change, this 'contract' becomes less valuable to society and professions can expect to see challenges to their identity, their role and their status as a result.[3]

Sociologists have also regarded professions as a subject of inquiry and have viewed them in a number of different ways. Bryan Turner describes the different approaches sociological observers have taken to the 'liberal professions'.[4] Some observers (for example, Parsons, Durkheim and Holton) have seen them as 'representing the institutionalisation of altruistic values . . . officially committed to various forms of personal service and community welfare . . . a disinterested commitment to community values'. The emphasis here is on 'the ethical character of the profession, its service to the person, and its basis in technical knowledge'. In the same tradition Donald Schön describes professionals as appliers of scientific knowledge, as a 'group who contribute to social well being, put their clients' needs ahead of their own and hold themselves accountable to standards of competence and morality'. He talks of professions being essential to the functioning of society, and says 'we look to professionals for the definition and solution of our problems and it is through them we strive for social progress'.[5] Not all are so convinced of the altruism of professions. Hughes talks of 'a group gaining material and symbolic benefits from a monopoly based on a licence to practise', notes that 'they claim to have extraordinary knowledge in matters of great social importance, in return for which they are granted extraordinary rights and privileges', and concludes that 'they misappropriate specialised knowledge in their own interests and in the interest of a power elite intent on preserving its dominance over the rest of society'.[6] Freidson too looks at professions as a form of 'social closure'.[7]

Turner suggests that it is to reconcile these two views that sociologists developed the notion of 'professionalization'.[8] Whether or not a professional group displayed the attributes of 'social altruism, professional competence, social responsibility and service would depend on the extent to which that group was fully professionalized'. Professionalization, in this view, illustrated by Millerson, takes place by the 'accumulation of attributes; whether an occupation is a profession will ... depend on the satisfaction and achievement of a number of traits, including theoretical knowledge as the basis of skill, the development of specialised training and education, the testing of the competence of members by formal examinations, the development of a professional organisation, the emergence of a professional code, and finally the development of an altruistic service'.[9] Turner points out, however, that the 'definitions of the content of these professional roles are based upon the official literature and ideology of the professions as developed by elites within the professional groups' and that this development of attributes is seen as a one-way street, with a particular end view in sight, whereas there are many variations in the 'specific and contingent historical contexts in which professions have developed', and this particular view represents at most one particular set of circumstances.

Taking all these views into account we have a picture of a profession as having a body of knowledge and set of skills that are valued by society, and acquired through a formal educational process, with a test of competence on completion. The asymmetry of skill and knowledge (and hence power) between professional and client leads to a need for some form of regulation of interests, either formally or through altruism, so members are bound by a set of norms and formal rules that they largely enforce themselves. The picture includes the fact that professions themselves (or at least spokespersons on their behalf, and often those involved in their education) lay claim to 'professional' attributes, which generally include service and altruism and an abhorrence of financial self-interest. It is interesting to note that other forms of self-interest are rarely condemned in the same manner as is financial reward, yet we know, from Chapter 1, that people are just as likely to be motivated by recognition, power, status and self-actualization, and it would be possible to imagine any of these skewing the priorities of a professional away from those of the client.

Now that we have some sort of picture of professions, if we are interested in HCPs we need an understanding of health and care.

Defining health and care

Defining health

All HCPs in their training learn to distinguish between a narrow view of health, as the absence of disease or illness, and a more holistic definition.[10] Perhaps the most holistic of all is the well-known WHO statement, first formulated in 1947, that 'health is a state of complete physical, mental and social well-being and not merely the absence of disease and infirmity'. Personally, I feel this means I have yet to meet a healthy person, and the definition strikes me more as aspirational than practically useful. However, we can agree with the philosopher David Seedhouse that 'to regard health and disease as intimately linked, as if on a continuum, so that the more disease a person has, the further away from perfect health he is, is to make a category mistake'.[11] He suggests that health is the 'ability to cope with, adapt to, the problems of life' and that 'any genuine theory of health will be concerned to identify one or more human potentials which might develop, but which are presently or likely to be blocked. Health work, however it is defined, will seek first to discover and then prevent or remove obstacles to the achievement of human potential.' Here, in Seedhouse's words, we have a picture of health as 'foundation for achievement'.

What do we mean by care?

Of the three words forming the term *health care professional*, 'care' is the one least often defined. I believe it is important that we retrieve it from the sentimental, woolly meaning it can so easily and hazily acquire and give it a more hard-edged and useful one.

In his book *The Road Less Travelled* (1978) M. Scott Peck, an American psychiatrist and psychotherapist, provides a definition of love: 'I define love as: the will to extend one's self for the purpose of nurturing one's own or another's spiritual growth.'[12] One of the interesting things about this definition is that it makes reference not to feelings but to intent. Peck goes further and suggests that love (longstanding and 'unselfish' love, which he differentiates from the romantically temporary state of desire – what the ancient Greeks termed *agape* as distinct from *eros*) necessarily involves the lover in work and courage. 'If an act is not one of work or courage then it is not an act of love. There are no exceptions.'[13] This is such a strong statement that out of context you will be tempted to dismiss it. But see if you feel the same after we have worked with it over the next few paragraphs.

If we consider love to be a more intense and narrowly applied form of the concept of care, then we could use similar definitions for the kind of care that as HCPs we owe to our patients, our colleagues and our staff:

Care is the will to extend one's self for the purpose of nurturing another's personal growth.

If an act is not one of work or courage then it is not an act of care. There are no exceptions.

Combining these two statements, we could define care as:

The will to engage in acts of work or courage for the purpose of nurturing another's personal growth.

If we further combine the definitions of health and care, we arrive at one for health care that looks like this:

Acts of work and/or courage undertaken with the intention of enabling the potential of patients.

Most HCPs would not argue with the notion that care[14] involves work. This work includes all the years of study and apprenticeship required to develop the knowledge and skills that HCPs bring to bear with their clients; it encompasses the direct care tasks undertaken by HCPs; but it also includes, for example, the effort required to communicate effectively with other disciplines and the time it takes to ensure that resources are deployed to best effect. But courage? I find that people do not immediately identify this as part of their caring role, yet they can often recognize that this is what is needed whenever there is bad news to tell, when they feel they need to argue for a treatment option they believe to be in the patient's best interest against opposition from other HCPs, when they reflect honestly and openly on their professional practice and, especially, when they realize they have made a mistake and have to decide how to remedy this.

Some HCPs find it difficult to see their role as enabling the potential of patients when they are suffering from degenerative disease or are terminally ill. This often provokes intense debate in a group who are thinking about it. Potential is just the right word here, though, because it looks at what is *possible*, and in this definition HCPs would seek to enable the best of the conditions that are possible for *this* patient. This would include enabling the greatest autonomy for the patient, even if this is diminishing, and providing the maximum level of comfort. It would also include enabling the patient to die as 'well' as is possible.

The role of 'a health care professional'

Now that we have come somewhat closer to understanding the meaning of the terms *health, care, health care* and *profession*, we can think more clearly about the nature of health care professions.

We have seen that a health care profession is a group of people who develop a specialized knowledge basis to tackle problems deemed important by society, who use that knowledge base and associated skills to engage in acts of work and/or courage with the intention of enabling the potential of patients.[15]

We can also see that a health care profession is a group that has some privileges, in return for the investment its members have made for the benefit of society, and that the very knowledge base that is of so great a benefit to us all is a source of power that can be abused. Methods of regulating the use of this power are therefore important, and professions have systems of regulation and registration to do this. However, we can also suggest that there is little agreement on the legitimate attributes of a profession, and that debate about this is, at the moment, left largely to members of professions, yet it is a valid concern to society as a whole. Although this last point has little impact on the way professions interact on a day-to-day basis (the subject of this chapter), it does have clear implications for the role of leaders of health care systems, to which we return in Chapter 7.

Differences in status between professions

One of the key factors in interactions between professions is their status. Members of lower-status groups find it difficult to express their views to those belonging to higher-status groups, and people respond differently to the same information and behaviours coming from individuals of different status.[16] Status pervades interactions in health care.[17] We all know that some professions have higher status than others. (Remember we are talking about status, a regard accorded by society, and not moral worth or likeability, with which, of course, there is no correlation.) Indeed, we recognize that, within a profession, different branches are accorded different status. Donald Schön, for example, observes that in any profession there is a gradation of status down from the academic researcher, to the specialist practitioner applying that research knowledge, to the generalist practitioner using a range of research knowledge bases but wearing them more lightly. So we can describe how status manifests itself, but when it comes to specifying exactly what it is that leads to these status differentials we find it more difficult to agree.

When I ask workshop participants what determines the status in which a profession is held, the answers typically start with power, money and gender.

Yet if we think carefully about these we can suppose that these are the results of the status of a profession, rather than the causes, although of course once a status has been established it can be further nurtured by the manifestation of power, wealth or the gender balance. Another popular suggestion is about the 'importance' of the decisions made by the professions in our daily lives. Hence the medical profession is deemed critically important by us because it often involves matters of life and death, and the legal profession is important because it involves decisions about the redress of wrongdoing, ownership of property and other types of rights. However, people also feel that decisions about whether you can be trusted to bring up your own children are important – yet few place statutory child protection work on a par with law and medicine. Longevity of the profession is sometimes mooted, but again clergy do not fare well in the status stakes compared to, say, accountants (a much more recent profession). Scarcity is proffered as another factor, and initially appeals until we remember that there are far fewer speech and language therapists than doctors – so it is not the scarcity itself but perhaps something to do with its causes that is relevant. It becomes apparent that although we recognize status differentials we don't yet fully understand the reasons for them.

Which literatures might we turn to for enlightenment here? Economics and sociology again make some claims. Economists might argue that the division of labour moves through the following stages:

1 The use of individual skills and talents.
2 The development of specialized trades.
3 The subdivision of those trades into specialized aspects.
4 The further subdivision of these aspects into processes.
5 The mechanization and automation of processes.
6 The computerized control of automatic processes.

They would further argue that the status of a group is highest during stages 3 and 4. Thus, the argument goes, any profession is somewhere on this pathway and its status will depend to some extent on how far along it is. This never feels, to the people I work with, like the whole answer, but it does raise an important point that we will return to shortly.

Economists also point to 'barriers to entry' as significant. They suggest that the more difficult it is to acquire the skills of a profession (because the entry criteria are high, and/or the length of training is long), fewer people will undertake it and the resulting scarcity attracts status. This begins to feel more satisfying as an explanation (although it may again be more of a description[18]) but it doesn't account for the differences in status between people of similarly long training programmes and identical entry criteria.

We saw earlier that some sociologists refer to processes of professionalization, suggesting that professions acquire more and more professional attributes on their journey towards being fully professional. Status, they suggest, attaches to the degree to which a group is professionalized, and we might suppose that the longer a profession has been in existence the more opportunities it will have had to acquire these attributes and the higher status it will have. This is often intuitively appealing, in that many of the higher-status professions are also the older ones. But there are problems with this argument too.

The sociologists Hall and Oppenheimer[19] have 'suggested that in contemporary society there is a definite and widespread process of de-professionalization', and that there are three distinct processes through which this takes place. The growth of bureaucracy is one, in which 'professionals working in bureaucratic settings often find their autonomy undermined by the hierarchical structure of rules and authority'. Fragmentation into distinctive and separate groupings as a result of the development of knowledge is another. And the third is the 'pressure from new professionals and para-professionals to take over and encroach upon the domain of the most prestigious and established professions'.

Furthermore, according to Hall and Oppenheimer, professions working within bureaucracies are subject to the process of 'proletarianization', involving the following features:

1   An extensive division of labour in which the worker performs a limited number of tasks.
2   The conditions of work, the nature of the workplace and the character of the work processes are set and determined by a higher authority, rather than by the worker.
3   The wage is the primary source of income and this is determined by the market place rather than by individual negotiation.
4   The worker, in order to protect himself or herself from the transformation of their work, has to form some association or union to bargain collectively for improvements.

We can see that time gives opportunities for both professionalization and deprofessionalization and thus that the age of a profession is no predictor of status.

Two other sociologists, Jamous and Peloille, have suggested that 'the relationship between the patient and the client can be discussed in terms of an "indeterminacy/technicality ratio" '.[20] This is perhaps a confusing term, because apart from anything else it is not a ratio. However, it describes an idea that I think is helpful. It suggests that the nature of the knowledge base held by the professional is an important factor in their status. The 'harder', more definitive, more 'technical', it is, then the higher the status is likely to be. So if a profession can give definitive answers ('yes', 'no', '2.59 per cent') it is likely to have a higher status than one whose vocabulary relies on phrases such as 'it depends', 'in this context', 'let's wait and see'.

However, if a knowledge base is totally technical then it is possible for it to be codified into processes that can automated and mechanized (as described above by the economists), and hence carried out by a machine, as happened when cottage weavers were replaced by mechanical spinning machines during the Industrial Revolution. You might like, in this context, to reflect on the way in which the delivery of pathology services has changed in recent decades in the light of advances of technology. So if a profession is to retain a high status there must also be a strong element of indeterminacy: the knowledge base must be interpreted and applied differently in different cases. The highest-status professions will therefore have a definitive knowledge base and this interpretative ability. Neither alone is enough.

Now I am not suggesting that this is a definitive answer to the question of status differentials in professions across the board, especially when we look outside health care. Jamous and Peloille themselves were focusing on health care professions. But it seems to me, and often to the people I work with, that this does enable us to predict and understand some important dynamics between professional groups, and also to challenge the thinking of some of the professions attempting to raise their status.[21] I think this will become more apparent as we work on through this chapter.

It may also help us to understand the reactions of professions to initiatives of certain kinds. If we do try to deprofessionalize or proletarianize a professional group, by reducing the amount of interpretation we allow them when applying their expertise (by introducing strict protocols, perhaps) or by paying them on a piecework basis, then we can expect a reaction that may well include the withdrawal of other professional attributes, such as altruism.

So, while decisions of this kind may be desirable, as the needs of society change, they need to be taken with great care, and with some thought as to whether there are ways of achieving similar results in ways that do not jeopardize the good will of professionals.

Other ways of thinking about the dynamics within and between professions

Status certainly affects the way professions engage with each other, but there are other ways of visualizing the dynamics between professions and in this section we look at a few of them.

The hierarchy of clinical descriptions

Let us consider how clinical conditions are described. An individual may feel tired and thirsty; his family may experience this as 'Dad's always too tired to play football'; his doctor having performed a urine test will talk of blood sugar levels and diagnose diabetes. We already have three different ways of describing one clinical condition. We can expand this further, to a hierarchy of descriptions in which each lower tier is at the next level of detail:

> level +2 patient's community
> level +1 patient's family
> level 0 patient as a whole
> level –1 major body part (e.g. chest, abdomen, head)
> level –2 physiological system (e.g. cardiovascular system, respiratory system)
> level –3 system part or organ (e.g. heart, major vessels, lungs)
> level –4 organ part or tissue (e.g. myocardium, bone marrow)
> level –5 cell (e.g. epithelial cell, fibroblast, lymphocyte)
> level –6 cell part (e.g. cell membrane, organelles, nucleus)
> level –7 macromolecule (e.g. enzyme, structural protein, nucleic acid)
> level –8 micromolecule (e.g. glucose, ascorbic acid)
> level –9 atoms or ions (e.g. sodium ion)

In this 'hierarchy of natural descriptions', entities (or 'nominals') at one level combine together to form an entity at the next level up. So the nominals at one level become attributes at the next. However, they are not the only attributes at the higher level, as others emerge with the combination. This is an aspect of 'systems thinking', a means of identifying order in complex systems that was developed not only by biologists but by engineers and a number of other scientific disciplines in the 1930s and 1940s. The 'knowledge network' in Table 2.1 expresses the hierarchy of information statements, where the nominals are to the left and the attributes to the right of the // sign. The emergent attributes have been distinguished from the attributes that are simply the nominals from the next lower level in the hierarchy, by putting them in *italics*.[22]

The early systems thinkers identified a number of features that pertain to hierarchies of this kind.

- First, we can focus our attention on only one level (and those immediately above and below it) at a time. You may reject this as a proposition, knowing that you can consider all the different levels. However, their observation was that while we can track between the different levels, and experience of a particular hierarchy increases the

Table 2.1 Levels and structures of systems

Level	Structures
+2	tribe//family . . . *social rules* . . .
+1	family//father, mother, children . . . *customs* . . .
0	human//animal . . . *highly developed consciousness, complex language, complex tools* . . .
−1	animal//skeleton, organ . . . muscle . . . *integument* . . . *complex behaviour* . . .
−2	organ/tissue//cell, cell . . . *connective tissue* . . .
−3	cell//nucleus, organelle . . . *reproduction* . . .
−4	organelle//membrane . . . *ordered chemical synthesis* . . . *compartmentation* . . .
−5	membrane//structural protein, enzyme, *lipid layers* . . . *permeability* . . . *enzyme arrangement* . . .
−6	protein//tyrosine, alanine, . . . *tertiary structure* . . .
−7	amino acid//H atom, O atom . . . *vibrational states* . . . *covalent bonds* . . .
−8	H atom//proton, electron, *excited states* . . .
−9	proton//mass, charge, magnetic moment . . . quarks, elementary particles

speed at which we can do this, at any one moment our attention is fixed on one part of the hierarchy. So we are able to trace the path from hydrogen atoms to a cabinet reshuffle, from the effect of medication on blood electrolytes to the relief of a patient's discomfort, but we are only focusing on one level at a time. This feature is what allows someone to say, for example, that 'There is no such thing as society, there are individual men and women, and there are families.' The anger evoked when Margaret Thatcher expressed these sentiments arose from a belief, on the part of others, that important attributes emerge when individuals are combined into society.

- Second, as we ascend the levels, individuality increases and uniformity decreases. One electron looks very much like any other electron and is readily distinguished from a neutron or proton. However, classifying both a Chihuahua and a Great Dane as dogs and distinguishing between the class of dogs and that of foxes is much less straightforward. At the higher levels classes and terms are more ambiguous, more fuzzy, and open to different interpretations.
- Third, at each level we need a different level of language. If we use a lower-level language at a higher level, it is overdescriptive and tedious without adding anything. Describing the heart in terms of all of its constituent cells takes a long time and is not necessary. Conversely,

the use of a higher level language at a lower level results in confusion or nonsense because it is too rich; it tries to ascribe attributes that do not emerge until higher levels to lower level items (e.g. colour has no meaning at the molecular level; neither does sentience at the level of cells or of organs).

- Fourth, numbers are often useful at lower levels (blood electrolyte levels, for example). They enable expression of a degree of abnormality and a measure of whether things are getting better or worse. At higher levels, quantification is more difficult. Where high level descriptions are converted to numbers (e.g. activities for daily living scores), they should be used with great care, since they are attempting to represent a rich, ambiguous, fuzzy, multifaceted reality. Just as words need to be used differently at different levels, so do numbers. We cannot manipulate numbers referring to high levels in the same way as those at lower levels.

While the four features described above relate to all hierarchies of this kind, there are also a number that relate specifically to health care. To avoid confusion I continue the numbering.

- Fifth, different professions tend to have expertise at different levels; indeed, many of the health care professions emerged as knowledge of the different layers developed. For example, although there are exceptions, typically psychologists and occupational therapists will focus on levels 0, +1 and +2 and general nurses (say, working in intensive care) on levels −1, −2 and −3. Within professions, different disciplines also focus on different levels, so although the medical profession as a whole includes those with expertise at levels −1 to −9 (and the length of the medical training results from this), hospital-based consultants in many specialties concentrate on levels lower than their colleagues in general practice.
- Sixth, no level is right or wrong, or better or worse than any other level. Defining a problem completely involves consideration of all the levels affected. In a multidisciplinary situation, the 'clout' is often held by those operating at the lowest levels (they have higher status, because, as we have seen, this is where the knowledge base is most definitive, and because the length of training required by people operating at this level is longer), but each level requires expert consideration in its own right. Interestingly, where no lower level malfunctions have been identified (for example, in many mental health problems), the dynamics between the various professions involved are different. It will be interesting to see whether these relationships change if research correlates certain neuroendocrine pictures with

particular mental health diagnoses and starts to identify the mechanisms linking the intervening levels.

- Seventh, we do not need to understand everything about every level to be able to understand explanations of the links between them.
- Eighth, patients sometimes hold invented hierarchies that differ from those understood by their clinicians. These are rarely explored,[23] but they impede insight into the patient's condition, compliance and satisfaction with outcomes.

There are a number of implications that arise from this hierarchy and its properties.

First, if health care organizations are concerned with health (rather than only illness), then they have to address between them all of these levels. But individual HCPs can focus on only one level at a time and our organizational systems should not expect them to do otherwise. Somehow our systems need to encourage HCPs to fight a valiant battle at electrolyte level where appropriate, while still providing for the needs of patients as sociable humans and family members. These needs include dignity and meaning, and thus, at a particular time, the need for 'a good death'. This is one of the most significant challenges to health care organizations and we consider it again in Chapter 7.

Second, HCPs will naturally find communication problematic, since they use different levels of language. We need not berate each other for that, but we may need to ensure that interpretation is available. We must also recognize our interdependence and the virtue of patients receiving specialist expertise, rather than amateur intervention, for each of the levels that is malfunctioning. This will be easier if those concerned remember that it is not necessary to understand everything about every level to be able to follow explanations that track from lower to higher levels. Greater exploitation of such 'tracking' would enable multidisciplinary teams to work effectively, with each member being aware of the reasoning behind an opinion. If the team then gave the responsibility for taking decisions where there are conflicting opinions to the professional most skilled at the level manifesting the greatest problems, then we might move towards a system in which multidisciplinary teams are truly teams. Clarifying the familiarity required with each of the hierarchical levels also enables decisions to be made about how best to staff a service, which professions will be most able to contribute and what knowledge bases are necessary.

It is sometimes not realized that it is the hierarchical levels of which professions have knowledge that determine the uses to which they put their skills. These skills, particularly of those individuals intervening at higher levels, may appear nonsensically disparate to an outsider. An occupational therapist in mental health may appear to be very different from an occupational therapist working with young, physically disabled clients. However, they both share a core knowledge base and reasoning process, and this fact needs to be appreciated when decisions on skills mix are taken.

Third, if it is only at the lower levels that we can be definitive, then we need different research methods at lower and higher levels. The researcher's 'gold standard' of the randomized controlled trial, preferably double-blind – better still, double-blind and crossover – requires that the control group is matched precisely (i.e. that all the features of the entities in those groups are matched, leaving as the only variable the subject of the study). However, as we ascend the hierarchy, it becomes more and more difficult to match perfectly because of the increasing complexity and ambiguity. Whereas at lower levels we can ask a question and get a definitive answer ('yes' or 'no', or in 'x per cent of cases . . .'), at higher levels, unless very large sample sizes are used, the answers have to be qualified ('In *these* circumstances this is what we found'; 'If your circumstances are similar, then you may find the same'). Higher levels, then, are illuminated by qualitative research, research that rarely yields definitive answers applicable in all settings, but qualified answers conditional on context. That applying the wrong research method is dangerous is summed neatly in the phrase 'to even the most complicated of problems there is one simple, easy-to-understand, wrong answer'.

Qualitative research may be conducted as rigorously, independently and objectively as good quantitative research, or it too may suffer from poor design and execution. In the first edition of this book I wrote that:

> The fact that the results of even excellent qualitative research are qualified, as we have shown, can lead to it being written off as woolly and inferior by, in particular, the medical profession. This is unfortunate for two reasons: first, doctors' behaviours and judgements are not informed by such research and, second, the quality of the design and execution of such research is not subjected to the rigorous criticism at which the profession excels. This allows too much sloppy qualitative research (quasi-journalism in some cases) to be undertaken and disseminated.

I recognize that there has been much progress since then in the way qualitative research is viewed and used in health care – but there is still talk of the hierarchy of research evidence, with the randomized controlled trial at the top, when in many situations, especially in the field of health care management, this type of model and approach will not be the most appropriate or helpful. So I suggest that there is still some danger of us being wedded to one particular type of research 'paradigm' here (see also the next section).

The other aspect of the fact that we can be more definitive at lower levels than at higher ones relates back to what we have considered about status. We explored the idea that the more definitive the knowledge base a profession works with, the higher status it is able to have (as long as there is a large degree of interpretation that is needed to apply it to a particular case). If we combine these two ideas we can suggest that professions working at the lower levels of this hierarchy (or at least including those lower levels in their clinical gaze) will tend to hold higher status than those working at higher levels. We can also suppose that groups who expand their knowledge into lower levels will increase their status. You might like to reflect on the role of clinical nurse specialists in this regard.

The corollary to this is that status is unlikely to be added by enlarging a role with the addition of activities at the same level in the hierarchy, regardless of which professional group may have undertaken them before. For this reason nursing, for example, is unlikely to increase its status by taking over from junior doctors' tasks at the higher levels in the hierarchy. There may be (and are) many good reasons for nurses to consider doing so, but this should not be one of them.

The spectrum of views of disease

Just as different professions, or professionals in different care settings, concentrate on different levels of the hierarchy, so too do they gravitate towards different points on a spectrum of views of disease. Traditionally, there have been two contrasting views of disease, each with a long and influential history.[24] The first is that a disease is an isolatable entity having a life of its own; in other words, a disease is regarded as something that is pretty much the same whether it is experienced by one patient or another. This is the ontologic view and has been used for millennia; for example, Plato describes disease in this way. We adopt this view whenever we talk of the 'course of a disease', or when we describe a disease entirely in terms of its attributes and without any reference to patients. The second is that a disease is the change seen in a patient when not in good health. Here the sick patient is the focus of attention. This has been called the 'biographical' view of disease and can be recognized in the work of Hippocrates, famous for his highly detailed case histories. Over the centuries, both views have held sway. However, as we have come to understand more and more about humans and the diseases we experience, we recognize that neither view alone is satisfactory in all circumstances.

In practice, there is a spectrum of views of disease, with a few individuals operating at each end, but most HCPs somewhere between:

Ontologic view of disease	Biographical view of disease
Health economists and epidemiologists	Psychotherapists

The position of an HCP on the spectrum tends to depend on how well defined the disease is and on how well they know the individual patient. A general practitioner, for example, will operate further towards the biographical end of the spectrum than a hospital specialist. Similarly, doctors will tend to view patients more ontologically than nurses.

In ensuring that patients receive the most appropriate care, we cannot say that one end of the spectrum is right and the other wrong; we will need attention to both. However, there is potential for strife, when professionals involved with the same patient have different concerns and feel that those concerns are not being addressed by others.

Degree of structure in the clinical problem

There is a another cause of disharmony between different disciplines within professions, which arises out of the degree of structure inherent in the clinical problem with which they are presented. Blois represents this as a funnel (see Figure 2.2).[25]

When a patient first meets the clinician, the latter needs the maximum cognitive span, since the patient's concerns could turn out to be anything or nothing, one of thousands of diseases or none at all. The process that follows (of conversation, history-taking, physical examination, perhaps lab tests or special examinations, differential diagnosis) introduces more and more structure into the problem. At point A, the problem could be anything; at point B, the possibilities have been progressively reduced and the alternatives are now few.

People working at different parts of the funnel can sometimes undervalue each other's skills, yet the expertise required to funnel down from point A to point B is no less, just different from that required to offer specialist assessment

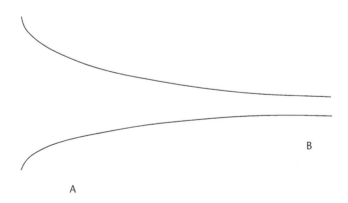

B

A

Figure 2.2 Breadth of cognitive span required of a clinician during a patient encounter.

and management once point B has been reached. The reverse is also true. Many of the communication problems that arise between primary and secondary or tertiary care workers appear to have at their root an undervaluing of the skills of the professionals on the other side of the boundary. Recognizing that different roles require different skills, rather than greater or less skill, is essential if 'seamless care' is ever to become more than just a slogan.

Causes of misunderstanding between professionals

The factors we have been looking at so far in this chapter are inherent results of the nature of health care needs and the ways that have evolved to meet them. However, there are other factors, more to do with the cultures of the professions, that also foster misunderstandings when they try to interact. These are where we turn our attention now.

Sets of ethical principles

What principles do you turn to when you decide whether a particular action is right or wrong? Philosophers have argued about these for millennia and students of ethics can describe a range of different approaches to answering the question. Most of us, however, have absorbed our ideas about ethical behaviour without being aware of any principles underpinning them, and in our professional lives much of that absorption happened early on in our professional education, as part of the 'tacit knowledge' that, Polanyi argues, is part of the paradigm or framework within which we operate.[26] That paradigm is invisible to us, because it is the way we structure our thinking, and not something we can easily bring into what Polanyi calls 'focal awareness' while we are actually in the process of using it. As Thomas Kuhn observes, 'scientists . . . never learn concepts, laws and theories in the abstract. Instead they gradually learn to think like their teachers.'[27]

Different sets of principles will lead us to different conclusions about the degree of right or wrong of a particular course of action, so if our set leads us to reason one way, while that of someone else produces a different rationale, and we have not been aware they were approaching this from a valid but alternative direction, we may be incensed and uncomprehending. It is helpful, therefore, to be aware of these alternatives and thus able to recognize not only our own beliefs but those of others.

One way of thinking about ethical theories is to divide them into three schools: utilitarian, deontological and virtue ethics. At its simplest, utilitarians are concerned with the consequences of an action. In making a choice, a utilitarian will decide between two courses of action based on which leads to the greatest good for the greatest number of people. If that requires the telling of a lie, or even killing one person to save twenty others, then that course of action can be justified. Deontologists, however, will find some actions unethical no matter what the consequences, because they believe that there are some rules (for example: do not lie, do not kill) that need to be followed in all circumstances. What these rules are depends: some believe they are those given by a deity, others that there are 'categorical imperatives' that can be derived from philosophical thought, others that they can be found in biological evolution. They will, however, be dear to the person concerned. Virtue ethicists suggest that an action is morally justified if it is the action that a virtuous person would take in those circumstances. Thus a person who possesses the virtue of honesty will not tell a lie, will challenge anyone who is dissembling, will make sure people involved have access to all relevant information and so on. The virtues, like the rules of the deontologists, may be described differently by different people. Aristotle's list, for example, focused on those character traits that a human being needs in order to flourish. However, virtuous people (and of course no fully virtuous person exists) are also painfully aware of the fact that in some moral dilemmas there are no 'right' actions, that even if one course can be preferred to another it may still cause harm, and thus even doing the right thing may cause the agent to feel wretched.

Consider the following. If a deontologist who believes they must never lie is discussing what information should be given to a terminally ill patient, they may well become furious with a utilitarian who is only concerned with what will lead to the best outcome. They may also become frustrated with the virtue ethicist who is agonizing over the choice. They could be seen as talking on different wavelengths, not in any way addressing the concerns and priorities that the others have, talking past each other, failing to comprehend each other's frameworks of reason. Trying to become aware of the underlying beliefs of all concerned will enable you to understand the logic and the emotional responses of others.

Group-think

There is a tendency in any group in which members share norms, values and deeply held beliefs to engage in a phenomenon known as 'group-think'. This was first described by a psychologist, Janis, who observed the behaviour in groups in which some disastrous decisions had been made by very able and well-intentioned individuals.[28] In particular, he looked at the ways in which the US Administration took decisions in relation to the Cuban missile crisis and the escalation of the Vietnam War. He noted the following characteristics:

- Group members are intensely loyal to the group and to its policies, even if some of the consequences of the policies disturb the conscience of each member.

- Members do not criticize the reasoning or behaviour of fellow members. In Janis's words, the group is 'soft-headed'. This is because members believe unquestioningly in the inherent morality of their in-group.
- Members are, however, 'hard-hearted' when it comes to members of out-groups. They hold negative, stereotyped views of these out-groups and their leaders.
- Individual members doubt and suppress their own reasoning when it conflicts with the thinking of the group.
- If a member does question the validity of arguments expressed, then other group members apply direct, albeit subtle, pressure to conform. Most censorship, however, is self-enacted.

As you can see (by thinking for a moment about your own reaction to members of other disciplines), very many of these behaviours are exhibited within the health care professions and their subspecialties.

Janis makes some recommendations to help to avoid the development (or worst excesses) of group-think, including:

1   Group leaders must validate the importance of critical evaluation of all views.
2   Leaders should require each member to discuss group deliberations with associates in other groups.
3   The group should invite outside experts to challenge the views of core members.
4   Members should be encouraged to play devil's advocate.
5   Whenever the group's deliberations involve relations with a rival organization, they should devote time to finding out as much as possible about their rivals and consider alternative ways of interpreting what the group perceives to be hostile actions.

Imagine, for example, a busy general medical practice in an inner city in England, with perhaps four GP partners, two salaried GP registrars, three practice nurses, a practice manager, three receptionists and a secretary. If the practice were in the grip of group-think then the team would feel very supportive and friendly. Anyone working within it would speak well of the team, would say that the friendliness of the practice is one of the things they most enjoy about working there and would see their practice as better than many others in this regard. They would ascribe all their problems (and there would be a fair few) to others outside the team – perhaps the PCT,[29] other practices, a few demanding patients, the government (for raising expectations and not providing enough money). So if you were considering whether you would enjoy working there you might well think that you liked the sound of the team but not the awful

PCT it was working in. At least in the practice, you might think, professionals are pulling together and working to a common purpose. Cosy, friendly, victims of incompetent or wicked people outside. Would you choose to work there? Perhaps.

Suppose the alternative is a practice where the members can be sharp with each other sometimes, where they challenge each other's views and practices and do not have nearly such a friendly feel about them. But they work effectively with their colleagues in other parts of the system, judging people on their merits rather than assuming them to be difficult or grasping, acknowledging the role of the PCT as necessary and finding ways of working with people there. All in all this team will see themselves as in charge of their own destiny rather than at the mercy of others, but it won't be cosy, and anyone joining it could expect to find it challenging. Which would you choose? Difficult to say, perhaps, because groups in the grip of group-think look so attractive, so friendly, but they aren't groups that are making good decisions, they are not groups that are working effectively and making the greatest contribution.

Ethical syndromes

At the risk of confusing you, I am going to introduce the word 'ethical' a second time, but in relation to a rather different concept. It is one that I personally find explains some dynamics and behaviours it would be difficult to explain otherwise, but I notice that other people are divided about its value. Some find it actively unhelpful and are suspicious of what they perceive as its political intent. I offer it to you, rather than insist on it.

The North American anthropologist Jane Jacobs suggests that we are short of a guide to ethics in the workplace. She points out that most work on ethics refers to the ethics of government, or the ethics of individual lives, and that there has been little attention to the ethics of working life. She observes that it is ethically possible to defend both honesty and loyalty, for example, but that often in the workplace they conflict and we must choose between them. In that case, how should we do so?

Her researches across nations and time periods suggest to her that there is a certain set of behaviours that is universally acclaimed. So wherever and whenever people have behaved with responsibility, cooperation, courage, moderation, mercy, common sense, foresight, judgement, competence, perseverance, energy, patience or wisdom, these behaviours have been valued.

However, there are other behaviours that are sometimes applauded and at other times lambasted. For example, if a shop assistant notices that shoppers are not buying a product because they don't like the colour then she will be praised for bringing this to the attention of the buyer or designer. Here honesty is seen as valuable, more valuable than any loyalty to the designer that might have prevented her from criticizing their work. But a soldier criticizing an order from an officer, even if he believed an alternative would be better, may find his honesty appreciated less than his obedience to his orders.

Jacobs observes that there are two distinct 'syndromes', two groups of behaviours, and calls these the 'guardian syndrome' and the 'commercial syndrome'. These syndromes arise out of the two ways, as humans, we have of surviving: one is that shared with other animals, of owning a territory and husbanding the produce of that territory; and the other is to trade with other people. However, these terms have a different set of values associated with them on different sides of the Atlantic, so I use the alternatives 'trading or innovative' and 'administrative or regulatory'. The behaviours within these syndromes are listed in Table 2.2.

Jacobs points out that in society we need both of these syndromes. Without the framework of law developed and enforced by 'regulators', 'innovators' would not be able to enforce contracts, reap the rewards of investment, and so on. Without the 'innovating traders' there is insufficient resource to fund the 'regulators' and a shortage of new ideas and inventions. She suggests, though, that the syndromes must be kept pure and not be corrupted by interspersing some attributes of one with those of the other. She cites the Mafia and the Nazi concentration camps as examples of the 'monstrous hybrids' that result if the separation is not maintained. She describes the two ways that societies have developed over the millennia to keep these separate: one is to have a caste system, which she does not defend, with the regulators ruling over the innovating trading system; and the other is to move with awareness from one syndrome to the other, depending on the kind of decision that is being made or the task undertaken. Jacobs further observes that as individuals and in groups we tend to have a 'cast of mind' that favours one of these syndromes, often seeing the other as reprehensible.

How is this relevant to working with other people in health care? Even after as brief an overview as the above, I suggest that there are four aspects of relevance.

One is that many of us in health care have a cast of mind (either regulatory or innovative) of which we are unaware, and we would be more effective if we were able to identify that and begin to value behaviours belonging to the other syndrome when those are appropriate. Another is that when we are deciding on our own behaviours we could usefully reflect on the role we are playing to make sure we are adopting the most constructive. A third is that when we design systems or organizations we avoid the development of 'monstrous hybrids'. And, finally, identifying casts of mind will enable us again to diagnose the causes of conflict, both between some individuals and within and between professional groups.

Do we really need to be able to move between the two syndromes? If we look at the lists of behaviours, I want to be sure that any HCP I consult as a patient is working very largely in the innovative syndrome. I want them to be

Table 2.2 Ethical syndromes

Commericial (Innovative) syndrome	Guardian (Regulatory) syndrome
Shun force: abhor the use of coercion to influence events	Shun trading: see anything to do with making money in a negative light
Come to *voluntary* agreements	Exert prowess
Be honest	Be loyal
Collaborate easily with strangers	Be exclusive, talk in terms of 'them'
Compete	Adhere to tradition, using methods that have been demonstrated to work
Respect contracts, these are what confer rights and responsibilities	Respect hierarchy: this is what determines rights and responsibilities
Use initiative and enterprise	Dispense largesse, rights or titles, or property
Be open to inventiveness and innovation	Be obedient and disciplined
Be efficient	Take revenge
Promote comfort and convenience, including good use of new technologies. Do not put up with things you don't like if you don't have to	Show fortitude and stoicism, put up with things and do not complain
Dissent for the sake of the task	Deceive for the sake of the task
Invest for productive purposes	Make rich use of leisure
Be industrious, invest now for productive purposes and reap the rewards later	Make rich use of leisure, taking pride in skills in these areas
Be thrifty	Be ostentatious, this is what conveys respect for authority
Be optimistic: believe something can be done to improve the future	Be fatalistic: believe that you cannot influence events. Guardian roles often involve personal risk and this allows individuals to say, e.g. 'If the bullet has my name on it', 'If I lose my seat at the next election', 'There's nothing I can do to cheat fate', without this becoming a disempowering thought
	Treasure honour and face, prefer to guard reputation over anything else

honest with me, to be enterprising and industrious, and not to be fatalistic about my prognosis.[30] At the same time, when those same HCPs are working together as members of a professional executive committee (PEC),[31] for example, making decisions about where to invest and disinvest resources, although they may argue until they are blue in the face until the decision is reached, I expect them to operate 'cabinet responsibility' once the decision had been made. In other words, to be loyal to each other and to the decision reached, by explaining and defending the decision, because no good purpose would come of doing the opposite. These are regulatory syndrome behaviours, suitable for a role that involves designing the framework for an organization. So the same individuals need to adopt different syndromes in different roles and situations. Yet some individuals find it very difficult to take on different ways of working depending on role and context – perhaps because no one has suggested the benefits of doing so, but also perhaps because they are operating from a cast of mind that can conceive of no other.

It is noticeable that many of the professional bodies in health care inhabit beautiful buildings, well endowed with paintings and beautiful artefacts, with gold-leafed lists of past presidents on the walls. This ostentation is reassuring, conveying history, longevity, a sense of the profession's place in the world. This is part of the regulatory syndrome. And professional bodies often need to be regulators, guardians of the processes of developing and regulating their members. But there can be a danger that the regulator cast of mind, with its stoicism and fatalism and lack of concern for convenience, may be adopted by longer-standing members of the profession, so that they behave in this way out in the workplace where the innovative syndrome is more suitable. It may also mean that professional bodies are not willing to consider new ways of working, of doing things within the profession, and not able to inform and support their members who are grappling with new initiatives and opportunities out in the field.[32]

Conversational rituals

Let us look now at the work of another North American researcher, Deborah Tannen. Tannen has worked for many years on styles of conversation and her research and that of others on whom she draws suggests that, in the US private sector setting with which she is familiar, there are two sets of conversational rituals, one associated with men and the other with women. This is also the theme of John Gray's best-selling book *Men Are from Mars and Women Are from Venus* (1992). Translating this research to the public sector in Europe requires us to take care, and personally I do not believe that in this setting these rituals can be attached to gender in this way. However, her suggestion that there are two distinct rituals and that they can cause major problems of communication is worth considering. For the moment I will continue to use the designation men and women to describe the two rituals, because I think it is possibly true that there are more women who adopt the 'female' ritual than adopt the 'male' and vice versa, so it can be helpful in picturing the behaviours, but it is important you remember the caveat above.

Tannen observes that rituals common among men include a spirit of opposition, including banter, joking and playful put-downs, and wherever possible avoiding being seen to lose (what she calls the 'one-down position'). Women, she notes, do not jockey for position in the same way and if they are superior in status to the person they are conversing with will seek to maintain an appearance of equality with them and downplay their own authority.

More specifically, the 'male' ritual involves not asking questions (finding out the answers in ways that do not make it evident that the person did not know), expressing confidence in their abilities, being direct and straight-forward, even where the news being given is bad, and expressing views more strongly than they may feel them (in the expectation that the other person will do the same and that a good verbal tussle will lead to a better answer than either singly). They will tend to believe they are being helpful by critiquing a piece of work, and if someone describes to them a problem they will attempt to solve it. They say sorry only if they are taking responsibility for something they personally have done, and express gratitude and thanks only if they are genuinely grateful.

The 'female' ritual is very different. Women, Tannen suggests, see asking questions as a sign of strength, not of weakness. They express less confidence about their abilities than they feel, and when they say they are sorry we do not know whether they are apologizing for something they have done or are lamenting a situation someone else is in ('I'm so sorry you've broken your leg'). Similarly, they thank routinely, whether they are particularly grateful or not (for example, when buying a bus ticket), and will aim to correct someone's performance by complimenting the better aspects of it, rather than critiquing the negative. They will express things indirectly, rather than directly, and if they talk of problems they are experiencing they are not wanting them to be resolved but are inviting a reciprocal offload about the problems of the person they are meeting. They will also express views more hesitantly than they feel them, expecting the other person to offer similarly tentative views that can be explored to reach a better result than either singly.

Tannen at no point takes sides. She does not place a higher value on one ritual than another, but records the kinds of problems that occur when people from one ritual try to communicate with those from the other. These problems include people not receiving good references because they were deemed not competent enough after they asked a lot of questions, women feeling their views are being overridden when men express theirs more vehemently and even aeroplanes crashing because of people using direct and indirect styles failing to understand each other. Her message is: diagnose the ritual of the people you need to communicate with and adjust your own style so that they can hear what you are saying.

I am sure we cannot link these rituals to men and women in this way, especially perhaps in our public sector (picture Margaret Thatcher and Prince

Charles, for example), but the principle that there are two rituals, and that there will be problems communicating with people using the other one, is, I suggest, worth testing out in your own experience. Why have I put it in this chapter and not in Chapter 6 ('Really managing yourself')? Because I wonder whether some professional groups tend towards the 'male' ritual and others the 'female'. We might suppose that professions with a more definitive knowledge base may adopt a more direct way of conveying information than those with a more contingent outlook. I think if I were about to interview a consultant surgeon I might rehearse my questions and arguments to ensure I could express them succinctly and confidently, whereas with community nurses I might make sure I was not inhibiting their input by doing just that.

Working effectively with other professions

At the beginning of this chapter we looked at the necessity of working effectively with other professions, the importance of taking responsibility across professional boundaries, and we have seen since why that can often be so difficult. Now we need to think about what we, ourselves, can do to work more effectively with other groups, and also how we can encourage others to do so.

Let's consider for a moment how we arrive at our feelings for other people. People are so complex that we can find characteristics in everyone that we can like, respect or admire. We may choose to concentrate on those characteristics when we call an individual to mind, and naturally we do that for our friends or colleagues with whom we have rapport. With others, however, we tend to do the opposite and choose to dwell on characteristics we dislike, particularly if they are in any way a threat to us. The fact that we can, to a large extent, choose how we feel about another person can be of great assistance as we go about our professional duties, interacting with a large number of other people and disciplines. If we choose to see the best in our professional colleagues, and to respond generously instead of jealously to their proposals, then our working lives become not only more enjoyable and less stressful but also more productive and fruitful. Extending good will to others in this way is what enables us to develop the open, honest, trusting relationships that are both satisfying and synergistic.

If we are going to choose how we feel about someone, we first have to become aware of just how we respond to them naturally, or automatically, before choice steps in. We need to become aware of our instinctive reactions so that we are able to analyse them: 'When that suggestion was made, how did I feel? Why did I feel that way?' Using material from this chapter and Chapter 1 we are well placed to analyse any feelings of discomfort, fear or anger that we notice.

You may find you are responding negatively to some of the ways the other person is behaving. They may be expressing concern about things of little interest to you, because their motivation profile is different. They may have dropped in to see you when you would have preferred them to make an appointment, or vice versa. Recognizing that these are just differences, and not fundamentally right or wrong, virtuous or wicked, will help you to reduce your irritation, and consider ways in which you can stop irritating *others*.

You may find you are angry because they are not caring – there are acts of work or of courage they could be undertaking and are not, and you are concerned about how their performance is preventing your own interventions from being effective. Or they may have more limited aspirations for the patient than you do (or vice versa). You may wonder if they are, implicitly, using a different set of ethical principles, or notice that they are behaving loyally when you think honesty would be more appropriate, or that they aren't hearing what you say to them because they are using the other conversational ritual. Becoming aware of the reasons for your feelings will help you to decide on the argument you want to make and the best way to make it.

You may also wonder if they are responding badly to your views because you are outside their cosy group and they are being hard-hearted as well as soft- headed. This will be more difficult for you to tackle, but at least you will know how to try – to drop your challenge to their thinking until you have convinced them of your motives and your friendly respect for the group.

You may feel anxious about discussing things with them because they belong to a higher-status group than you do, and you may feel that this is a harder problem to deal with. You will certainly not be able to wave a magic wand and elevate your own status or reduce theirs. But you should be able to make sure that you do not allow differences in status to lead to bad decision-making.

So if you observe that you, or others, are holding back from expressing contrary views, or deciding that there is no point in contributing your views because they won't be listened to, you need to act on that observation. What is it that is inhibiting you? Fear probably. Tackling fear (and fear is often at the root of our negative emotions, such as anger and resentment) requires honesty and clear thinking. What precisely am I afraid of? What is the very worst that could happen? Why does that matter to me? How does this fit with what I want to achieve with my life?

Caring for colleagues

Let us now imagine you are in the situation described at the beginning of the chapter, where you are one of the professionals in the responsibility cake[33] caring for a patient. Perhaps you are person A. You are worried that another HCP, perhaps person C, is not contributing as effectively as you expect and the care of and prognosis for the patient is suffering as a result. There is no overall team leader, and you account for your actions to different management structures. You wonder whether to say something but hesitate because there has been much emphasis within the team recently on the importance of respect. You have made yourself aware of your feelings and have analysed their origins and are now prepared to think constructively about intervening in the situation. How will you decide what to do?

First, you might reflect that caring for patients requires that the role of the HCP (as we have seen) is to remove any obstacles in the way of developing their potentials. So it may be appropriate to identify just what potentials are being blocked and what obstacles are not being removed as a result of your colleague's performance; in other words, checking that there is a real problem about her performance and that it is not merely that she is doing things differently from the way you expect them to be. Once you are sure there are needs not being met, then you can think about ways in which you can try to ensure that they are. In many cases there are several ways a deficiency of this sort can be remedied by other professionals involved, and you may decide to do this first while you reflect on how to tackle your colleague. Once you have done so, you may hesitate to say anything at all, now that you have put in place a system that reduces the patients' reliance on her input, and know that raising it with her will be uncomfortable for you and perhaps be seen as interference or lack of respect by her and her professional hierarchy. Of course you must make sure you observe policies where there are any that cover this situation, and this may involve reporting your concerns to senior members of her organization, but I suggest that effective working within and between professions flourishes when professionals constructively challenge each other directly. If we look again at our definition of care ('the will to engage in acts of work or courage for the purpose of nurturing another's personal growth'), then caring for your colleague requires you to engage in acts of work or courage to enable her to grow. The view is sometimes expressed, particularly within the medical profession, that our concern for her patients can conflict with the need to demonstrate respect for the clinician.[34] However, if we respect a clinician, we respect her integrity, her concern for her patients and her ability to use the information given to her constructively.

We looked at ways of giving feedback in Chapter 1, but you may also find it helpful to reflect on some further suggestions from M. Scott Peck. He suggests that whenever we are in possession of information and are considering withholding it, we should:

- Never speak a falsehood, so we may choose to withhold the truth but not to tell a lie.
- Remember that in each instance in which truth is withheld a moral decision is required, so doing nothing is a deliberate act.
- Never base the decision to withhold truth on personal needs (for power, to be liked, to avoid discomfort).
- Base this kind of decision entirely upon the needs of the person or people from whom the truth is being withheld.
- Remember that the assessment of another's needs is so complex that it can only be executed wisely when one operates with genuine care for the other.
- Make the primary factor in the assessment of another's needs the assessment of that person's capacity to utilize the truth for his or her own growth, and be aware that our tendency is to under- rather than overestimate this capacity.

Peck also points out that we should approach this task with humility, checking and rechecking the validity and reality of the truth as we perceive it.[35]

Of course your colleague may respond defensively or angrily, particularly if you have expressed your concern ineffectively (usually through a lack of genuine care for her, or out of an undue concern for yourself), or even if you have expressed it with great empathy and concern, because something like this can be very difficult to hear. But if you have prepared your presentation carefully, remembering to address your colleague's goals, preferences and styles (see Chapter 1), rather than your own, and with genuinely constructive intent, then this is less likely. Even so, it will require courage on your part as well as on hers.

Of course it may not be your colleague who is on the receiving end of this kind of challenge, but you. It is now up to you to respond generously in a situation where you are bound to feel hurt. You will almost instinctively want to reject what you are hearing and justify yourself, but you will be doing yourself no favours if you do so without listening first to what is being said. Listening is so important that it is worth thinking about this further.

Listening

Perhaps the most effective way of working with others is the most obvious. It is to listen, to find out how they are seeing the world and see how that feels to them. When I suggest that listening is a skill that needs to be developed, HCPs always protest that they spend all their day listening, and indeed many of you do – but it is a different kind of listening that is required. At work most of us listen purposefully. We look for themes or key facts that enable us to diagnose a problem and suggest a solution. All the time we are listening we are actively processing the information with a view to making a response. In our social lives, we adopt a similar listening pattern, although sometimes with different intent.

As Roger Gaunt, in his book *Personal and Group Development for Managers*, says:

> To listen well is to begin to manage well. Yet somehow the essence of listening eludes me. For it has to do with a transparent openness to the speaker that is only achieved at cost. 'I so easily only hear the resonances within myself when you speak. I don't listen to you at all, but only to the memories within myself that your words activate. I so deeply want confirmation of myself that I hardly hear you at all.' Yet when a person does grow sufficiently to give unconditional attention to another, then there exist the conditions of significant change. *Development* may then take place.[36]

If we are to understand another person well enough to empathize with their needs in the complexity and richness in which they exist, then we need to listen in a different way. We need to focus our attention entirely on the other person, letting go of our sense of purpose, not doing anything with the information we are given other than absorbing it: not judging it, not organizing it, but experiencing it, feeling it. This 'bracketing'[37] of ourselves with the person we are listening to engenders empathy and insight in a way that no other kind of listening can. It is an essential element of any really close relationship, at work or at home. It requires (but also nurtures) a genuine interest in the other's position, a considerable amount of work in the form of concentration, and self-discipline in overcoming the urge to switch back into our more normal listening mode. Similarly, the philosopher Martin Buber suggested that in authentic dialogue something much deeper is going on than in ordinary conversation.[38] In true dialogue, he argued, there is a genuine openness of each individual to the concerns of the other. Participants do not selectively screen out views they disagree with or busy themselves with summoning up arguments to rebut the other person's, all the while only half listening to what the other person is saying. This kind of dialogue is not something we can usually sustain for a very long period of time but it is an important component of working successfully with others.

Concluding thoughts: synergy

When we reflect on the content of this chapter, it becomes clear that the keys to working well with others are self-discipline and generosity. The *discipline* to take the time and trouble to become aware of our responses to other people and professions, to analyse the dynamics of a situation and to understand the needs of colleagues. The *generosity* to choose to behave towards them in a constructive way, and to listen well enough to interpret their motives and behaviours positively.

We have seen that differences in status are part of forces that are as wide as society and thus outside our control. For this reason appeals for 'respect' between professions will always be limited in their success. But if decisions are to be informed by the most relevant knowledge or experience we may need to give more air time to a lower-status professional than to a higher-status one. Indeed, we may find ourselves in the position of being that lower-status individual. This will not be easy, but recognizing and challenging inappropriate use of status is one of the most important roles of the real manager.

We consider some ways of challenging inappropriate use of status when we look at behaviours in Chapter 6. For the moment the message is: diagnose the status differentials among any group of professionals and heighten your awareness of the contribution each is making and the way this is received by the others. If you notice that the content is receiving more or less support than you think (thinking as dispassionately as you yourself can) it deserves, then note that this needs to be challenged.[39]

The real payoff in working with others comes when you gain more from the collaboration than is necessary because of your interdependency, when you gain more from joining forces than together you put in, when the whole is greater than the sum of the parts, when there is synergy. Synergy often occurs where it is least expected. In 'know-how' industries like health care, it usually takes the form of cognitive leaps and there can be no leap if there is not a novel situation in which a particular way of thinking can be applied. Such situations cannot be predicted. The development of synergy therefore requires an openness to new ideas and technologies, to approaches from other individuals or departments. It also requires a generosity with your own ideas that runs counter to the culture in many academic settings. Being clear about what it is you are trying to achieve can be helpful here, as can an appreciation that people who work well with others can achieve so much more than those who insist on working alone.

This runs counter to many of our formative influences in education, where working alone was the norm and it was the task completed that was assessed. It takes a huge shift in attitude to accept that the choices about how we work with others deserve as much attention as the choices we make about the tasks we undertake ourselves; that these 'process' issues are tasks in themselves and have a valid claim to our working time.

Our ability to care for and manage others is ultimately dependent on our ability to take responsibility for ourselves. Only then are we likely to work amicably and productively with others. It is only when we choose how we ourselves behave that we begin really to work *with* others and allow others to work effectively with us.

Notes

1 See Jones, S. (1994) *The Language of Genes* (London: Flamingo).

2 Since no single uncontested definition of a profession exists so far, one way to approach this issue is to come at it from two different, complementary perspectives, in order to build up a constellation of features that characterize a profession. For argument's sake, I am going to look at the concept of 'profession' through the perspectives of the economist and the sociologist. I might use any other number of perspectives, including those of the philosopher or the educationalist, but these first two encapsulate many of the dynamics and issues – including 'human capital', altruism and self-interest – that are particularly important in health care.

3 We can see the changes to accreditation, revalidation and accountability in response to the Bristol, Shipman and Alder Hay events in this light.

4 With the exception of Schön, the sociologists quoted in the following paragraphs are cited in Turner, B. (1995) *Medical Power and Social Knowledge*, 2nd edn (London: Sage).

5 Schön, D. (1995) *The Reflective Practitioner: How Professionals Think in Action* (Aldershot: Arena), p. 4.

6 See Hughes, E. (1975) 'Professions'. In G. Esland, G. Salaman and M. Speakman (eds) *People and Work* (Edinburgh: Holmes-McDougall and Open University Press).

7 See Freidson, E. (1983) 'The theory of professions: state of the art'. In R. Dingwall and P. Lewis (eds) *The Sociology of the Professions* (London and Basingstoke: Macmillan).

8 See note 4 above.

9 See Millerson, G. (1964) *The Qualifying Association* (London: Routledge and Kegan Paul).

10 It is again interesting to look at the way sociology defines some of these terms: *disease*, malfunctions of physiological and biological character; *illness*, the individual's subjective awareness of the disorder; *sickness*, the social role adopted by the individual.

11 Seedhouse, D. (1991) *Liberating Medicine* (Chichester: John Wiley and Sons).

12 Peck, M. S. (1979) *The Road Less Travelled* (London: Arrow Books). Many people I have worked with have found the first two-thirds of this book to be profoundly helpful.

13 Ibid.

14 Jonathan Richards points out that 'HCPs are trained to focus on and prioritise *cure*, care is the better, more comprehensive word that includes palliation. There is *always something* that can be done to care for another.'

15 We can suggest that a health care profession should be a group whose members 'work to enable the development of potentials which will enhance the life of clients', which is the way that Seedhouse describes the role of doctors. And, as Seedhouse again suggests, those members will 'work to identify obstacles in the way of the development of those potentials and choose to help with those they are best equipped to assist with'.

16 One example of the difficulties caused is when members of high-status professions believe that their own time is more important than anyone else's. Sometimes, of course, they will be right, but often they are not, and this attitude will waste resources, slow down decisions and generally frustrate effective organizational life.

17 I find that although some managers are oblivious to this, it is completely evident to people working *within* organizations, especially to members of groups that are not of the highest status (broadly, people other than doctors).

18 As with power, money and gender, it may be as much the result of status, and hence the ability to set high entry standards and increase the length of the training.

19 Cited in Turner (1995); see note 4 above.

20 Jamous, H. and Peloille, J. (1970) 'Professions or self-perpetuating system'. In A. Jackson (ed.) *Professions and Professionalisation* (Cambridge: Cambridge University Press), p. 198.

21 Especially if we combine it with the barriers-to-entry argument.

22 Blois, M. (1984) *Information and Medicine: The Nature of Medical Descriptions* (Stanford, CA: Stanford University Press), provides descriptions of natural objects allocated to appropriate hierarchical levels to produce a knowledge network, p. 47.

23 Tuggett, D., Boulton, M., Olson, C. and Williams, A. (1985) *Meetings Between Experts* (London: Tavistock). A fascinating description of qualitative research into the nature of doctor–patient conversations and the factors that influence recall.

24 Succinctly described by Blois (1984); see note 22 above.

25 See Blois (1984), note 22 above. Hierarchical levels of medical descriptions, see p. 113.

26 Polanyi, M. (1959) *Personal Knowledge* (London: Routledge and Kegan Paul).

27 Quoted in Wulff, H. R., Audut Pedersen, S. and Rosenberg, R. (1990) *The Philosophy of Medicine* (Oxford: Blackwell Scientific), pp. 2–7.

28 Janis, I. L. (1971) 'Groupthink', *Psychology Today*, 5(6), 43–4, 46, 74–6.

29 Primary care trust: at the time of writing this is the organization that manages the contract between general medical practitioners and the NHS.

30 Of course, they may need to use some regulatory behaviours too, e.g. notifying the public health authorities about certain infectious diseases. Since writing this chapter I have come across the work of Dr. Richard Bohmes, Ass. Prof at Harvard Business School who suggests that the clinical task can be divided into two aspects: discovery and delivery. Discovery involves exploring with a patient what is wrong, experimenting with treatment options etc. Delivery is the implementation of a pre-formulated, evidence-based care protocol. We can suggest that the discovery aspect benefits from 'trading/ innovative' behaviours, and the deliverary aspect from 'regulatory' ones. These two ethical syndromes could prove to be of far-reaching importance in health care.

31 PEC (UK): a sub-committee of the board of a primary care trust (PCT), composed of HCPs who consider PCT decisions from a clinical perspective.

32 I have not done justice to Jacobs's ideas in this short introduction, and understand if you reject them as irrelevant. I am not sure myself of the theoretical underpinnings, but I do observe these casts of mind, I have noticed that the syndromes help to explain why some behaviours sometimes feel right and sometimes wrong, and I certainly observe the frustration when HCP innovators confront the regulatory upward loyalty of some senior managers. I think Jacobs is on to something that is worth exploring further.

33 You may prefer to think of this as a patient pathway.

34 See, for example, Smith, R. (1994) 'Medicine's core values', *British Medical Journal*, 309, 1247–8.

35 See note 12.

36 Gaunt, R. (1991) *Personal and Group Development for Managers* (London: Longman). This book is highly recommended to anyone wishing to develop skills in action learning or in mentoring.

37 'Bracketing' is the phrase used by Peck (1979) to describe this activity; see note 12 above.

38 See Buber, M. (1923) *I and Thou* (Edinburgh: T & T Clark), reprinted 1970.

39 Status can, of course, be used to good effect. For a good example of this look at Julian Tudor Hart's description of how he practised 'enlightened despotism' within his general practice for many years, in Tudor Hart, J. (2002) 'The autonomous patient: ending paternalism in medical care', *Journal of the Royal Society of Medicine*, 95, 623–4.

3 Really managing people
Working for others

Almost all of us work for someone else, even if we are self-employed. There are very few people who have the resources to be able to take decisions and implement them without having to convince someone else of their validity. For the rest of us, taking any action that requires additional money, people or premises requires us to gain the approval of resource allocators either within the organization or outside it: boards of directors, bank managers or major customers. In other words, we depend upon the approval of others to be able to achieve our own personal goals. This is not interdependency of the kind discussed in Chapter 2, where different specialists rely on each other to undertake tasks that, together, form a complete service for the patient. This is straight dependency.

As we saw in Chapter 1, people differ in their response to dependency. Some like it, some tolerate it, many (those with strong power or autonomy goals) hate it. Since it is often individuals in that latter category who rise to leading positions in the health care professions, it is not surprising that there is often tension between senior clinicians and management boards. Individuals choosing primary care as a career, and the relative autonomy of independent contractor status, also fall into this category, and we can therefore expect that there will always be tension between them and their local contract holders.

This chapter is intended for: people who dislike dependency; people who find it difficult to achieve their own goals within their current organization or contractual arrangement; people committed to effective care of their patients who find their resource allocators unsympathetic to, and ignorant of, the needs of patients, and how they can best be met; people who find that working in their current post induces anger, frustration and demotivation; and people who experience a conflict between their role with patients, where they are a specialist carer with a credibility that inspires confidence and trust, and their role in the organization or system, where they feel undervalued. Its aim is to help you to achieve what you believe is important, and to assess whether you can do that where you are. It takes the form of a number of self-assessment or stock-taking questions for you to ask.

Are my aims congruent with those of my organization?

If you are going to be satisfied in your organization your own aims need to fit in with those of your organization, and these will be different for every organization, depending on its history, its environment and its cast of characters. So one of the first things you will need to find out is what these organizational aims are. They are sometimes expressed as a mission statement so this is not a bad place to start, although many mission statements consist of a set of 'apple pie and motherhood' statements that are not particularly helpful here.

The aims or mission of an organization depend to a large extent on the concerns and emotions of key opinion-formers and decision-makers within the system. If you have worked in your organization for some time, you will know who these key opinion-formers are and perhaps something of what they care about, but if you are new or have not considered this before you will need to identify them. Looking at an organizational chart will help you do so, but it is often not possible to detect from these where real influence lies, so observing the way people react to the mention of individual names and paying attention to what people say about them is often more reliable. Once you know who they are, you will be able to find a means of meeting them, and of using the listening skills described in Chapter 2 to try to understand properly their interests and priorities. You may feel unattracted to the prospect of wasting your time with these people, and if you do feel like that, remember that you do not have to like them, or admire them – you only need to obtain information that you can then analyse to get the best deal for your patients. They will not, of course, provide you with the information you need if you express antipathy or perhaps boredom when you meet, whether in word, deed or body language, so you will need to prepare yourself in advance to be empathetic. Somehow you must bring to this meeting an open mind, an ability to concentrate on what is being said and to take it at face value, without interpreting it in the light of past events and the anger these have induced. Only in this way will you be able to empathize sufficiently well to succeed in obtaining the information you need.

Am I labouring this point? Of course you would naturally have approached such a meeting with this openness of mind and language. Well, my experience suggests otherwise. Observing such conversations, or debriefing participants later, suggests to me that actions and attitudes perceived by the actor (you) as open are often interpreted by the receiver (them) as prejudiced, or as hostile or defensive. So it is worth taking special care here about the impression you give.

When you have identified the priorities and perspectives of the organizational decision-makers, you will be able to compare these with your own. To do so, however, you need to clarify just what your own priorities are. One way of doing this is to try to write down a statement of your aims and values – a kind of individual mission statement. I can almost see you thinking that this is not necessary, that you know what your aims are without writing them down, but a lot of people do find it helpful. So even if you don't take time right now to do so, it is worth mulling over for a few weeks what you might write, and then jotting it down when you have a moment. You may want to think about what your talents are, and how you can realize them to the full; what you most care about and how you can translate this into action; and how you want to behave. There is more about writing personal mission statements in Chapter 6.

Clearly, any incongruity of aims is going to cause problems. If you believe the greatest contribution you can make is through research, and your organization is interested only in efficient service delivery using existing technologies, then both you and they will be unhappy. Perhaps more common is the case where your wish to offer specialist care to a particular group of patients conflicts with the organization's wish to meet the more generalist needs of a wider group. You may also come across a situation in which senior managers are focusing only on meeting governmental targets that you question, and are borrowing resources from your own service, which has no relevant targets, to do so. While there is always bound to be *some* lack of fit between the aims of the organization and the people within it, if there is a genuine disparity between your aims and those of the organization that you cannot see being resolved in the medium term, then you are ready to move on to question 3 or even question 5. If there is not, the next question becomes relevant.

Are my values and beliefs in harmony with those of my organization?

There are lots of ways of defining values, so let me explain that I am using the word here in the following sense: values are the beliefs that drive our actions. Now the beliefs that are shared by members of an organization make up its culture, and another way of describing an organization's culture is 'the way we do things round here'. Since one of the things you will want to consider is whether 'the way they do things round here' is the way you want to do them, we need to explore the notion of culture a little further. We do so again in Chapter 7.

One way of thinking about it is to consider culture an invisible framework through which people see the world, which influences how they feel, behave and think. It is the way people make sense of what is happening and is manifest in the way people weave stories to describe what is happening to them and around them. Thus cultures are acquired through apprenticeship, and absorbed as part of the tacit knowledge that we looked at in Chapter 2, and within an organization there will be several cultures, some of which pervade the whole while others are specific to groups within it.

Paul Bate,[1] writing about culture, draws attention to the fact that cultures can have careers, suggesting that they start as healthy ways of looking at, responding to and engaging with a set of circumstances, and over time they degenerate into an unhealthy form. He describes the latter in a way that we can recognize only too well:

> Not only has the culture lost its creativity and vitality and its ability to touch hearts and minds, it has also lost its direction. What was once a progressive linearity of development has become a regressive circularity of development. The virtuous circle with its infinite capacity for generating new combinations of the cultural material has become a vicious circle – a spiral of narrowing options and endless repetitions of constantly failing solutions; a framework of opportunities has become a framework of constraints. The [culture] has become a straitjacket; the solution has become the problem; the vision has become blind, short-sighted dogma unable to see the wood for the trees.

Being trapped in an unhealthy culture is a miserable place to be, but being anywhere where the values and beliefs are very different from yours is not much fun, so understanding the culture in your organization is very important if you are trying to decide whether to stay or go. There are various interesting tools for identifying a type of culture[2] by allocating it to one of a generic set of options, but these are not going to be helpful to you in this situation. Bate's approach is more useful here – it involves identifying the stories that are being created (woven) and told within the organization, and distinguishing those that are helpful (and that if necessary you can help to support and develop) from those that are unhealthy (and would need to be transformed if you are going to be happy and effective here). So, identifying the stories being told will indicate the framework of values and beliefs through which people in your organization are looking at the world and engaging with it. These will rarely be expressed in writing (and if you do find a written set of values for the organization they are usually those espoused by the small group people writing them[3] and will not be generalizable to the organisation as a whole), and again you could look at an organization chart and find out the narrative being told by people in senior positions. But while this is important you can also notice the stories that have the greatest currency in corridors, in coffee rooms and in team meetings, and trace them back to their source. This will tell you who the real opinion-formers are, and their value framework and beliefs. You may find it helpful to write down what you think those beliefs are; for example, what do these senior people and these key opinion-formers believe about the following? And do these weave together into a picture that you are happy to be part of?

- Patients.
- The population served by the organization.
- Staff.
- The resources available.
- The way resources are being used.
- The performance of particular teams within the organization.
- The performance of the organization.
- Other organizations in the health economy.
- Their own performance.
- What the future will bring.

Where you come across beliefs that you will find it difficult to work with, you may find it helpful, drawing on the first two chapters, to try to distinguish between beliefs that spring from individual traits, such as motivational drivers ('Security is more important than relationships or creativity, so we mustn't take risks') or preferred behaviours ('Being straightforward is better than being indirect, so I have more confidence in person x than person y'), and those that derive from professional norms. This will help you to assess whether a set of beliefs will live in the organization only as long as a particular individual is in post, or whether they are longer lived and more enduring.

Needless to say, the opinions you form about these people and the way they approach the world must be your own. The opinions of others will be interesting, but you cannot assume that (no matter how much you may like the person who is giving you their opinion) your own assessment would be the same. Whenever you are tempted to accept an opinion from someone else, it is important to look for evidence that supports or contradicts that view.

Identifying the beliefs of these senior people and key opinion formers will help you to assess their level of confidence and maturity. The more genuinely confident individuals are about their own abilities, the more generous are their beliefs about others and the more able they are to work effectively with others, to give credit where it is due, to encourage, respect and develop others by offering them opportunities and assistance.

In his book *The Seven Habits of Highly Effective People*, Stephen Covey describes what he calls a 'maturity continuum'.[4] At one end of this continuum is a mode of behaviour he labels *dependency* (see Figure 3.1). In this mode, individuals believe that their feelings, their behaviours and, to a large extent,

Dependency ——————— Independency ——————— Interdependency

Figure 3.1 Maturity continuum.

their fortunes are entirely caused by factors outside their control. These factors could be genetic, psychosocial (their upbringing) or environmental (the situation in which they find themselves). Dependent individuals are essentially reactive. The language of the reactive person is peppered with phrases like: 'There's nothing I can do', 'He makes me so angry', 'They won't allow me to do that', 'If only'. Covey draws a distinction between this reactivity and proactivity, which he defines as 'more than merely taking initiative, it means taking responsibility for our own lives'. Proactivity is rooted in the concept that we choose our thoughts, feelings and behaviours, they are not dictated to us by circumstances or conditioning but are within our control. In other words, Covey quotes Victor Frankl 'between stimulus and response we have the freedom to choose'.[5] The language used by reactive and proactive individuals can be contrasted as follows:[6]

Reactive language	*Proactive language*
There's nothing I can do	Let's look at our alternatives
That's just the way I am	I can choose a different approach
He makes me so mad	I control my own feelings
They won't allow that	I can create an effective presentation
I have to do that	I will choose an appropriate response
I can't	I choose
I must	I prefer
If only	I will

The midpoint on the maturity continuum is *independency*, when individuals decide to take responsibility for themselves. Further still to the right, at the other end of the continuum, is a state of *interdependency*,[7] where individuals recognize that they can achieve very much more if they take responsibility not only for their own life but also for collaborating effectively with others.

Reactivity correlates with a lack of a sense of personal agency, a lack of belief that what I think, say or do will make a difference. So we can suggest that self-esteem and self-belief increase as the position on the spectrum moves to the right. The values held by individuals with a firm sense of inner security will differ from those of their less mature colleagues and they will be more likely to live by them. Insecure individuals are more concerned about how others see them than they are in making valid judgements about how to help others to optimize their contribution. Their devastating wit, scapegoating of others and constant criticism of peers will shape an organization in which they are influential. The values they espouse may well sound attractive (although they are likely to talk of rights and respect rather than of contribution and growth), but their behaviour is often at odds with them. Such individuals will find it very difficult to accept any criticism, preferring to shoot the messenger rather than reflect on the message. Their mature counterparts treat criticism as an opportunity to learn and grow. They find it inappropriate to shoot the messenger because they take the trouble to understand their point of view even if they disagree with it. Empathy is not in the nature of insecure individuals, who are too concerned with their own needs to get close to other people's.

Diagnosing an individual's maturity or genuine self-confidence is not always straightforward, because we are sometimes misled by arrogance or complacency. Both of these are features of insecurity rather than confidence but can be confused with it. Confident individuals take pride in their own achievements, as do arrogant individuals. Their attitudes to the achievement of others differ, however: the former delighting in them, taking an interest, making recommendations and so on; the latter belittling, criticizing, finding fault. Similarly, confident individuals are sure enough of their integrity to want regularly to test their view of reality, their understanding of themselves, their responses and the filters through which they see the world. This may look like self-doubt and the preserve of the insecure, but it is far from it. Its opposite is complacency and the belief that there is only one way of seeing the world. People who care more about whether you like them or admire them than they do about what they can do to help you to achieve your objectives (and in so doing achieve theirs) are ineffective managers. Working for them is going to be a miserable experience, unless you, yourself, are very mature.

Being big when working with or for little people is not easy. All too often we find ourselves responding in a way that disappoints us, makes us feel diminished: when we join in hostile gossip, for example, or when we 'give as good as we get' to critical colleagues at a meeting. Sometimes, if we cannot rely on our temper or our tongue, the mature course of action is to avoid the meeting, avoid the coffee room. Acting with integrity in an organization without discipline and generosity, where gossip is not discouraged, where meetings are not kept to task, where individuals are scapegoated, where constructive criticism meets defensive anger, requires great strength of purpose.

Your role as a real manager is to develop the maturity of your part of the organization by developing the confidence of the people in it. Max de Pree describes maturity in an organization as 'a sense of self-worth, a sense of belonging, a sense of expectancy, a sense of responsibility, a sense of accountability, and a sense of equality'.[8] The essential question here is: are you going to be able to do that in this organization?

Where does the power lie in this organization?

Many writers and researchers have considered the nature of power in social groupings, the ability to influence the way others behave. French and Raven[9] describe five sources of power, three of which derive from a person's position within an organization and two from their personal characteristics. The three kinds of positional power are:

- *legitimate power*, the authority granted by an organization to someone in a role;
- *reward power*, the ability to decide who is entitled to a pay increase, a training opportunity or any other form of reward;
- its counterpart *coercive power*, the ability to decide who warrants punishment by not giving a pay rise or reprimanding in some way.

Personal power comes in two forms:

- *expert* power, which arises because of the individual's specialist knowledge or skill, which is recognized and seen as relevant;
- *referent* power, aspects of personality that others respect and admire.

This question overlaps with questions 1 and 2, but is worthy of consideration in its own right. Identifying who has what legitimate power, reward power and coercive power (i.e. positional power) is, on the whole, easier than ascertaining those with personal power (expert or referent), but both are important. Understanding who are the most influential individuals or groups in your organization will help you to predict how conflicts may be resolved, and in whose interests. If you combine this knowledge with your insight into their aims and their values and beliefs you are well placed to analyse the interactions and dynamics around you.

Who is likely to succeed in this organization?

It would be comforting to think that the people who do the best job are those who succeed in organizations, but if you look around you do you observe this to be the case? When you think about it, how *could* it be true? Decisions about advancement are made by people, and we know that people are bad at judgement.[10] People, we know, often don't use their own judgement but rely on those of others, and these latter judgements can be both generally held and at the same time very wide of the mark. They are impressions created and sustained as a result of events that are built into a narrative, which then forms a baseline that is adjusted slightly (but not greatly) as further events take place. In other words, once we have a picture of someone as reliable, funny and warm we interpret their actions against that image, and may amend it slightly if they do something arbitrary and mean spirited. However, we will tend to judge them less harshly than we might do if we have previously formed the view that they are suspicious or selfish or have no sense of humour. So anyone wanting

Table 3.1 Analysis of political influence of stakeholders

Politically aware

	Integrity
	Wise Owl
	Has an active awareness of purpose and tends to follow a set of guiding principles (not always explicit)
	Interested in harnessing power in pursuit of that purpose
	Can cope with being disliked, if that serves the purpose
	Good interpersonal skills, strong personal values/ethics
	Thinks before speaking, assertive, tactful
	Emotionally literate Plans actions in pursuit of purpose
	Checks grapevine, excellent listener, aware of other viewpoints
	Uses coalitions of people with similar interests
	Knows how formal processes work
	Non-defensive, learns from mistakes, reflects on events
	Can make procedures work for them
	Open, shares information
	Gets support, with integrity
	Recognizes and works with key interests of others involved

Ability to read a situation

Clever Fox

Interested in power and in associating with people in power

Interested in meeting own needs rather than being guided by a set of ethical principles

Wants to succeed, if necessary at the expense of others

Thinks before speaking, and chooses words with care, masking feelings of aggression

Charming veneer, can simulate feelings

Does not display genuine feelings spontaneously

Plans actions in pursuit of own goals

Checks grapevine, aware of other viewpoints

Uses coalitions of people with similar interests

Knows how formal processes work

Insecure at heart, but well defended

Always leave jobs before mistakes come to light

Gets support, good at ingratiating with others and at bargaining

Recognizes and exploits key weaknesses in allies and opponents

Self interested game playing	
Presence or absence of game playing	Presence or absence of game playing

Table 3.1 continued

Inept Donkey

Not skilled interpersonally, unprincipled

Hates to be ignored, likes to associate with authority

Seeks to meet own needs and wishes

Plays psychological games but does not read those of others

Emotionally illiterate, concerned with own feelings and not those of others

Predisposed to projection and paranoia

Makes judgements based on feelings rather than knowledge of bureaucracy or organizational procedures

Inept at making alliances and coalitions

Does not listen to others, tries to be nice but does not know how

Innocent Sheep

Principled, ethical, tends to rely on authority

Does not recognize political purpose

Does not network, does not know how to get support

Listens but does not hear (because doesn't understand difference)

Sticks to rules: ethical, professional, organizational

Understands content but not process of procedures

Exaggerated respect for rationality

Literal-minded, doesn't recognize double messages

Believes in expert and position power

Thinks you are powerful if you are right

Open, shares information

Ability to read a situation

Politically unaware

to succeed in an organization will need to be aware of the press they are getting, and in what quarters, and decide what they can do to adjust it favourably.

One study[11] of the relative success with which individuals in a large local government organization achieved their objectives suggested an interesting way of categorizing the behaviour of the people involved (see the matrix in Table 3.1). In this matrix the vertical axis is the ability to read a situation or an organization. The behaviours on this axis range from politically aware, at the top, to politically unaware, at the bottom. The horizontal axis represents the degree of psychological game playing involved, ranging from a position of integrity on the right, to one of self-interested game playing on the left.[12] People's behaviours and values can be seen as falling into the four boxes that are described, and each of the four clusters is characterized as an animal (the wise owl, clever fox, inept donkey or innocent sheep). The researchers found that owl and fox behaviours were more successful in achieving desired objectives than were those of sheep or donkeys. I invite you to look at the matrix and reflect on which of the four animals tends to match your own behaviours and values. But before you do so I want to nudge you out of any potential complacency by suggesting that you are more than likely to have a sheep tendency. Why do I say that? Because very many HCPs I come across use so much of the language and behaviour of the sheep box that I would happily position them there, yet they claim to me that they behave like owls. An owl is what we need to become if we want to achieve what we think is important, and we can't improve our owl skills if we believe we already have them.

If you have located yourself in either of the bottom boxes, you are at least being honest with yourself. But I hope you will want to consider how you might begin to move into one of the upper quadrants, and naturally I hope you are aiming for the owl box rather than the fox. As you look around your organization, which box do you think the behaviours of the key opinion-formers and resource allocators are in? Most important of all, what about people who have a direct influence on you and your service?

It can be tempting to put someone we don't see eye-to-eye with as a donkey or fox, and I hope that the concepts we explored in Chapters 1 and 2 enable you to resist this and to think carefully and perceptively. Sometimes, however, we come across genuine foxes, people for whom winning a career game is more important than anything else, and if you are dependent on a fox in the organizational structure then your life can be difficult. Even here, though, you can take the opportunity to develop your owl skills, looking for owls you can engage with, encouraging sheep who support you to become more owl-like.

You may also be asked to join the campaign team of a sheep who is fighting a fight you sincerely support. Here it is worth thinking clearly about your position and contribution, because ardent support of a cause bound to fail is not much good to anyone – least of all you. Your analysis of the people ranged on both (or all) 'sides' in this debate, using as many as possible of the concepts in this book, should indicate where power lies, and what arguments and behaviours are most likely to convince. Deploying this knowledge and helping your 'sheep' colleague to think about the dynamics of the situations in this way will be a hundred times more valuable than your simply swinging in behind their banner.

Are there other ways of achieving my aims?

A few pages ago you (perhaps) jotted down an idea of your personal mission. Having now analysed your organization and thought about how you might increase your chances of achieving your aims if you stay, you also need to consider whether you could achieve them more satisfactorily elsewhere. There is more information about how to capture and challenge your thinking about your personal mission in Chapter 6, so you might like to turn to that before you finalize your reflections in this chapter.

When you identify alternatives you can certainly start by looking at other organizations that are currently in existence. However, it is a good idea to think much wider than this. Imagining the kind of organizations that may be around in five years' time can be instructive (as well as fun), and thinking about how you would design these if you were a patient, or a government minister, can yield new ideas about needs or wishes that you can help to meet, or about the direction organizations may be required to take.

You might also find it thought provoking to look outside health care. Sacrilege? Your values are associated with public service and helping others? Impractical? You don't have skills needed in commerce? Bear with me for a few paragraphs before you ride off on your moral high horse.

Your talents, your training, the ways in which you handle information, people and pressure, your skills at diagnosing the needs of others, of working with members of other professions, are very useful in a range of settings. In the voluntary sector certainly, in the commercial sector too. Of course you would need to acquire some additional skills but these are not beyond you and there will be people willing to help you do so. So it is not at all impractical. What about fitting with your values?

You may believe that couldn't possibly work in the private sector, in industry, in anything other than pubic or voluntary services because the former are only interested in making money, being entirely driven by 'the bottom line'. You are, you may say, more interested in helping people, in meeting needs, in making society a healthier place. That is in fact what many HCPs routinely tell me, yet when we take a look at the kinds of things that help them to enjoy life, help them to realize their potential, and support relationships and other things that give meaning to their lives, we find that very few of these things appear to be provided by public servants. Mostly they seem to be provided by commercial companies. I would argue that there is nothing inherently superior about being employed in the public health and social care sector compared to being in a company making films or computer software, importing wine, publishing books, making furniture, designing hiking boots or running ski resorts. These goods and services aren't inferior to health care, they are simply catering for different parts of the same picture: our lives. Are companies offering the above sorts of product driven entirely by the profit motive? Some of them will be. Ultimately they will have to demonstrate a profit; in other words people will have to want to buy their products (value them) at a price that is higher than it costs to make and distribute them. To be successful, then, companies have to be very customer oriented, they need to understand what customers need, what they want and how much they value these. They will also have to be efficient in their operations so they will have to be able to encourage staff to work well and creatively at a rate that is determined by the market.

Does this sound hugely different from the pubic sector? Well, yes, but not necessarily in a negative way. Commercial companies cannot get away with caring more about what their staff want to do than their customers want or need. My own experience and the feedback I receive from others suggests that the public sector can and does. So when you say it is your values that keep you in the public sector, are you sure it is that? Or is it that only here can your own wishes take precedence over those of your clients? Does this suggest to you that I have a political agenda, that I am castigating public services per se? Well that is not my intention. What I want to do is challenge certain assumptions and casts of mind, as Jane Jacobs would phrase it. I hear so often the motives of people in commercial companies being dismissed as profit driven, often by people who are very good at making sure their own research proposals are put forward whether or not the resources needed to support these could be better spent elsewhere. There is a good argument that the public sector offers an essential opportunity for the development of virtue that is needed to correct market failures, but we would be naive to think that it does not degenerate into forms of self-interest in many cases. Similarly, we know there are companies that behave unethically, exploiting information asymmetries and being overly concerned with financial rewards. If you are committed to 'public sector' values then you probably won't feel happy working for one of these; indeed, I hope you won't want to work for either of these degenerate forms. But it would be wrong to assume that all private sector companies are the latter any more than free market evangelists are right to berate incessantly the public sector.

We saw in Chapter 1 that we all have a range of motivational drivers, and that is true of people everywhere. So we can imagine that many people in the private sector will be just as committed as you are to quality, to service, to using their talents in the interests of the customer. They may even have decided to opt for the commercial sector because they find they can do that more easily than in the public sector. One way of thinking about this is to suggest that in the commercial world the people at the top are worried about making money, while in the public sector the people at the top are worried about getting re-elected. Neither of these is inherently superior to the other, and both can distort behaviours in unwelcome ways. In both cases it is the job of managers within those organizations to make sure that the company makes money or politicians get re-elected as a result of excellent services that meet real needs.

So your options may be wider than perhaps you assume they are. The world is full of places where you can use your talents to the benefit of others and yourself, and you will add more value to society if you can find where you can best use your talents than if you stick with the public sector out of a misplaced sense of duty. If you want to stay in health that is wonderful, but don't think you are a better person because you do. I hope you find this line of argument potentially empowering and that you will look widely and openly at other alternatives, because if you decide to stay you want to be sure this is absolutely the best place for you.

Do I want to stay?

When you have appraised all the available options, you will be able to decide whether or not you wish to stay where you are. You may find that, even though your goals and values do not coincide with those of your current organization, those of the alternatives are even more dissimilar. If this is the case, you will decide to stay in full knowledge of the disadvantages but prepared to work to overcome them. With this positive intent, the skills that you develop to do so will undoubtedly increase your own maturity and that of your staff. It is an opportunity for the real personal growth that springs out of difficult, challenging circumstances.

You may find, when you get closer to the decision-makers, that your aims and values are similar and that you are happy to stay where you are. You may, however, come to realize that you are not in the best place for you to achieve your objectives and that you must, in your own interests and that of the organization, devote energy and time to moving on. This is a very different situation from that where, infuriated by another setback, you march into the office of the person who has made your life difficult and hand in your resignation. It is a constructive response to the situation rather than a destructive one. The difference between them may not be apparent to the organization you leave, but it will be to you and to the organization you join. In the latter case, you will find there the same old problems you thought you had left behind; you will have taken them with you.

Concluding thoughts: staying on

If you fall into the category of people to whom this chapter is addressed, the considered decision to remain where you are is an important step, but only the first step. The next is to reflect on what it is you want to achieve and identify precisely what or who in your organization or system is preventing you from achieving them. Very often the problem lies in interactions with the gatekeeping departments. By these I mean departments such as finance or personnel whose approval is required before decisions can be implemented.

Often there are individuals in these departments who are genuinely interested in supporting you. Equally often they are staffed by people who believe their concerns are of paramount importance to the organization, without appreciating the balance that is essential – necessity without sufficiency. Budget containment is necessary, as is observance of employment law, but they are not sufficient. Often our problems in dealing with these departments arise because we adopt a similarly unbalanced attitude. The development of clinical practice, the introduction of an additional and beneficial service, the adoption of a new approach whose clinical value has recently been demonstrated, these are all essential, but they too are not sufficient. They must not be allowed to jeopardize the financial viability of the organization or expose the organization to risk of employment litigation.

Internalizing the importance of this balance will help you in your dealings with gatekeeping individuals or departments. Overt recognition of it ('We realize that the financial aspects of this are critical. Would you help us to think them through?') and a request for help at an early stage can often prevent problems from arising. Where there is a history that makes such conversation difficult or unproductive, or where you find the arguments for your proposals so compelling that you flare at the prospect of having to justify them again, at a cost to you of considerable time, then you may find it worthwhile to ask a colleague to write the business case for you. A couple of briefing sessions to a peer who understands your reasoning and concern but who is not directly involved, and thus who is not as passionate as you, can be time well invested. Naturally, you would reciprocate the favour. Once our emotions are disengaged, insurmountable problems often become interesting puzzles, so the time spent on them is enjoyable rather than infuriating. Even if you decide to write the case yourself, testing out the arguments with someone slightly removed from it often enables you to make them more convincing. It would be very sad if clinicians were not passionate about their practice and their patients, but this essential emotional commitment is bound to make dealings with gatekeeper functions fraught. All concerned need to realize this and find ways around it, rather than personalizing the situation.

When presenting a business case you are basically answering the following question: 'I have limited resources to invest, why should I choose this particular project?' The case should therefore specify how investment in this project will help the decision-maker to meet *their* objectives. It should spell out the benefits to be reaped from the investment; for example, better clinical outcomes resulting in more contracts; reductions in future costs and how these will be delivered. It must also detail the full costs. If the case can be supported on these grounds, then approval will rest on whether you are judged capable of delivering the benefits. The case should therefore also describe your strengths and how this project exploits them, how this project fits within the strategic direction of your service and your track record in managing investments of this sort.

If, despite your investment of time and energy, your case is not approved, how do you respond? One way is to express your anger to all concerned – to the decision-maker(s), your staff, your patients – explaining indignantly to them all that your ability to care for your patients is being hampered by others. This can be momentarily satisfying, yet what impact does it have? Your staff are further demotivated and less able to provide the care or support your patients need. Your patients lose faith in your ability to meet their needs and have to cope with anger and frustration as well as their clinical condition.

Another way is to ask for the reasons why your case failed, and why other cases have been supported. Work on the assumption that all concerned are reasonable people, that if the evidence convinces you, it can convince them if you present it in a way that meets their needs. Invite them to discuss with you their reservations, hear them out, reflect on them and address them. If, for example, they feel that you already have sufficient resources within the department to develop this project, invite them to discuss how they have come to that conclusion. If their view is based on faulty information, then correct it; if not, then consider whether there may be some justice in their position.

As a general rule, whenever you are tempted to blame someone else, stop for a moment and reflect on whether there is anything you have done or are doing that is exacerbating the problem, or whether you are actively trying to resolve it. As Eldridge Cleaver stated, 'If you are not part of the solution you are part of the problem.'[13] All of us, if we are honest with ourselves, will find many instances every day when we have been part of the problem rather than the solution, when we have acted little rather than big, when we could have been effective rather than angry. Dwelling on these mistakes does not help at all, but neither does ignoring them. Recognizing them and learning from them is the way forward. It is very difficult to do this unless we learn to lose our anger. While we are angry with someone we are less effective. The impact is on us. It does not touch them, does not harm them, does not reduce their effectiveness – only our own. We can choose our feelings about people, we can choose to see their virtues and disregard their vices. Even when this is difficult, we can choose not to let them get the better of us by making us angry. Here again generosity and self-discipline are required. Keeping in mind our purpose will once again help.

Perhaps as important as anything else is our recognition of our own role in influencing the mission and values of our organization. As far as the organization is concerned, are we part of the problem or part of the solution? If we think about Paul Bate's suggestion that the culture of an organization is manifest in the stories woven by people within it, then we can see that (as he also suggests) people who rewrite some of those stories are leaders, whether they are in formal positions of power or not. Using the content of this chapter and the previous two you will be able to decide which stories you want to support and which you believe need to be changed – and you will be able to start to do so. You can help to create an organization you *want* to work for.

Notes

1   Bate, P. (1994) *Strategies for Cultural Change* (Oxford: Butterworth Heinemann).
2   See, for example, Mannion, R., Davies, H. and Marshall, M. (2004) *Cultures for Performance in Health Care* (Maidenhead: Open University Press).
3   Sometimes, for example, the board.
4   Covey (1990) *The Seven Habits of Highly Effective People* (New York: Simon and Schuster). A number of people I have worked with have found this book to live up to its title; namely, it has helped them to become more effective. It has also helped them to assess the development inputs required by others in their organization. I find this book complements Peck (1979); see Chapter 2, note 12. Peck's book introduces the territory, whereas Covey's book is a 'how to' manual.
5   The full quotation from Frankl's *Man's Search for Meaning*, Beacon Press, Boston 1963, is 'Between stimulus and response there is a space. In that space lies our freedom and power to choose our response. In our response lies our growth and freedom.'
6   Taken from Covey (1990).
7   Note that this is a different use of the term from that employed in Chapter 2.
8   de Pree (1989); see Chapter 1, note 16.
9   French, J. R. P. and Raven, B. (1960) 'The bases of social power'. In D. Cartwright and A. E. Zander (eds) *Group Dynamics* (Evanston, IL: Row, Peterson and Company), pp. 607–23.
10   Discussed in Laming, D. (2004) *Human Judgment. The Eye of the Beholder* (London: Thompson).
11   Baddeley, S. and James, K., *Owl, Fox, Donkey and Sheep: Political Skills for Managers. Management Education and Development.* Vol. 18. pt. 1. 1987, pp. 3–19.
12   Psychological game playing is a term taken from Transactional Analysis. See Berne, E., *Games People Play*, chapter 6, note 8.
13   Quoted in Peck (1979); see Chapter 2, note 12.

4 Really managing resources

Managing people and relationships, the subjects of the first three chapters, are often what service leaders find the most difficult aspects of taking on a management role. However, managing the performance of the service against targets, and finances against budgets, has also been known to keep them awake at night, and in this chapter we consider how to make the very most of the resources you have available.

Making the most of resources

Let us make sure, first of all, that we are talking the same language. Figure 4.1 expresses a very simple idea: that your service has an aim (or set of aims) and a certain amount of resource you can use to try to achieve that aim. Those resources (people, materials and so on) deliver outcomes that we can think of as the performance of the service. When we are interested in how well we are managing resources we are really answering two questions: is the performance very similar to the aims; and have we stayed within the resources available to us? Typically HCPs tend to think they can answer 'yes' to only one of these, and find it agonizing to choose between them. But we need to be able to think about them *both* at the same time. In other words, to think about using resources both effectively and efficiently.

The schools of thinking that have most to offer here are those of quality management and management accounting, so we will look at key elements from both of those. However, we will start by thinking a little further about efficiency, since it is a term that has had a very bad press in many health services as they have struggled to limit increases in costs.

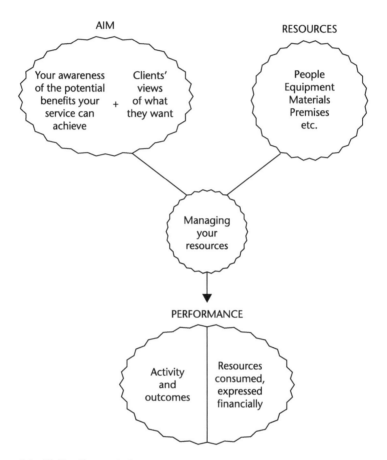

Figure 4.1 Making the most of resources

Efficiency

Efficiency is about achieving as much as you can with as little as possible, so that you can do more, or spend less, or both. In most areas of life it is a good thing, although, of course, not the only thing. In health care many people have developed an aversion to the very idea because it has become synonymous in many people's experience with 'cuts'. The 'efficiency savings' that have been required in many services have all too often been achieved, not through efficiency at all, but by making cuts. Managers may have seen those cuts as efficiencies, as means of achieving the same results with a smaller resource, especially if they involved axing staff posts away from the frontline. But staff left behind have had to absorb workloads or do without support from which they previously benefited, so unless they had previously been underemployed or were enabled to approach their work in a different, less labour-intensive way, these were definitely cuts. This is no way to approach efficiency savings.

Efficiency requires a mindset that focuses on improvement, an emphasis on quality, a genuine concern to do the best for the customer. Cuts come from a manipulation mindset, a style that could be described as *command and control*. While cuts involve *zero-sum* thinking, in which it is assumed that there is a game to be played, in which if I win you have to lose (and vice versa), efficiency needs *abundance* thinking. This takes as its starting point the assumption that if we work together to try to meet all our aims we will probably find a way of doing so, or at least get much closer to it than if we fight. Efficiency needs a good understanding of the processes of providing a service and of the way costs are structured. Cuts just need a change in a budget. Cuts are much easier, but ultimately self-defeating. Efficiency is hard work but yields long-lasting positive results. It is a tragedy that, in my opinion, many politicians and managers in the 1990s could not tell the difference, and that it has led to alienation of clinical professionals in a way that was quite unnecessary.

Managing resources, then, requires you to understand processes, understand the way costs change with different levels of activity and understand the dynamics at play between people within the system. It also requires the courage to prompt people of high status to think constructively about changes they can make in the ways they work – not at all an easy thing to do. We will start by looking at what we can learn from the strand of thinking that started in the manufacturing industry, about quality.

Quality management

The field of quality management has a history of eclecticism. Several strands of thought have fed into a large armoury of approaches and tools available to us today and the choice can be bewildering. As many advocates of particular approaches can be single-mindedly evangelistic (and surprisingly often have a vested interest) and are thus not able to help you make a judicious selection of different tools for different situations, I am going to take you back to some of the essential elements to help you do so. These elements are: wanting to improve; finding out what your customers want; measuring how good you are; and focusing on processes rather than events.

Wanting to improve

If there were no other thinking or tools available to you, you could get a fair way to improving quality if you genuinely wanted to. We will see later that by itself this is not enough, but the desire for improvement is still the basis of everything else. If you can work together with other people who are equally genuine in their desire to make changes for the better you will, naturally, be able to achieve greater improvements than you can on your own. And without a desire to improve, no matter how many other tools you deploy, you will change almost nothing for the better.

If you don't care about how your service performs then you may be able to maintain the service levels where they are, but improving performance will happen only by accident. Even if you are instructed to reach a target of some sort the likelihood is that, if you do not accept that the target is important, you will only achieve it by reducing service in another area.

But perhaps we are getting ahead of ourselves, because we haven't yet established what we mean by 'quality' and hence 'better' and 'improve'.

Knowing what we mean by quality

Box 4.1 lists a number of definitions of quality, with the earlier ones first. Does anything strike you about them? You may find the dotted line indicates a change. The difference is only one of emphasis: none of the definitions actually contradicts another, so we can see that they all convey a sense of being 'fit for purpose'. However, later definitions suggest that the purpose is identified by the customer, whereas in the earlier ones it is more likely to be defined by the provider. This difference is important. As beauty is in the eye of the beholder, so quality is in the eye of the customer.

It is easy to confuse quality with luxury, and thus to assume that quality costs money. When we appreciate that it is about meeting particular needs we can see that this is not necessarily so. A car is a useful example. It is primarily for transporting people and luggage from A to B safely. So any car that does that reliably could be thought of as a quality car. However, the different needs of a large family (lots of room), a city driver (small parking spaces), a senior business person (credibility/status), a motorway driver (robust in case of accidents at speed), a student (cool design) and someone hiring out cars for fancy weddings mean that what is quality for one is not necessarily quality for another. Anything for which we don't have a purpose is luxury. Paying extra

---

Box 4.1 Definitions of quality

Fitness for use
Conformance to requirements
Meeting the needs of customers
. . . .
Satisfying customers (meeting the expectations of customers)
Delighting customers (exceeding the expectations of customers)

for it is extravagance. So paying more does not guarantee higher quality. Meeting the needs of customers as they see them does. Of course, there are times when that does require greater expenditure, but we cannot assume it will, and noisily arguing for more resources without first having done any analysis or measurement is simply irresponsible.

So when I say that the intention to improve quality is fundamental, it is *your* intention I am talking about, not that of other people you can blame for not giving you more resources. I do know, though, that for you to *want* to improve your service you have to feel *able* to, and that there are a number of reasons why you may not. One of the most frequent is that you have to persuade other people to change the way they are doing things, and some of these people will be difficult (in ways we have looked at in Chapters 1 and 2) and some will have higher status than you do. I hope you find that using the learning from this book will help you to tackle this, but you may feel you need additional support. This is just the kind of situation where you could find an action learning set or a good coach or mentor invaluable. It is worth remembering, too, that even without influencing others there will be a lot you can do if you want to. It would be unrealistic to deny that sometimes the situation you are in will limit how much you can achieve, but even here you can always consider what you *yourself* can do to improve quality.

Finding out what your customers want

Wanting to improve your service and feeling able to do so are essential, but you will also need a sense of direction about what it is that most needs improving. You could decide that for yourself, based on your knowledge of the purpose and potential of your service. But if quality is in the eye of the customer, you will also need to find out what your customer needs or wants. Who do I mean when I talk of customers? Do you have in mind a patient or client? Are you irritated by my choice of term? I have used it deliberately, to encompass patients or clients, whom we can think of as 'external customers' in that they have nothing to do with the provision of services, being consumers of them, and also 'internal customers'. These internal customers are people who are part of the service process but rely on you to provide them with something they need if they are to fulfil their role. If you call to mind the activities you undertake in the course of a day, some of them are directly for patients, some are for other people in your organization and some may be for people in other health or care organizations. Most will be concerned with the same client group as you, and if you sketch out a map of the patient journey through the service you will see that every health care worker on that chart fulfils a 'triple role' – they are a customer, a processor and a supplier. For an illustration of this please see figure 4.2.

If the service is to be of acceptable quality overall, then every customer

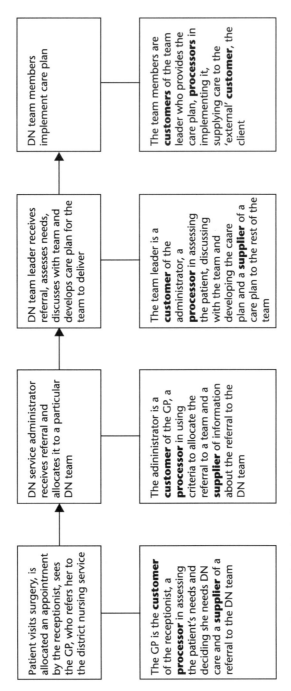

Figure 4.2 Triple roles in the referral of a patient from a GP to a District Nursing Team

along the pathway should have their needs met by the person who is their immediate supplier. For the service to be good, customers must be exacting and suppliers obliging. As you yourself will be both customer and supplier, are you able to say that you are an exacting customer (gracefully exacting) and an obliging supplier? This is worth thinking about because most of us, most of the time, concentrate on being an effective processor, and while that is important, it is not enough.

You can probably see that the story is more complicated than this – that in every interaction between customer and supplier the customer needs to receive something from the supplier if they are to be able to be a good customer. For example, if the District Nursing Service inform the GP how to access the service, the information they will need to process the referral quickly and the response time they can offer, and they make this available in a form that is easy to retrieve, then they help the GP to be a much better customer. In turn they will be able to be more effective suppliers. Thus, identifying customers is important, and not as straightforward as it might initially have seemed, but the step that will make all the difference is discussing with them what you each want or need from the other.

Depending on who you are, on your credibility or authority with the other HCPs on the patient journey, you may feel you can go no further than that – establishing and then working to meet the needs of your internal customers and suppliers, and the patient as you are directly working with them. You might, however, want to take it further and look at quality across the whole journey.

There is a lot of information and help available now on 'process mapping', so there is no need for much detail here, but the principle is to bring into one room all the people involved in the care of one carefully defined group of clients, and try to represent in a visual way the pathways actually taken by clients through the service. The most commonly used tools are rolls of wall-paper and self-stick notes, and typically the discussion will start with a description of what *should* happen to a client entering and moving through the service. As individuals start to voice their observations that, in practice, what happens to the patient is something quite different, the discussion usually becomes more heated. A facilitator is useful in containing the emotions and directing them along useful channels. Once each step along the pathway is written on a note and there is general agreement (which can involve checking data or other evidence) that the way they are placed on the pathway represents what happens in practice, it is possible to think about how to redesign it. As existing pathways have rarely been designed in advance, but have evolved over many years, they usually include a number of steps that are unnecessary and can be eliminated with little argument. Typically there will be some points on the pathway where opinion is divided as to the most appropriate course of action, and now that this difference of view is out in the open, evidence can be sought about their relative merits. Sometimes the evidence will be sufficiently compelling for agreement to be reached easily. Sometimes it will not and the clinicians involved will have to agree with the rest of the team (and especially their immediate 'customers') how the different views can be accommodated in practice. Bottle necks can be identified and means of releasing pressures at that point can be devised. If this is done with everyone present then the usual danger, of the solution to one problem causing another, can be avoided.

The most valuable part of the exercise is often the realization of just what the pathway involves. Participants are usually well aware of their own section of it, and innocent of the rest. Hearing the frustrations of clients and other HCPs can have a profound impact on the way individuals see their own role and behaviours.

Even well run redesign projects can run into the ground, however, and it is often tempting to blame particular individuals as intransigent, or groups as arrogant or complacent. While this may occasionally be the case it can be more helpful to try to identify the levels of energy available for redesign and see if those are what is causing the problem.

What do I mean by energy? Well, not what we mean when we talk colloquially about energy levels. Soft systems methods is the term given to a group of processes that illuminate energy best and the simplest tool of these is to view the 'system' as seen by each of the participants. The key system components are the inputs, transformation processes, outputs and 'wider system' within which the 'system of interest' nests.

You will see what I mean if we look at an example. Let's take an outpatient clinic that was causing problems on a maternity services pathway a few years ago. We know it was a problem because mothers-to-be regularly complained at being kept waiting, and because the service was not meeting its target for clients seeing a midwife within 30 minutes of arriving.[1] When asked about why this was happening the clinic nursing staff explained that the medical staff were always late, and the medical staff, when approached about their lack of timeliness, explained that they must give priority to their wards, where they had cases more urgent than those in the antenatal clinic.

After much heated discussion agreement was reached that a different rota system would be implemented, and that the outpatient sister would give feedback to the consultants about the timeliness of their junior doctors, and this would then form part of their appraisal. After six months, however, nothing had happened, and if we look at how the same outpatient clinic can be seen as a set of completely different 'systems', in Figure 4.2, we can see why.

You may be surprised to see that the energy in the outpatient sister's system was low, but this was because she was just as, or more, interested in friendly relations with her clients as in meeting their needs. Because she was able to explain to them that the problem was due to the doctors being late she remained on those friendly terms. We can see that the energy for change is to

Table 4.1 Key system components

System as seen by	Inputs	Transformation processes	Desired outputs	Wider system	Energy for change
Mothers-to-be	Pregnancy Appointment	Examination Ultrasound Discussion with midwife and obstetrician	Reassurance or knowledge of any problems and how they will be dealt with	Nine months of pregnancy Day-to-day life at work and home Other family and work pressures	High
Outpatient sister	Clients Clinic resources Midwives and obstetricians	Greeting clients Getting clients in to see clinicians	Friendly relations with clients and clinicians	Antenatal clinic all day every day Working with the clinical staff on an ongoing basis	Low
Consultants and junior doctors	Large numbers of mothers-to-be so that they can identify the small percentage that will need their input	Assessment of and discussion with clients	(Abnormal births) Cases that require their specialist expertise	Their wider obstetric practice on the wards Their research Their medical careers	Low
Service manager	Targets set in Patients Charter Clients arriving at the clinic	Clients being seen	Percentage of clients seen within 30 minutes conforms with target	Pressure to meet targets in order to protect career and reputation of organization	High

be found among mothers-to-be and the service manager, but the change was to be implemented by the outpatient sister and the medical staff. As we must always work with human nature rather than against it, this change needs to be rethought. Either we need to find a way of increasing the energy of those who are due to implement the changes (by which I mean increasing the difference between their desired outputs and their actual outputs) or we need to design a change that uses the energy in the systems of mothers-to-be or the service manager.

In the case on which this fictional, simplified version is based the service manager resolved the matter to his satisfaction by introducing a 'hello mid-wife' who greeted mothers shortly after their arrival, thus meeting the target, and perhaps offering a small amount of additional reassurance, but not fundamentally improving the service. Once this happened, the only people who cared deeply about improving it were the clients. Given the lack of support from the obstetricians and nurses, not because they were wicked people but because there was no energy in *their* systems that pushed them to make any changes, it was probably the only thing he could do. I would like to think he used his solution as a breathing space that allowed him to invest the energy needed to introduce further changes himself, monitoring their implementation and making sure that everyone received feedback on just how welcome the mother found the changes to be. But I doubt it. He will have had other fires to fight.

Does it frustrate you that I don't castigate this behaviour? If so, just think. The service manager has a limited amount of time and he can't waste it bashing his head against a brick wall if there are other areas where he will be more successful, unless there is a danger in leaving something unchanged. In this case inconvenience isn't danger, so what would you do? I hope Chapter 2 will have given you some tools the manager here didn't use. But you too will sometimes have to decide where you can invest your time most successfully.

Measuring how good you are

So far we have said that wanting to improve your service, feeling able to do so and deciding on what to aim for are all important. There is another factor that is essential: measuring how well the service is doing. Unless you measure you won't know and, unless you know, you won't be able to step in and address any problems. Of course, you could rely on informal measures (the number of patients who seem appreciative, the number who don't) but we are very unreliable interpreters of this kind of feedback, and tend to give greater weight to evidence that confirms our own views than to any that challenges them.

So, if we can agree that measuring is important, I would like to introduce you to two factors it is important to remember. Trade offs and variation.

Trading one measure for another

Imagine you are manufacturing widgets that are the shape and dimensions given in Figure 4.3. If the role of the widget is to fit into a larger piece of kit (a super-widget) then it must conform to dimensions that will allow it to do so. These dimensions will be easy to measure and so it will be easy to determine whether the widget conforms to the specification, and is fit for its purpose. You might perform the measurement on a sample of widgets taken either at random, or, say, every hundredth off the production line. If there was a problem of some kind with the machine making them and one particular aspect of the widget was proving problematic (perhaps the distance between A and B was fluctuating between 10 per cent too long and 8 per cent too short, when you need it to be within 1 per cent of the mean), then by making alterations to the machine you could increase the reliability of the positioning of A and B and ensure that that measure conforms to its specification. However, there is now a good chance that the machine is delivering widgets that do not conform to one of the other measures. If, when you were worried about the AB problem, you decided to concentrate only on the AB measurement you are now in real trouble, because you have a different problem with quality and you do not yet know that you do.

We can always improve performance against one target if we do not mind missing others, if we are prepared to trade off one aspect for another. And sometimes this may be appropriate, but often not, and never blindly.

As we move from simple goods to simple services we see that the measures change but are still straightforward. Imagine a widgetburger and the measure that might be relevant there: Figure 4.4.

As we think about producing goods and services that are more complex the measures are more difficult, but the principle is still the same: because of the dangers of trading off one aspect of quality for another we need to measure all of them. Of course, they will not all need the same amount of attention,

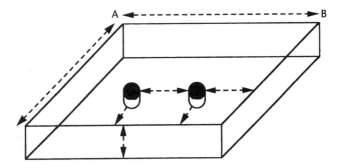

Figure 4.3   Shape and dimensions of a widget

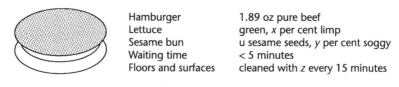

Hamburger	1.89 oz pure beef
Lettuce	green, x per cent limp
Sesame bun	u sesame seeds, y per cent soggy
Waiting time	< 5 minutes
Floors and surfaces	cleaned with z every 15 minutes

Figure 4.4 Measuring the quality of a widgetburger

because some are more difficult to get right than others, and because some cause greater problems than others. So we can tailor the way in which we measure and the intervals between measurements so that we do not waste unnecessary time, but we do need to ensure that everything *is* measured. This will become clearer when we look at an example.

What is it that we are measuring in health care? Robert Maxwell[2] suggested twenty years ago six measures of any health service, and made this very point that it would be all to easy to score highly on one at the expense of another, and that all six needed to be kept in mind. Certainly these six are still important and relevant, and worthy of reflection and attention by managers at all service levels. On a more day-to-day basis, though, something more is needed, something that reflects more directly the kinds of thing patients need and care about as they use the service.

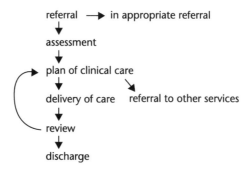

Figure 4.5 A patient's pathway through the clinical process

Every service can be thought of as a series of stages through which the client progresses. This is not exactly the same as the patient journey but could be thought of as a simplified version of it. Typically it looks like Figure 4.5. We will see this being used again in Chapter 7 when we think about information flows; here we are going to use it to identify the kind of things about a service that need to be measured. You can probably see that at each stage in this progress through the service there are several standards or objectives that you would like to meet. You wouldn't want to keep the referrer waiting very long before you respond to their call, for example, and you want the treatment prescribed to be in line with good evidence. For every stage there will be some aspects that are wholly within the control of the service (these can be called standards) and there are some that rely on the involvement of others, usually other services (and these can be called objectives). Of course you could call them all targets, but I think it is helpful to distinguish between those things you control and those you can only influence.

Where do these standards and objectives come from? You will have a good idea of the kind of service you would like to provide, and of what is possible. The patients too, and referrers and the other services to which you refer people on, will have views on what is important. So asking these stakeholders will give you useful information. Does this sound familiar? It is not dissimilar to the kind of conversations we talked about before, when we thought about being exacting customers, effective processors and obliging suppliers.

Once you have decided *what* to measure you will need to think about *how* and *how often*. The least critical and least problematic need be measured much less frequently (though still regularly) than those that have a more profound impact or are more likely to go wrong. All need to be measured in as unobstructive a manner as possible, and some could be as simple as a question to everyone who calls the service on a particular day every six months about how long it took them to get through. Some, though, will need more careful measurement and ongoing attention. All the measurements should be recorded, so that any patterns can be identified and action taken if necessary. It can be tempting to try to take too much action or too little and, to understand why that is, we need to look at the second factor I mentioned earlier: variation.

Variation

Although all the widgets you produced, when you were manufacturing widgets a few pages ago, may have looked the same, they definitely were not the same – not exactly. Many of them will have been similar enough to fit into the super-widget, and that is what they are needed for, so that is fine. Some of them will have been too different and they will have been rejected as imperfect. Variation is inherent in any system of producing anything. I found that idea difficult to accept fully when I was first introduced to it, and I notice that others find it difficult too. We pride ourselves in tailoring care to individuals and think of variation as a good thing in that sense, but the idea that it is present even when we want things to be the same takes a while to absorb. We need to acknowledge it for two reasons, or to avoid two mistakes. One mistake is to intervene in systems too much and the other is to intervene too little. Let's find out more about the nature of variation.

If you can bear to think back to the manufacture of widgets we can see that widget production is a process. How many of the widgets that are produced are of the right quality (fit into the super-widget) depends on the nature of that process. If we noticed that not very many of the widgets are fitting the super-widget, what might we do? Suppose last month nearly 30 per cent of the widgets were not the right shape for the super-widget, and the remaining 70 per cent were. We could decide to set ourselves a target, that 85 per cent of the widgets would be the right size. That is probably more acceptable as a figure, so that might be what we want from the process. But do we know whether it is what we will get? We could look back at the figures over the past six months, find that the percentage of defective widgets fluctuated between 90 and 70 per cent (90, 80, 70, 70, 90 and 80) and decide that we need to find out more about what was happening in the months when the figures were poor, so that we can fix any problems and increase the quality overall.

That is what we would do if we did not understand about variation. If we fully accept that variation is inherent in all processes we will know that some of the difference in these results is just a manifestation of that variation, it is not because anything about the process itself was different in those months when the quality was lower. However, those low results may indicate that there was indeed a problem with the process, not explicable by normal variation at all. So how can we tell which is the case? We need a way of knowing how much of the difference in these figures is 'noise', variation that will happen inevitably, and how much is a signal that something different is happening in those months. The way to distinguish between noise and signal is to use a control chart. Control charts were first devised by Walter Shewhart in the 1940s and made popular by W.E. Deming and the total quality management school. In essence they consists of a graph on which you plot, let us say, the average number of defective widgets for every month. When you have eight or nine plots on the graph you can take the mean of these figures and draw a line on the graph that will be central to the figures depicted so far (see Figure 4.6). Now you calculate an upper and lower natural process limit[3] and plot these parallel to the central line.

If the figures on the chart are mostly within the upper and lower lines then the process can be said to be in control; in other words it is producing results that behave predictably. It may not be producing the results you want it to, but at least you will be able to predict what it will produce. If the figures fluctuate outside of these limits then the process is said to be out of control, and the results will be unpredictable and inconsistent and will change over time, so you will not be able to predict its output. Or you can predict that it will fluctuate and in random directions. So 'a process is said to be in control when, through the use of past experience, we can predict at least within limits how the process will behave in the future. Thus the essence of statistical control is predictability.'[4] This is what Shewhart called the 'voice of the process, the process talking back'. So we now have two 'voices', the voice of the customer,

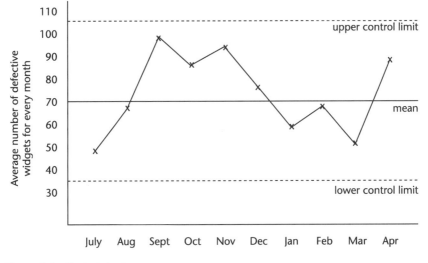

Figure 4.6 Control chart

the person feeding the super-widget who wants only x per cent of defective widgets, and the voice of the process telling us that we are likely to produce between y and z per cent defective widgets. It is our job now, as the manager of the process of making widgets, to see that those two voices are as close as possible, and that may well involve changing the process so that the super-widget feeder can rely on only x per cent defective widgets.

So the role of statistical control of processes (otherwise called statistical process control or SPC) is to help you as the manager of a process to intervene to improve it whenever, but only whenever, improvement is needed. Without SPC it is all too easy to make changes unnecessarily (because you assume a low reading is significant when it is just random variation within the limits of the process) and to ignore changes that need to be made, because you are not recognizing readings that do indicate a problem in the process. In practice you will look out for points that lie outside the upper and lower control limits, or for three or four consecutive values that are closer to one of the limits than to the central line, or for eight or more successive values on the same side of the central line.

Who should use SPC? Anyone who controls a process. So you need to be devising control charts for any process that you control. As we saw above, not all measures need to be frequent, but they do need to be regular. And if you do this you will find you are much more likely to be in control of what is happening, and perhaps to feel really in control for the first time – you will be able to predict what will happen, be able to intervene if necessary and know before anyone else if anything is going wrong. It is important that you do it, and that you share it with the people who are part of the process, because, as George Box puts it,[5] the purpose of SPC is 'so that everyone can improve the process, not so that some people can control other people'.

We have seen that if we want to improve quality we have to want to do so, to feel able to do so, to find out what our customers want and to measure how we are doing. There is one other fundamental to improving quality and that is genuinely to believe that it is systems that lead to outcomes, and not individuals, that when we are analysing what needs to be changed we need to reflect on processes and not events.

Systems, not individuals; processes, not events

Let us look at defective outputs from a whole range of industries (manufacturing and service industries in private and public sectors) and consider that a defect could have been caused either by someone who should have known better and does something that another person in that situation would not have done, or by someone who behaved in just the same way as anyone else in that situation would have done. In other words, in some cases individuals are to blame for the defect, and in others the system is to blame. Figures from across a range of industries show what percentage of defects are caused by individuals and what percentage by systems, and you might like to estimate what those percentages are before I tell you in the accompanying note.[6] So whenever we are investigating an adverse incident of any kind we must certainly consider if there are any individuals who should justifiably be seen to be at fault, but we should probably spend eleven times as much effort on analysing where the processes should be improved.

Chris Argyris and Donald Schön[7] refer to this in their concept of distinguishing between single loop and double loop learning. Single loop learning is where we identify something that is going wrong and we step in to fix that particular thing. So if referrer A fails to give HCP B the information B needs in order to assess the urgency of a particular case and someone suffers as a result, then we can learn from this that A needs to be taught or told what information is required.

Double loop learning takes place when we look more widely than an individual or an event and see whether there are systems or processes that need some attention. In this case it may be that the service of which B is a member has no arrangements in place to make their referral process widely known, and double loop learning would involve setting up such arrangements.

We could think of double loop as a deeper level of learning than single loop, and there is a third type of learning that we could see as deeper still, and this is called deutero learning. Here we ask the questions: 'How is it that we never noticed, or didn't care, that these arrangements were not in place? What do we need to do in order to ensure we notice something like this in future?'

There are occasions where single loop learning is enough, where a quick fix is all that is needed. However, there are many more when it is not, and we do no harm if, in every case, we ask ourselves whether there is any double loop or deutero learning to be done.[8]

An improvement mindset

I said, on page 91, that efficiency needed an improvement mindset and I hope that by now you can see what that involves and feel excited by it. But we can't pretend that money isn't important too; of course it is. In the next section we will look at how money behaves when you introduce any changes, and how to monitor your performance in a different way – against a budget.

Understanding money

Does the following sound familiar? 'A survey has revealed that approximately 70 per cent of the responding organizations used questionable financial information as a basis for decision-making.'

HCPs can get a bad press about money. Surveys can show that they don't understand financial statements, don't use budget statements to influence their decisions and wait to be told at the end of the year whether they have come in on budget or not – caring little either way. But it is time for 'financial skills' and their perceived shortage in health care organizations to be put into perspective. The quote above refers not to health care but to UK manufacturing companies.[9] It may well be the case that HCPs cannot read financial statements with any comprehension, but no one has satisfactorily demonstrated a link between this and the ability to manage money. Indeed, in many industries, any 'failure' in such circumstances would be acknowledged by the finance staff who had prepared the statements.

Managing money owes more to an acceptance of the guidance of Mr Micawber (the penurious landlord in *David Copperfield* who lives in the eternal hope that 'something will turn up') than to anything else. It requires recognition of the fact that if you have only one pound to spend, and towards the end of the financial year you are confident that you will spend only Mr Micawber's nineteen shillings and sixpence, then you (like him) will have the happiness of sixpence to spend as you wish; but that if you spend one pound and sixpence the result will be the disaster of outside interference in the way you allocate your resources. Once this belief is firmly embedded then the greatest financial skill required is the ability to turn over to the back of an envelope, to do your calculations. This all-important belief is endangered every time any department or service or organization is 'bailed out', and judging the difference between a genuine (and genuinely unforeseeable) need for extra funds and arrogant or undisciplined profligacy is one of the reasons chief executives, and their most senior staff, must spend so much time out and about in their organizations.

Contrary to the wishful thinking of many, improving your financial skills will not in itself make any more money available to you. Nor will it allow you to achieve any more with the money you have – that is the result of the skills discussed earlier in this chapter. It will, however, help you to understand the impact on your financial position of a particular proposal, increase your ability to calculate how much your services are costing and allow you to monitor how you are managing your money.

There are two sets of users of accounting information: people inside the organization and agencies outside it. Generally the internal users require it for decision-making and the external for regulatory purposes. The two sets of users and uses have given rise to two kinds of accounting: financial accounting (for external parties) and management accounting (for internal). A set of financial accounts is generally required once a year, in a statutory format, prepared in accordance with accepted accounting principles, referring to the past year and encompassing the organization as a whole. Their emphasis is on precision rather than speed. Normally they are written by accountants for accountants, or at any rate for people with some specialist expertise in deciphering them, analysing them seeing behind them and knowing what questions to ask of the organization's top management. If you are ever required to help to put these together, or to read them, then you will have specialist advice and assistance available. A failure among HCPs to make head or tail of a set of financial accounting statements is to be *expected*. It will be the norm, and rightly so.

Management accounts are produced for use within the organization. They are outside statutory regulation; they can be presented, commissioned and used entirely at the discretion of the organization and the people within it. In many respects, they are the converse of the financial accounts. They are produced not once a year but on an ongoing basis; they refer not to the past but to the present and future; they describe parts of the organization, rather than the whole; and they occasionally sacrifice precision for the sake of speed. We could perhaps use the distinction we have been drawing on throughout this book and characterize the difference between the two kinds of accounting by suggesting that financial accounting is the 'complicated easy', whereas management accounting is the 'simple hard'.

The aim of this part of the chapter is to arm you with sufficient understanding of the principles of management accounting for you to be able to have a sensible discussion with your director of finance, finance department or management accountant about the kind of information you require from them if you are to manage your resources. Incidentally, you may be interested to know that accountants are taught that part of their role is to 'motivate desirable individual performances by communicating performance information in relation to the targets set' in the budget.[10] I have yet to encounter a HCP who finds their monthly budget statement motivational, and this major difference in perspective may go some way to explaining why accountants, even those with talent and good will, find health care organizations so challenging and exasperating (and vice versa).

If you enhance your financial skills in the ways outlined in this chapter, you will improve your ability to do three things:

1 Calculate your costs.
2 Look at the impact on your financial position of any clinical or managerial decisions.
3 Set up mechanisms for monitoring your financial performance, so that you can then decide what to do about it.

All of these are far too important for you to leave to someone who does not understand your service the way you do. You cannot leave this to the finance department – I am sorry, but it is *your* job. If your response to this is that you did not enter health care to become an accountant, then think clearly, because this is not what you are being asked to do. In any setting, anywhere, the use of any resource has to be justified, and health care is no exception. The resources you use or commit must be justified; either by you, or by someone else who will then have the right to tell you what you can or cannot do. No one is asking you to concentrate *solely* on financial figures; those figures are only one way of capturing what you and your service are doing and you will be much more interested in the kind of figures we have been looking at in relation to quality, but unless you give them your attention someone else will give them theirs.

Calculating costs[11]

Calculating costs, even in industries where the products are much simpler than those in health care, is not as straightforward as it may seem. To find the cost of a 'widget' we are manufacturing, or a patient contract we are providing, we divide the total costs associated with producing it by the number of 'widgets' or patient contracts that we produce. That sounds simple, but let us consider exactly what we should include in these 'total costs'.

Imagine for a moment that we *are* producing widgets. Clearly, we must include all the costs of the materials used up in the manufacture of the widgets. Also the costs of the labour hours spent on making them. But if the machines used in their production also produce other goods, then any costs of maintaining these machines cannot be borne entirely by the widgets. And yet, if the other goods were to go out of production, then the entire machine maintenance cost would have to be recouped from the widgets. The widget-making machine will be housed in factory premises that incur rates. Should these be included in our 'total' costs? And what about the expense of the staff canteen? Already we can see that there are different kinds of costs.

The cost of any goods or service can be thought of as made up of three parts: direct costs, indirect costs and overheads. *Direct costs* are those that are used only for, and entirely by, the product we are trying to cost. In our widget example, these would be the materials and labour. *Indirect costs* are linked not solely to one product but to several. Machine maintenance would fall into this category, as would any holiday pay for the operator. *Overheads* are incurred on an organization-wide basis; in our example, the building rates and staff canteen are overheads.

If instead of trying to cost a widget we were attempting to calculate the average cost of all the products made by the widget-making machine, then clearly the machine maintenance switches from being an indirect cost to a direct cost. So whether a particular cost is direct or indirect depends on the *cost objective*; that is, exactly what it is we are trying to cost. It is therefore not possible to say that study leave, for example, is invariably a direct or an indirect cost, since it will depend on whether the individual taking it is engaged in providing more than one service and on what is the cost objective.

Indirect costs must be allocated to the cost objective, but normally the means of doing so are not contentious and require only the deployment of common sense. Machine maintenance costs, for example, could be split according to the ratio of the number of widgets produced to the number of other products produced on the same machine. Alternatively, the machine hours spent on each could be used. Another possibility would be the weight of the materials used in production. A knowledge of the machine and its propensity for malfunction would be needed in order to choose between them, but to someone with this knowledge the appropriate option would be self-evident.

When it comes to overhead costs, however, the allocation process is almost invariably a two-stage process, the alternatives are greater in number and the option selected can have an impact on the decision-making behaviour of departments and budget-holders. In the widget example, the building rates and the costs of running the staff canteen need to be allocated. A sensible rationale for apportioning the rates would be the floor area each department occupies. Using floor area as the basis for allocating canteen costs would be ridiculous; instead, the number of employees would make more sense. The canteen will also have received its portion of the rates bill and will be passing this on when its total costs are allocated. Suppose that when the rates, the salary of the chief executive and the renovation of the building's exterior are included in the canteen costs, they exceed the prices on offer elsewhere. Suppose departments could feed their staff more cheaply by giving them an allowance to buy meals at a local cafe. If the canteen closed, the rates, chief executive's salary and renovation expenses would still have to be paid, so should they be included in the 'total costs' of the canteen? Is the answer influenced by the fact that the chief executive spends no time at all worrying about the canteen service or management, or that the canteen is in an interior room with no exterior walls? Management accounting is not simply a question of knowing where to wield your calculator; it requires careful consideration of behaviours.

The different ways in which overhead costs are allocated may all have their basis in logic but lead to very different figures being produced. The same widgets manufactured in the same way can be presented as costing very different amounts. The same is true for patient contracts or any particular pathway of care. Their costs can legitimately be presented in a number of different ways.

How costs behave when activity changes

Sometimes we need to know how costs will change if we make changes to our level of activity, or to the list of services we offer. We need to know how costs 'behave'.

Cost structures

In the previous section, we saw how costs can be divided into direct costs, indirect costs and overheads. To investigate cost behaviour, we need to use another classification, this time fixed, variable, semi-fixed and semi-variable costs. You may be tempted to try to equate the two classifications (fixed with indirect and overheads, variable with direct). Remember, though, that they have two different purposes, one to calculate costs at a given level of activity, the other to explore their behaviour at different activity levels.

Variable costs change in direct proportion to your activity level (see Figure 4.7). You double or treble your volume of activity and your variable costs double or treble accordingly. They include all the materials used in the production process. Variable costs therefore remain the same per unit as activity levels rise or fall. The total expenditure on variable costs of course rises or falls (varies). Fixed costs remain the same regardless of activity levels. The salary of the chief executive is a fixed cost. Fixed costs, on the other hand, rise per unit if the activity level falls, because the number of units that must bear them has fallen. Similarly, they fall, per unit, if the activity levels rise. The total amount remains the same, however.

Staff salaries are not a variable cost, since a rise or fall in activity levels does not precipitate an immediate and consequent change in salaried hours. But if volume increased or decreased to the point where an extra post could be justified, or an existing one jeopardized, then the salary figure would change. Such costs are called semi-fixed costs, or step-fixed costs, since they remain the same over a given range of activity levels and then increase or decrease in

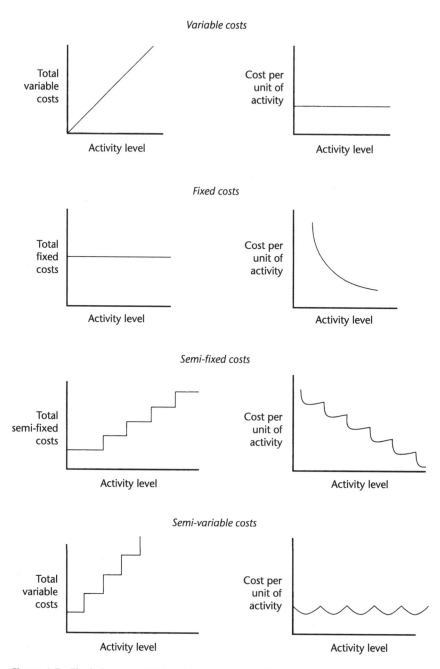

Figure 4.7 The behaviour of different kinds of costs with changes in activity level

steps. Equipment maintenance costs, which are incurred with greater frequency as activity increases, are not fixed costs, but neither are they variable, since they do not increase or decrease with every unit of activity. These are semi-variable or step-variable costs.

Imagine the range of activity levels changing from zero to ten times the current level, and you will see that almost no cost is completely fixed. Ultimately all staff can be made redundant and premises sold; conversely, staff numbers could increase tenfold and a new site be acquired. So when we consider the breakdown of costs into fixed and variable, we are doing so over a limited range, otherwise known as the relevant range.

Identifying which elements of the costs are fixed and which are variable enables us to differentiate between the average cost and marginal cost. The average cost is just what it says: the fixed plus variable costs divided by the number of units of activity. The marginal cost is that of providing one more unit. Unless you are right at the limit of a step cost, the marginal cost is the variable cost. Obviously, once you have recovered all your fixed costs, you are able to afford to offer your services at a price lower than the average cost, without losing money, as long as you recover at least your marginal costs. Sometimes when the costs discussed between two health care organizations look very different (for example the cost of a community diabetic service run by a hospital or by a community care provider) it is because one is using average costs and the other marginal.

Understanding how costs behave in relation to changes in activity levels enables us to answer such fundamental questions as:

- How many units do we need to sell at price *y* in order to break even?
- What must our price be if we are to break even on a given number of units?
- If we can only sell *x* units at price *y*, what must we reduce our fixed costs by (usually staff numbers) if we are to break even?
- How many more units would we need to sell to pay for an extra member of staff in the department?

As long as all the variables except the volume remain constant, the costs can be accurately divided into fixed and variable components and the question falls within the relevant range, then the *breakeven point* is where the cost of the units sold is equal to the income from those units:

$$\text{number of units sold} \times \text{variable costs} + \text{fixed costs} =$$

$$\text{number of units sold} \times \text{sale price}$$

Whatever price is charged, as long as it is in excess of the variable costs, it will make a contribution to the fixed costs. The amount of contribution is known as the *contribution margin*:

contribution margin = sales income – variable costs

Thus an alternative way of calculating the breakeven point is:

$$\text{number of units at breakeven point} = \frac{\text{fixed costs}}{\text{contribution per unit}}$$

These calculations are simple and the value of the answers relies on the validity of your forecasts about demand, prices and fixed and variable costs. *Sensitivity analysis* is the term coined for investigating the impact on the final financial picture if your assumptions and forecasts turn out to be incorrect. In essence, it asks the question 'what if?' about every element of costs and revenues. Tedious and time-consuming manually, it is usually undertaken on a computer spreadsheet.

In addition to the questions posed above, you may find that you want or need to consider such issues as:

- Should we 'make or buy' (i.e. undertake a service ourselves or buy it in)?
- Would a new piece of equipment help us to reduce our costs?
- What will happen to the costs of service *x* if we stop offering service *y* from the same department?
- If a commercial company would like to buy services from us, but at less than the average cost, should we supply them?

In order to answer these questions satisfactorily, there is another concept that must be understood. When it comes to these sorts of decisions, not all costs matter.

Relevant costs
Whereas when you are calculating costs all elements of the cost are *relevant*, when you are making decisions about different options some of them become *irrelevant*. This is because they have been incurred anyway: they are irretrievably committed, they are unavoidable. No matter what you do you cannot influence them. These costs are termed *sunk costs*. You can ignore them, no matter how big they are, because nothing will change them. Since your decision cannot change them, it must not be influenced by them. I stress this because emotionally this can be difficult. The fact that a million pounds has been spent on a piece of equipment would be difficult to ignore. If, however, using that equipment is going to cost you more money for a given outcome

than a different alternative (once you have included all purchase and related costs in your calculations), then you must be able to say goodbye to the million pounds. The decision to purchase that machine may have been absolutely the right one at the time, or it may have been a misguided one; but whichever is the case, insisting on its use when there are alternatives that will be cheaper for you now, that give clinical results that are just as good, is indisputably wasteful.

When you are financially appraising different options, you need to consider only the costs that differ between them. If both options require the additional employment of a member of staff, or if they can both be accommodated within the existing establishment with neither permitting any staff reduction, then staffing costs are irrelevant to your decision: they do not need to be included in your calculations. You compare the position with and without that option and write a *with/without* case.

The staff costs mentioned are irrelevant costs, but they are not sunk costs. Thus all sunk costs are irrelevant, but not all irrelevant costs are sunk.

Irrelevant costs, despite being ignored in your calculations, are real in that they have been spent. There is a class of costs that are *relevant* even though they are only ever hypothetical, and these are called *opportunity costs*. Whenever you have any money to spend (or any other resources to allocate for that matter), there is always something else you could choose to spend it on. The benefits of this alternative are closed to you if you choose the option under consideration. An opportunity cost measures the opportunity that you must forgo when your selection of one option means you cannot pursue another. If you can pursue both, then there is no sacrifice of opportunity, so opportunity costs are only incurred where there is a scarcity of resources (so there are a lot of opportunity costs in health care).

Moving away from imaginary costs back to real ones, let us now look at ways of monitoring the costs actually incurred by individuals and departments.

Monitoring costs

The first stage in any monitoring exercise is to set targets against which performance can be measured. When you are managing money, the targets take the form of the annual budget. The budget-setting process largely determines the robustness of the budget produced and its likelihood of being delivered. It should include all of the following stages:

1   *Framework.* Top management describes relevant details of budget policy and provides guidelines to the individuals in each department, who will be responsible for preparing their budgets.
2   *Limiting factors.* Any factor that restricts performance can be described as a limiting factor. In the manufacturing sector this is usually sales

demand, but it could be a restricted number of staff with particular skills, or a capacity limit on a machine. The next stage in the budgeting process is to identify what these limiting factors are. Since these determine the activity levels, only when they have been highlighted can achievable activity levels be set.

3 *Activity level budget.* Activity levels determine expenditure, so these must be agreed before sensible discussions can take place. Agreement on the activity level requires discussion between the service involved, the finance department, and sometimes senior management. The discussions need to be informed by data from previous time periods, knowledge of any new developments, etc.

4 *Bottom-up preparation of budgets.* When departments know what activity they are expecting to achieve, they can use their detailed knowledge of their services and their cost structures to put together a schedule of expenditure.

5 *Negotiation.* Human nature being what it is, departments are likely to set budgets that they believe they will achieve without too much effort. Some negotiation needs to take place between these departments and an individual with experience of managing individuals in similar settings, who will know where any 'padding' can be found. This individual is usually the line manager of the departmental heads, and this closeness to budget detail is another reason why such managers should have had significant operational experience and should be in close contact on a regular basis. The ability of the individuals concerned to negotiate fruitfully and not emotionally requires a relationship between them of the kind described in Chapter 7.

6 *Coordination.* Only when all the budgets are brought together can the total costs be projected, and they may be unaffordable as they stand. There may also be inconsistencies between departmental assumptions. Thus a coordination phase is required and this may necessitate a second or even third or fourth reworking of stages 4 and 5 before a feasible, affordable organization-wide set of budgets can be finalized.

7 *Acceptance.* When the budgets have been agreed by all parties, they are summarized into a 'master' budget.

8 *Monitoring and review.* In the master budget, all costs should be allocated to a responsibility centre as close as possible to the individual who commits these costs. Thereafter at monthly intervals reports can be generated that compare predicted expenditure with actual expenditure.

We now come to the fourth (and final) classification of costs in this chapter. Where costs can reasonably be expected to be regulated by the individual to whom they are allocated, then those costs are *controllable*. Clearly, overhead costs (e.g. the canteen), although they need to be apportioned for cost calculation purposes, must be awarded to their own managers when it comes to monitoring and review. Costs outside the control of anyone in the organization (e.g. many supplies) are known as *non-controllable* costs. They must also be monitored, but their uncontrollable nature acknowledged. In practice, this means holding a contingency fund centrally once the scale of the uncontrollable element is known.

Any disparity between actual and predicted expenditure or income is known as a 'variance'. Most variances are due to one or both of two factors: the price paid per unit of activity and the activity levels. A projected spend of £10,000 on material A will give rise to a favourable variance of £2000 when only £8000 is spent. However, if the activity level on which the £10,000 projection was based is 100 and only 70 cases have been treated, then the picture no longer looks so rosy. For this reason, budgets should not be *fixed* but be *flexible*. They should change the expenditure projections as any changes in activity levels occur. Frankly this is asking too much of most finance departments in the complex world of health care. Since you are the one who needs to know how well you are doing at keeping within your budget, you need to keep a record of expenditure committed and activity undertaken. You will probably not want to do the variance analysis yourself, so give your figures to the finance department so that they can do it for you.

Counting your own money is an important aspect of real management. You understand better than anyone else how your costs are incurred, the factors that influence them and the *cost drivers* (those activities by which it makes most sense to monitor costs). You also know better than anyone else your workload. You could, of course, wait for the conventional monthly reports based on information you and your team have given to the finance department (in one form or another), presented in a form that you find unhelpful if not unintelligible, in which costs are analysed under headings that are not meaningful in the context of your services. You could, but it would take less time than deciphering and analysing these to do the counting yourself, detailing someone in your team or department (or everyone) to enter details of costs and activities into a dedicated program.

You could do neither, stuffing the budget statements in a drawer unread or barely skimmed. But then you would not be managing money, it would be managing you. You would be at its mercy, being forced to reduce activity because of overspends, or to do without support staff while there is no let-up in workload. This is so intolerable a position for the responsible HCP that you really have no choice. Managing money is part of the professional role and requires the kind of effort described here.

Concluding thoughts: Using resources effectively and efficiently

At the beginning of this chapter Figure 4.1 was used to indicate that *really* managing resources requires us to answer two questions on an ongoing basis: 'How close is our performance to our aim?' and 'Are we keeping within the resources available to us?' I hope the concepts we have looked at since leave you feeling able to tackle both of them, so let's expand on this in Figure 4.8 to see how this looks in practice.

The toughest decisions HCPs have to make centre on shortages of resources, so the only way to reduce the number of times those decisions have to be made is to ensure that every resource is used to its optimum. That is what *real* management is about.

There will probably be many occasions on which you feel that you can't do all you want to do (offer all the care you want to offer) within the resources available to you. This must be true, because there are always good ideas to

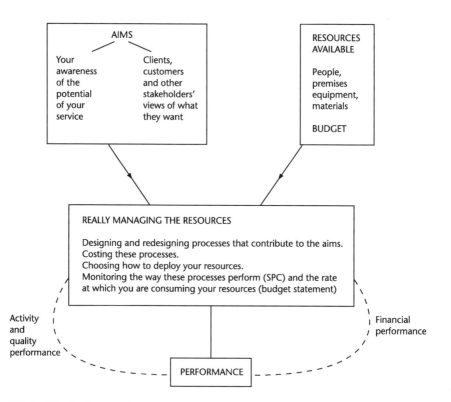

Figure 4.8 Really managing resources

pursue, and new developments that you want to explore.[12] Whenever this is the case there are two questions a real manager can legitimately ask:

1   How can we organize our own resources differently so that we can offer this care?
2   Can we get hold of some more resource?

Although these are both legitimate, they are only legitimate in that order. Furthermore, you will find that you and others will put much more energy into answering the first if you forget about the second, at least until you have exhausted all the possibilities of the first. This will be true not because 'they won't give us any more money anyway', a most de-energizing thought, but because 'we want to make the very best of everything we've got and then we may be able to free up resource to do this new stuff, and/or we will be able to secure the most we can out of any new money coming in'.

None of the concepts in this chapter is complicated; conceptually they are all relatively simple. Once again, implementing them is hard, again because they require you to be disciplined in the way you *think* about them and in acting to keep on top of them, and also to be generous in your attitudes.

Discipline and generosity will help you to avoid a common enemy of improvement and efficiency: complacency. Complacency that everything is as good as it can be, or that there is nothing you can do. This is an ever-present enemy, ready to attack at any time, especially when you have been working hard on improvement activities. The antidote is surprisingly simple, a single question to be asked daily: 'How have I managed my resources better today?'

Notes

1   This refers to performance targets set by the government of the day within the Patient's Charter for maternity services. The Patient's Charter was abolished as part of changes to the NHS implemented in 2000 under the NHS Plan.
2   Maxwell, R.J. (1984) 'Quality assessment in health', *British Medical Journal*, 288, 1470–2.
3   The means of doing this is as follows. Plot a graph of the *differences* between one month's average defects and the last's. This is called a moving range chart. Construct a central line for this by taking the average (just as you did for the chart of the individual monthly values). Multiply the average of this moving range chart (where you have just drawn your central line) by 2.66 and this will give you the natural process limits, i.e. the appropriate amount of spread for the graph of the individual monthly values. To plot the upper process limit add this figure (average of the moving range × 2.66) to the average of the individual values chart, and for the lower limit, subtract it from that average. If you want to calculate the upper and lower limits for the moving range chart,

instead of multiplying by 2.66 you multiply by 3.27. To understand more about this, and how these specific calculations are arrived at, a good place to start is Wheeler, D.J. (1996) *Understanding Variation: The Key to Managing Chaos* (Knoxville, TN: SPC Press).

4 Ibid.

5 In Berwick, D.M., Godfrey, A.B. and Roessner, J. (1990) *Curing Health Care: New Strategies for Quality Improvement* (San Francisco: Jossey-Bass).

6 Ninety-two per cent of defects are caused by system faults, and only 8 per cent by individuals. Frustratingly, I have mislaid the reference to the particular survey from which these figures come, so if any reader can provide me with it I will be most grateful.

7 Argyris, C. and Schön, D. (1996) *Organizational Learning II: Theory, Method and Practice* (Reading, MA: Addison Wesley).

8 Although frankly those terms aren't very user friendly and you will probably want to devise alternatives, e.g. 'Learning to notice when we're not learning', instead of 'deutero learning'.

9 From a survey conducted by Drury and co-workers. Reported in Drury, C. (1994) *Costing: An Introduction* (London: Chapman and Hall). This book is an accessible introduction to management accounting.

10 See Drury (1994).

11 I am going to use here a generic example of manufacturing widgets. You will probably find you learn more from this section if you translate the principles to a product or service you are involved in delivering.

12 And, of course, in a productive economy this is true in every field, not just health care.

5 Really managing change

What is it that prompts us to make changes? When I ask service leaders this they give me the following answers:

1 Something goes wrong and I want to prevent it happening again.
2 I come across a good idea and want to try it out.
3 An opportunity presents itself and I want to exploit it, especially if it may disappear if I don't.
4 I want to offer better services.
5 I want to offer additional services.
6 I want to be a success and run a successful service.
7 I am told to meet a target and can't do so if we carry on the way we have traditionally done.
8 I have been told to make efficiency savings.
9 Something challenges the way I see the services we are offering: a patient satisfaction survey, a complaint, feedback from other services, seeing the way other services operate.
10 I am instructed to make a change.

In all these cases (I will refer back to them as 'prompts' throughout this chapter) people want the changes they make to have real benefits; they don't want them to have only superficial or cosmetic effect. And they want them to go on yielding these benefits after they have stopped putting time and energy into them – they want them to be sustainable.

This chapter is titled 'Really managing change' and is about how *real* managers encourage beneficial and sustainable change. There are people who dislike the term 'managing change' and their concerns are valid, although (I believe) their prescription, of insisting on using other terms instead, is not, so it is worth exploring these concerns a little. They centre on whether it is really possible to manage change, so let's think about that.

The increasing specialization of society that we looked at in Chapter 2 has had another major impact on our lives – the rate of change grows faster and faster. As the wag said, 'Change isn't what it used to be.'

Is it possible to manage change? Of course, when we think of a lot of the change around us, the answer is no. But when we decide to respond to some of these changes, by changing the way we ourselves do things, we can begin to use the term more meaningfully. Even here, though, some people are highly sceptical. They note that, except in the simplest of situations, change is never straightforward, never goes entirely to plan, always includes an element of unpredictability, so 'managing', they say, is not the verb to use to describe the process that takes place. While I don't disagree with them, this seems to me to imply a more limited definition of the term managing than the one I picture, and the way in which I use the term, especially when I talk about *really* managing, encompasses a whole range of approaches that together prompt and encourage change in a way that should lead to sustainable improvements.[1] So perhaps we need to agree that when we talk of really managing change we are thinking not that we will be in control of every single aspect of it, but that we are prompting it and influencing it in a direction of our choosing.

In this chapter I first introduce you to three different theoretical approaches or schools of thought about change, and then look at how to use them to address the prompts for change listed above.

Three schools of thinking about change

The three schools of thinking can be termed *planned, emergent* and *spontaneous*, and I will introduce them briefly to you now. Then we will look at a matrix that indicates how to bring them together, and finally we will apply this matrix to those prompts for change.

Planned change

The planned approach[2] to change advocates carefully analysing our situation, using some specific tools to do so, identifying key priorities, devising a plan of action to address those priorities, implementing that plan, monitoring progress along the way and finally evaluating the outcomes against our intended achievements. Of course each stage is not as simple as this sounds and there are more or less sophisticated analytical techniques for each of them. The key to the approach is to make sure that the initial analysis is rooted in bringing together three elements: your goals, the resources you have at your disposal and the environment in which you are operating. All three are essential and leaving any of them out renders the analysis and the subsequent planning and implementation very much less useful. Skilful military and political leaders have been thinking this way for centuries, and the approach was brought into business thinking when management first became an academic subject in the early twentieth century. The SWOT analysis, first codified by Igor Ansoff,[3] is an example of this school.[4] Undertaken well, the analysis at the heart of this approach can be revelatory, and can lead to the development of a sound strategic plan. In order to achieve this, there is an emphasis on high quality thinking, on good analytical skills and on identifying the best strategic option, and this has required a valuing of bright people often with good quantitative skills, who can move from organization to organization and industry to industry, taking these transferable skills with them.

Emergent

Contrast this with the emergent school. The very term 'emergent'[5] was coined by Henry Mintzberg, a commentator critical of US business schools, operating in Canada at McGill University.

Mintzberg compares a manager with a potter, crafting a strategy for change in the way that a potter works with the clay on the potter's wheel: setting out with an intention but making minor adjustments in response to the way the clay is handling, and sometimes even major changes as an opportunity arises that hasn't been visible before. In place of analysts being bussed in from outside with good skills at applying an analytical framework to explicit data and information, Mintzberg talks of the importance of authenticity and intuition, born of longevity in an organization. He describes the importance of tacit knowledge, knowledge held by people as a result of their interactions with and within an organization over many years, knowledge that is not always available to be put into words, knowledge that gives an intuitive sense of whether a proposed action is right or not.

Mintzberg also talks of managers sensing patterns, spotting trends in a set of events or opportunistic actions, that allow them to weave a story round what is happening. Rather than writing the story in advance (as the planning schools does), these managers write it as it emerges, or even afterwards. Thinkers in this school (Weick, Bate and others) suggest that a strategy narrative is still important, that people will always want to feel part of a journey in a direction that they can understand. They recognize that people in organizations always do weave stories of their own to interpret events, and that one of the roles of the real manager is to weave stories with and for people that give them this sense of direction and movement.

Spontaneous

There is another way of thinking about change, and that has its roots in thinking about complex adaptive systems. There is a classic question asked by people teaching complexity theory: who runs the food system in New York?

The answer of course is no one, yet somehow all New Yorkers eat, and the majority eat well (including a proportion of those excluded from society, such as the homeless). Every part of the 'system' that delivers food to New Yorkers is subject to change: the deli on the corner may change hands or close, a new supermarket will open, the wholesalers and their suppliers will also change. None of this is planned, it isn't part of any one organization: it is all spontaneously the outcome of groupings and regroupings into a system that is *complex*, that is made up of individual components that all *adapt* to the situation around them; and somehow it all works. Could we predict today exactly what it will look like in six months' time? Probably not. We may imagine that if we knew in detail exactly what each part of the system looked like, and we knew the factors that would determine what would make them expand or contract their business, start up or close down, change suppliers or increase their orders, we would be able to enter that all on to a computer and run the program, just in the way that meteorological systems do to forecast weather. But even if we could (and in practice, of course, we can't, there are just too many variables and the links between them are too difficult to capture), we know from chaos theory that even very small changes to the initial figures we entered on the computer could change the results drastically. We could, though, be reasonably sure that it will still work, and that to an outsider it would look roughly the same.

We can think of health care organizations as complex adaptive systems in the same way. The elements of the system are people and departments, including you and me. And we can't predict exactly who will be in the organization and exactly what they will be doing in six months' time, although we can be pretty sure it will look roughly the same. Change theorists who draw on complexity theory suggest that it is just not possible to predict the outcome of any particular intervention in even a simple system, and certainly not in a complex one. So the notion of analysing a situation, designing an intervention, implementing it and expecting this to result in a particular desired outcome looks rather fanciful. Instead, say these change theorists, we need to concentrate on the nature of the relationships between the key components of organizational systems: people. And we have to realize that when we are trying to manage change we are as much part of the system, part of the loops of feedback and influence that result in new events and behaviours emerging, as anyone else. Thus our attention, according to this school of thinking about change, must be on the quality of our own relationships with other people, and on the ways in which we influence the quality of relationships between others.

Bringing the three schools together

At first sight it appears that each of these approaches contradicts the others, and that if we choose to adopt one we must reject the others. However, each has a coherent theoretical underpinning and some supporting evidence of success.[6] So it would be hard to justify jettisoning any of them in favour of the others. What we can valuably do is find a way of using all three, but in ways that exploit their strengths and do not expect more of them than they can reliably deliver. The matrix in Table 5.1 is an attempt to do just this.[7]

The three schools of thinking are represented in the three columns, with the planned on the left, the emergent on the right and the spontaneous in the middle. The rows are three different time periods: *prospective* (when we are thinking about what we are going to change); *real time* (while we are in the process of making changes); and *retrospective* (as we reflect on the experience later). The matrix is described in more detail in Table 5.2.

My suggestion to you is that at each stage all three boxes in the corresponding row are important; however, one of them tends to dominate. This does not matter as long as *sufficient* attention is given to the others; if any box is completely ignored then the change is much less likely to be effective or sustainable. The boxes that tend to dominate in the three rows are those numbered 1, 5 and 9. If you stop and reflect on this thesis for a moment, you will, I think, recognize this pattern of preferences in your own experience.[8]

Working with managers on the use of this matrix also suggests to me that we each have a tendency towards one column (one school of thinking) and find it difficult to value the others, and this means we are less effective at managing change than if we could use ideas and techniques from all three. For instance, if you have a penchant for planned change you may gravitate to boxes 1, 4 and 7, which means you may be less sensitive to real-time

Table 5.1 Matrix to summarize kinds of activities to be undertaken when managing change, drawing on the insights of three different schools of thinking

	Strategic approach		
Time	Planned or deliberate	Spontaneous	Emergent
Prospective	**1** Analysing situation and designing intervention	**2** Engaging players in developing a spirit and purpose	**3** Encompassing tacit knowledge and recognising patterns
Real time	**4** Implementing it	**5** Living it	**6** Active awareness/ aware opportunism
Retrospective	**7** Evaluating the implementation	**8** Learning about dynamics	**9** Weaving a story into a longer narrative

Table 5.2 Matrix to illustrate in practice the kinds of actions to be undertaken when managing change, drawing on the insights of three different schools of thinking

Time	Strategic approach		
	Planned or deliberate (analysis followed by plan and implementation)	*Spontaneous (events, actions and behaviours emerge spontaneously from interactions)*	*Emergent[a] (foster, craft, discover things, detect patterns)*
Prospective	**1** Undertake a rigorous analysis, that leads to a list of critical issues that need to be addressed, and some form of implementation programme. *Key skills:* analytical and clear thinking	**2** Engage with a wide range of people, encouraging them to contribute their perspective and to take responsibility for playing their part in shaping the analysis and the design. *Key skills:* listening, being comfortable with ambiguity.	**3** Work with the people with 'tacit knowledge', authentic and intuitive understanding of the organization. Experiment with different ideas and look for patterns in the experience of the organization. *Key skills:* spotting patterns, identifying authenticity.
Real time	**4** Project manage the implementation programme, using sound, proven methods for monitoring progress.	**5** Keep in mind, and voice for others, the spirit of the programme of change, help others to behave in the spirit of this plan, while engaging in the everyday world of interactions between people, events, behaviours and feelings – all of which lead to new events and behaviours which were not foreseen in the change programme.	**6** Make all your usual everyday decisions that appear to have little connection with the implementation plan.

Key skills: developing cascades of interlinked objectives for depts, teams and individuals; using critical path methods, milestones etc; contingency planning; reporting on progress.	The more association people have had with the plan, in box 2, the more their emergent behaviours will be within the spirit of the plan. Attributes needed: dynamic poise, attentiveness, flexibility and responsiveness.	Take opportunities as they arise, fostering and crafting choices to make the best of each unforeseen situation. Interpret all sorts of knowledge and information, tacit as well as explicit, and bring meaning to events as they unfurl. Key skills: sensing, interpreting, using tacit knowledge and intuition, helping others make sense of things!
Retrospective **7** Compare actual events and outcomes with those of the plan, and with the analysis that led to the plan. In practice this can have a developmental intent (enabling better analysis and planning in the future) or a judgemental one (performance management).	**8** Try to understand what actually happened and how, by considering the events and processes, behaviours and relationships that emerged as time went on. This gives a better understanding of the dynamics of the system and enables the design of development programmes that will influence the way people respond in the future. Tools used: facilitated reflection, informal reflection, non-blame feedback, systems thinking.	**9** Tell stories: help people to make sense of what has happened, by selecting some events and decisions and weaving them into a coherent story that is recognised by others as having authenticity. This engenders a sense of meaning and of belonging to a longer narrative, which can become part of the history of the service or organization.

Note: Although presented as a matrix, the horizontal axis (strategic approach) does not reflect a single concept that differs only in degree as we move along it. The vertical one does in that it represents time changing, but the three schools represented in the three columns are discrete schools of thinking, each rich in its own right, and there is no single attribute or occasion or use that indicates that one column is more or less of anything than the others. The placing of the three in this order is therefore rather arbitrary, except that, although the boxes in each row take place in the same time period, they can perhaps be summarized as intent, being and awareness. We can suggest that conceptually intention comes before being, which in turn comes before awareness.

[a] The words emergent and emergence appear in both the middle and right hand columns but with slightly different meanings. One way of distinguishing between these, for which I'm indebted to Beverley Slater, is to call them crafted emergence (right hand column) and spontaneous emergence (middle column).

opportunism (Box 6), less concerned about engaging others in the spirit of the plan (boxes 2 and 5) less open to learning retrospectively about the dynamics involved in the change intervention (box 8) or less alert to the value of explaining to others what went well and not so well (box 9).

Since all the boxes in one row take place at one and the same time, we need to be able to pull together a set of activities that allows us to fulfil the needs of all three boxes in that row. We also need to ensure that each of the boxes receives the attention it deserves. We now look at how we might do this in a number of different situations.

Leading a service through change

Imagine you are the head of a department or team (perhaps the manager of physiotherapy services, within a trust, managing 35 staff on a number of sites) and you know it is not performing as well as you would like it to. You are under pressure to meet performance targets, to make efficiency savings and to address the fact that a recent patient satisfaction survey showed some unhappiness about your appointments system. So you want to make changes that will improve the quality of your service, and you are also being required to think about changes that will save money and achieve some specific objectives. You will almost certainly also want to be seen to be running a successful service. So of the list at the top of this chapter you are addressing prompts number 4 (perhaps also 5), 6, 7 and 8 and 9.[9] You are going to use the matrix to help you decide what to do and how to do it. We will look at the way to approach each of the boxes in turn, and then at how to bring them together. In doing this we are going to pay proportionately more attention to the first box, for one main reason. This is because box 1 forces us to stop and think in a deliberate way about change. All too often changes are introduced by enthusiastic management teams without adequate analysis and evaluation of the costs, benefits and risks associated with different options and investing time in box 1 helps avoid this. The importance of doing so is clear if we consider that in any change that affects job security, one of the greatest costs of that change is its impact on the ability of staff to respect and care for others, while they feel under threat themselves. Since this is at the root of all health care, it should be jeopardized only with great caution.

Managing in box 1

First we will look at the kind of analysis that will identify your key change priorities. This is very easy to do badly and when this happens it is not only a waste of the time and effort invested, it can give a distorted picture of what the priorities are and lead services in unhelpful directions. For that reason we will look at this in some detail, and so the next nine pages are devoted to box 1. You will probably be relieved to find that the other boxes can be grasped much more readily. As we saw on page 120, the analysis needs to bring together three elements: the goals (or 'mission') of the service; the resources available to it; and the environment in which it is operating.

Goals, direction, mission [10]
To articulate a mission for the service you will need to think carefully about what it is that the service is there to achieve. All too often in health care we define our mission in terms of what we *do* rather than what we are here for, and it is worth reminding ourselves of that. As the physiotherapy manager you may express this as 'increasing the mobility of patients'. A pharmacy department might do so as 'enabling effective and efficient use of medication'. Speech and language therapists may talk of 'enhancing the ability of patients to communicate'. Now that this has been articulated you can list the most important ways in which you are going to achieve it. Normally you would include your main clinical tasks, but you also need to mention aspects such as ensuring your service is financially viable (by doing what?), and has the support of key organizational decision makers (how?), and so on.

Mission statements have had a bad press, and understandably so. Many have been politically correct waffle, often far too long and not representative of anything that the organization or service really cares about or lives by. What you are thinking about here is a mission statement that you can use in your analysis, not for putting on the wall or even in an annual report, so there is no point starting your analysis with a mission statement that isn't real. This means that you will have to reflect on what people in the department genuinely care about – and in particular what the key opinion formers want to achieve, since their views are what shape the way the rest of the service sees the world. It is because people are different, and services are in different contexts, that it is not possible to be prescriptive about what the mission statement for a particular service should be. Many HCPs find this counterintuitive so let's think about it for a moment.

If a key opinion former is interested in research then energy and resources within the service will be being consumed in this direction and if you don't include it in the mission statement it won't feel real to people who know how the service 'ticks'. Similarly, if they are most interested in the service being seen as 'leading edge', and applaud members who speak at conferences and write for journals. Or if they are most concerned about treating patients in a friendly and respectful way; or if the pervading spirit is of wanting to treat as many people as possible, if necessary at the expense of niceties of relationships. We saw in Chapter 1 that we are all motivated by different things and when writing a mission statement that captures the genuine essence of your service you will need to find out what it is that motivates the people within it who lead opinion and influence that essence. You may be thinking that your service is trying to do all of these things, and, of course, it is. But you will care more about some than about others and these will shape the service in ways that may be invisible to you.

Let us look, for instance, at the aims of different GPs working in a small geographical area of inner London. An outsider might be tempted to think they would be fairly undifferentiated. The following list of statements contributed by real GPs illustrates how diverse they can be:

- being, and being recognized to be, a leading edge practice;
- being a friendly practice, part of the community, where patients are almost friends;
- meeting the health care needs of a very deprived population without burnout;
- being primary carers, adopting a holistic perspective, being concerned with health rather than only health care;
- making a reasonable living for the partners in an enjoyable and interesting way;
- working towards the best possible health for patients, not only treating them but persuading them to take responsibility for their own health, while, at the same time, developing partners and staff to the full.

Often, indeed *usually*, when the members of a clinical team come together to discuss a mission statement, they find that individual members have different views of what the service contribution could/should be. Gaining agreement on direction is a very valuable outcome, especially where differences were previously unrecognized or unacknowledged. On some occasions it becomes apparent that the current mission of the service is not one that is appropriate, that it cannot be justified, and then you, as its leader, are going to have to find ways of challenging this.[11] Boxes 2 and 3 give us some useful approaches for doing so.

Resources and environment

When you have articulated the mission you are ready to think about the service itself and its environment. There are a number of tools for doing this and many of them work very well. However I find that one of the most effective, in that it keeps people very clear in their thinking at every stage, is a very old one. This is the SWOT analysis, informed by two other analyses: the Seven S and PEST. PEST has been in use for as long as SWOT, and the Seven S dates from the early 1980s.[12] Can these really be the most useful, you may ask; haven't they been superseded? I don't think so. I find that if people use them clearly and carefully they yield results as valuable as those of any of the alternatives.

Seven S model

The seven Ss are simply a list of different aspects of an organization, that need to support each other. They are depicted in Figure 5.1. The way to use the seven S framework, is to refresh your memory with your mission statement, and then ask yourself this kind of question:

- If we are to achieve our mission what kind of people (*staff*) do we need in post? How many do we need, of what kind of grade and profession or specialization? What kinds of *skills*[13] do they need?
- What kind of people do we *have* in post? What numbers, what specializations and what kinds of skills?
- Do we have the people we need, with the skills we need? If we do then we can see that as a strength, if we don't then it is a weakness.
- If we are to achieve our mission, what key *systems* will we need to have in place? These will be very different according to whether we are most interested in research, in building our profile, in offering a friendly service to patients or in trying to achieve the best clinical results.
- Do we have these systems in place?

Now that we have thought about three of the Ss we can compare them not only with the mission but with each other. So we ask:

- Are these the right systems for the kind of staff we have?
- Do they have the skills to operate them?

By continuing to think through all seven of the Ss and comparing what you *need* in order to achieve the mission with what you *have* in place, and then looking at how the Ss support or inhibit each other, you will be able to build up a good idea of where the service is strong and where it is weak. Be careful to think clearly though. Many is the occasion when I have heard that good team work is a strength of a service. When we look more closely at how it contributes to the mission we find it doesn't. Indeed, because team members so dislike confronting and challenging each other the service to patients is actually suffering. So, as we saw in Chapter 2, the team feels cosy but is not productive. Instead of a strength this is a weakness. When you come to the Structure S it is important that you think clearly about the advantages and disadvantages of different kinds of structures, and you will find these described on pages 239–241, in Case Study 2.

PEST

Hardly anybody has not heard of a PEST analysis yet it is often used neither wisely nor well (see box 5.1).

I find that when people first start to think about the PEST headings (see

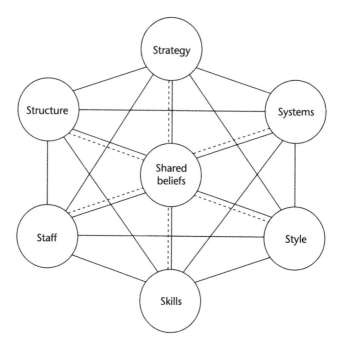

- **Strategy:** the actions that are being planned.

- **Structure:** who is accountable to whom, for what.

- **Systems:** the procedures that make an organization 'work'

- **Staff:** how many people work here, what professions, what seniority etc.

- **Skills,** in four categories: clinical or technical; interpersonal or behavioural; managerial; research or evaluation.

- **Style** of management: autocratic, participative, paternalistic, laissez-faire, empowering, supportive etc.

- **Shared** beliefs, or culture: often beliefs about the kinds of things listed on page 76.

Figure 5.1 Each of the Seven Ss must support and be supported by all the others (based on Waterman *et al.* 1980; see note 11).

box 5.1 on page 131) they come up with very little, and most of what they describe are government initiatives. However, as they think further, especially by thinking 'What lay behind that initiative?', they identify all sorts of underlying economic, demographic and sociological trends of which they are so well aware that they have forgotten to notice them. The most common 'mistakes' at this stage of the analysis are to forget the small 'p' political factors or what

---

Box 5.1 PEST factors

The term PEST is an acronym, abbreviated from Political, Economic, Social and Technological, each heading referring to factors in the environment surrounding an organisation.

- **Political** factors might include initiatives stemming from central government, from your local health community and from the 'small p' politics within an organization.
- **Economic** factors might include finances, and also the different markets that parts of the organization operate in. For example, a particular department may be competing for staff in the local labour market.
- An increasing interest in work–life balance, the ageing of society, and its impact on caring responsibilities for women, and multicultural aspects are just some of the trends you might think relevant under the **sociological** heading.
- When it comes to **technologies** you need to think more widely than new kinds of equipment and use the term in its original sense of 'an approach'. So you might think of clinical audit, quality management, aspects of learning organizations and various change management tools.

---

some analysts call 'the micro politics' (e.g. the organizational politics, the personality clash between two people who have an important say in your service, the fact that someone on the board has a low opinion of physiotherapy, perhaps) and not to think widely enough about the technological ones. There is just so much useful thinking around that we can describe as technology,[14] from redesign methods to concepts about communities of practice, work on organizational learning, to particular approaches to audit and clinical governance.

If we can identify which of these will help the service to achieve its mission we can think of these as opportunities, and those that will impede or inhibit the ability of the service to achieve this can be seen as threats. Again, being precise about how these factors will help or hinder will ensure that you are thinking clearly and are not including as opportunities things that you happen to find interesting or 'nice', and that you are not identifying people you happen not to like as threats when their challenge or their ambition may be just what the service needs.

SWOT

Both Seven S and PEST enable us to think clearly about aspects that are relevant to a service but they are even more useful when we draw on them to conduct a perceptive and rigorous SWOT analysis. SWOT is an acronym for Strengths, Weaknesses, Opportunities and Threats, in which strengths and weaknesses refer to your use of resources within your organization, opportunities and threats to the external environment.

The purpose of the SWOT analysis is to identify a small number of issues that are the most important for you to address. So any SWOT that does not finish with a set of such issues and a means of addressing them is a poor one. In practice most SWOTs are poorly conducted, a poor use of the time and energy that went into them. If you feel you have wasted your time on SWOTs in the past please do not reject it as a tool. SWOTs can be immensely useful: they can help you to see your service in a different way, and to persuade others in your service of the direction you all need to take. Conceptually they are very simple. You write the mission at the top of a sheet of paper (so that you keep it in mind at all times during the SWOT thinking) and then list the strengths, weaknesses, opportunities and threats of your service. Then you scan across all four boxes (and the mission) and see what strikes you. In practice you will find it very difficult to be anything other than superficial if you try to do it in that way, and I suggest that instead you use a three column approach. For each of the headings (S,W,O,T) you draw three columns. In the left hand column you write down the features you identified from your Seven S and PEST analyses and in the middle you answer the question 'How will this affect our ability to make progress towards the mission?' If you find that you can answer that satisfactorily (and this again helps you to weed out those pleasant but irrelevant factors from your strengths and opportunities), then in the right hand column you think about another question. For strengths and weaknesses this is 'Is there any underlying cause for this?' and for opportunities and threats it is 'Is there anything we need to do about this right now?' Tables 5.3 and 5.4 illustrate this.

It is important to keep your thinking clear here. It is not unusual to find the kind of thinking shown in Table 5.5. If you look at this you will see that it is not at all clear that the lack of strategic direction mentioned is a weakness. Morale is such a fuzzy and immeasurable concept that it can always be claimed to be high or low, and there is no indication of how this translates into an ability to achieve the mission. It is also all too easy to find a fuzzy diagnosis (lack of management skills) that is entirely unhelpful and often inspired by

Table 5.3 SWOT analysis (strengths)

Strengths	How will this affect our ability to make progress towards the mission?	Is there any underlying cause for this?
Range and diversity of services offered, e.g. in physiotherapy or midwifery	Meets diverse client demands and makes service attractive to both clients and commissioners	Imaginative responses by individuals x and y to outspoken advocacy service

Table 5.4 SWOT analysis (threats): a trust wishing to close a local hospital identifies the following threats

Threats	How does this impede our ability to achieve our mission?	What do we need to do about this?
Concern of local community	May lobby to prevent closure and this will not allow us to free up the resources we need to invest in good community care	Keep community informed about our reasoning and keep abreast of local opinion
Interference of local MPs	May take position based on own political needs and prevent us closing, and liberating resources	Assess political needs and give MPs information that will help them to meet their needs as well as those of the trust

blame rather than a desire to work out what to do about it. The weakness may indeed turn out to be the lack of certain skills, but we need to be precise and perceptive when we identify them.

Now you will find scanning these SWOT boxes and arriving at your critical issues much easier. You will find that the most useful boxes are often those in the right hand columns, and you will be able to spot issues that have one element in the strengths and another in the weaknesses, and that perhaps also enable you to respond to an opportunity or to fight a threat. This is an imprecise art and the value of the results will depend on how perceptive you are at this stage and on how disciplined and clear thinking you have been up to this point. Altogether you should find, in this way, that there are three or four issues that require some quality attention if you are to be successful. You may also find that there is one additional factor so significant that although it occurs in only one box you decide it is an issue that needs to be declared a priority. You may have a weakness that means you simply can't achieve your mission, or an opportunity you can't afford to miss (or a threat that could blow you out of the water). This list of about four critical issues is your change agenda.

Table 5.5 SWOT analysis (weaknesses)

Weaknesses	How does this affect our ability to achieve our mission?	What lies behind this?
Strategic direction unclear	Low morale in the team	Poor management skills on the part of the team leader

If you care about your service and are knowledgeable about it, and are prepared to stand back from it sufficiently to think very clearly about it, this stage will be interesting and satisfying. It will almost certainly take one person at least half a day, probably more. Two people will take longer. It is unlikely that you will be able to persuade an entire department or practice to be object-ive enough to complete this satisfactorily, yet we know that if we are to apply the thinking from boxes 2 and 3 we will need to, so we shall consider how to approach this conundrum shortly.

If you would like to see an illustration of the whole sequence (mission, seven S, PEST, SWOT, change agenda) you will find one in *Developing Change Management Skills*.[15]

Action plan

Now you have your change agenda you can devise ways of making sensible changes. To help you to do so, however, it can be useful to think first about a goal for each of the issues you have identified (what would it look like if this wasn't an issue any more, if you had sorted it out?). When you have done so you can brainstorm as many ways as possible of trying to get there. This is your first attempt at an action plan.

Typically I find that at almost every stage in this analytical process people have tried to draw up an action plan, ('Right, so what we need to do about this is . . .') and the greatest advantage of the process is that of slowing you down so that you don't launch into action until you are sure it is the most helpful way forward. Even now, though, I suggest a further step before you draw up your action plan. That is a stakeholder analysis.

Stakeholder analysis

There will be a number of people who have an interest or stake in the changes you are proposing for your service, and they may be able to ensure the success of the change programme or wreck it. So it is useful to list all of these, together with an indication of how important it is that they support the changes. Three categories are sufficient: those who must actively support and champion the changes, those who must concur but whose active support is not necessary, and those whose views are not going to influence the success of the pro-gramme. These individuals can also be categorized according to whether they are strongly in support of the changes (lions), are strongly opposed to them (mules) or will go along with the opinion-formers (sheep). It is helpful to construct a grid, as shown in Table 5.6.

A scan of this grid soon makes it clear just who are the people you need to spend time and energy convincing. If in your situation you find you have C, a mule whose active support is essential, and you do not try to persuade them of the virtues of the change (using the material from Chapters 1 to 3), then the change programme will almost certainly fail, and the blame for it doing so will

Table 5.6 Stakeholder analysis: example

Stakeholders	Must support	Must acquiesce	Can be ignored
A			Lion
B		Sheep	
C	Mule		
D		Lion	
E	Sheep		
F			Mule

Table 5.7 Empty Gantt chart

	Week							
Action	1	2	3	4	5	6	....	n

rest almost as much with you as with C. It will, of course, be much more agreeable to spend your time with the inoffensive, non-threatening individual A who strongly supports you.

Your action plan now has a lot on it, and it is worth thinking about how to organise it so that you can monitor your progress. For this purpose a Gantt chart is often helpful (see Table 5.7).

So now you have undertaken a rigorous analysis that has brought together your goals, your resources and the environment and you have developed a programme of action. In other words you have finally completed box 1. However, we have said that we need to try to use approaches from the other two boxes (2 and 3) at the same time, so let us now have a look at these.

Managing in box 2

If you refer back to the matrix in Table 5.2 on pages 124 and 125 you will see that in this box you are concerned about engaging other people in the analysis that we've just looked at in box 1, so that they are genuinely part of it and it reflects their interests and behaviours. You are encouraging a wide range of people to contribute their perspective and take responsibility for playing their part in shaping an understanding about what change is needed. Ways of doing this might include:

- Taking time to do the analysis, and keeping your thinking open to all sorts of new perspectives from the people you work with. This will certainly involve being out and about with people in the service and outside it.
- Hearing messages, not being oversensitive to criticism, encouraging people to participate in the analysis, listening well, reflecting back to people, dealing with *what* it is that people are saying and sometimes choosing to ignore *how* they say it.
- Understanding emotions but not getting pulled into or down by them.
- Stating realities that people may not want to hear. Being consistent.
- Acting with authenticity, clarity and honesty.

Managing in box 3

In box 3 you are trying to identify existing strategies by identifying patterns and weaving stories around them. You are also finding the people with the greatest tacit knowledge, people whose understanding of the situation is intuitive rather than (or as well as) analytical, people who have authenticity because they have been in the organization for a long time and have remained constructive members of it. When you have found them you want to unlock their tacit knowledge and their dreams for the future so that the sense of a direction of change emerges.

Here you might try:

- Developing a real intimacy with the service, knowing the service from the inside, finding out for yourself what its prevailing values, beliefs and myths are;
- Telling a story, such as 'If my mother were having this physio I would want her to find . . .';
- Finding out other people's aspirations for the service, working with the people who are or can be passionate about what the service can offer;
- Not being blown off course, being purposeful but also properly hearing what people say;

- Living out the values and picture you describe;
- Respecting other people's tacit knowledge and intuition; listening to what they say, how they say it, what they don't say.
- Sitting down with patients and with other providers on the patient pathway;
- Building on previous successes, helping people to see them as successes if they are sceptical.

Boxes 1–3 are in the same row of the matrix, so they are taking place in the same time period. In other words, we need to undertake the activities described in them concurrently. This means that as the manager of the physiotherapy service you will need to engage other people, especially those with great tacit knowledge, in the analysis for box 1, both to inform the analysis and so that it forms part of the narrative they are developing about the situation, and so it will inform their behaviours when it comes to the next stage. You can see that thinking ahead about what changes you want to make will take time and involve a lot of robust relationships and personal emotional commitment, as well as a clear head and disciplined thinking. In practice it will mean that although you may be tempted to do all the analysis yourself, based on your (perceptive we hope) interpretation of the mission, Seven Ss and PEST factors, you will not be successful if you do not actively engage others in the process. This is where the complicated easy meets the simple hard, and you will need to use a high level of both sets of skills. It is why really managing change, encouraging sustainable change, can be so challenging. I mentioned, for example, that it will take you half a day to draw up your SWOT and identify the critical issues, that it will take two people much longer and that it is often not possible to get a whole team to stand back sufficiently to do this. That sounds as though I am advocating their exclusion, and I am not. It is important, though, that high quality thinking *is* done and you can valuably go through this analytical process yourself or with a couple of others, and use your findings to prompt thinking across the wider department. If you do this over a period there will come a time when you can reflect back to them the thinking you have engaged in with them and the messages you have heard, and work with them to build a direction of travel they can support.

Managing in box 4

Now we have arrived at the stage of implementing our change programme, of enacting it, of living it out. If you have conducted the thinking ahead stage (boxes 1, 2 and 3) well, you will by now have a programme of action, developed with the people who understand the service best, and who will be involved in the change processes, so that they understand what will be happening and why.

The activities of box 4 encourage you to implement it effectively using sound project management and performance management principles. These include drawing up a detailed project plan, with tasks and time frames clearly allocated to teams and within them to individuals. Very often this is through a cascade of objectives, so that every team member has objectives that together comprise those for the team. There will be a comprehensive reporting process with all concerned reporting their progress against their objectives on a regular basis, with the consequences of their success or failure to achieve these made clear in advance. Where the programme is highly complex (for example, if it were building a new hospital or decommissioning an old one) there will be a need for computer-assisted monitoring of tasks against milestones, particularly those that lie on the critical path (this is another project management tool, similar in function to a Gantt chart, which uses a set of diagrammatic conventions to identify and display the dependency of some tasks on others, and those which must be completed on time, as well as those tasks that can be delayed for a while).[16] The programme you develop as the physiotherapy manager in our hypothetical example will not need such sophisticated tools, but you will still want to monitor progress and ascertain the causes of any 'slippage'.

One interesting point arises here, about the ethical syndromes we encountered in Chapter 2: in all the other boxes you would expect to operate in the innovative syndrome. However, in box 4 you might think the regulatory syndrome is more appropriate. In other words, while you encourage everyone to be completely honest about their views of the plan in the other boxes, especially in boxes 1–3, and inventive so that it can be as good a plan as possible, once articulated you may want to display loyalty to it, support it and point out its positive benefits, rather than encourage continuing criticism of it. How we marry this with behaviours from boxes 5 and 6 we explore below.

Managing in box 5

Box 5 is the everyday world of interactions between people, events, behaviours and feelings, with a multitude of tiny interactions and reactions shaping the way the change programme is enacted in practice. Integrity and credibility are important, and having robust relationships with a wide range of people will be necessary if you are to identify and encourage behaviours that support the change programme and discourage those that don't.

It is the quality of our behaviours in box 5 that determines how effective we are as real managers. You may want to think about the following:

- Living out the plan yourself;
- Adopting in action the values you advocate;
- Keeping people refreshed and engaged;
- Modelling non-anxious responses to unpredictable and ambiguous situations ('We'll be able to work this out');

- Trying to maintain dynamic poise;
- Being aware of your own reactions to others, others' feelings, behaviours and actions;
- Taking issues seriously but not being defeated by them;
- Identifying other people's emotional responses and heeding them, but not necessarily changing your direction;
- Leading with questions, not answers, autopsies without blame;
- Keeping in touch with what is important to you;
- Monitoring progress in ways that are meaningful to you, so that you have a valid sense of how things are going that you can use to support or counter the views of others.

Managing in box 6

In box 6 you are doing two important things, characterized in Table 5.1 on page 123 as aware opportunism and active awareness. These are taking (and encouraging others to take) opportunities that arise, that may look as though they have nothing to do with the plan in box 4. (In this way you are not allowing the plan to inhibit your ability to act.) And you are also identifying trends or patterns in the opportunities that are being taken, and in the way the plan is being implemented, so that you can build these into a story about the plan and the changes that are happening. Moreover you do this as much through your intuition and conversations as you do through your analytical skills.

Here you may need to:

- Give people the limits within which they can act without any further authority;
- Exhibit and support creativity and innovation;
- Build and encourage a sense of responsibility;
- Sense patterns;
- Formulate and ask the questions that turn people's minds;
- Identify the stories being told, and challenge when a different narrative is more helpful.

As an example of the last item, I have come across several teams who have been given fantastic new premises and other resources, yet complain about how badly the world is treating them. They have somehow managed to weave all this support into a story of imposition and pressure. They are much happier and more effective if this can be challenged.

Once again we need to enact all of these boxes at the same time and it will not be easy. Once written, the plan becomes only one of many agendas people will be pursuing. So, as the service leader, you will need to ensure its profile remains sufficiently high. One way of doing this is to use the three rules of

Chapter 1 when allocating or agreeing responsibilities for the tasks within it. You will also, though, be modifying the plan in the light of events and so you will be constantly refreshing your expectations of others (rule 1) in discussion with them. Of course you must not let deadlines slip unnecessarily, but amendments of the plan in the light of experience shouldn't be seen as failures if they are contributing to greater sustainability of the change in the longer term. Perhaps the most important of all is to try and live out the behaviours suggested in Box 5, and you may find that to be able to adopt them requires some work on really managing yourself – which we shall look at in the next chapter.

Working in box 7

The final stage is that of evaluation and reflection, and all the boxes in this row tend to receive much less attention than they warrant. Box 7 is often practised as an exercise in post-event rationalization. If it is done honestly, however, it can be a very useful review of what the situation is now, how the plan was implemented, how it was not and whether the initial analysis was borne out by subsequent events. In other words, the aim of this box is to build your ability, and that of the service, to analyse, to plan and to implement a plan: all important tasks.

This requires:

- Honest evaluation of where you are and what you have done, keeping as factual as possible;
- Comparison with the project plan, and with the stakeholder assessment;
- Assessment of the analysis in the light of experience.

Having considered these, do you still believe the issues highlighted were the critical ones? Is there anything in the way you approached the analysis that seems to have led to skewed results? Is there a gap between where you hoped you would be and where you actually are? Does this matter? What do you need to do about it?

It is worth noting here that we need to revert to innovation syndrome behaviours in this box (since in Box 4 you may have chosen regulatory), so we are back to honesty being more important than loyalty.

Managing in box 8

Box 8 is about understanding behaviours and relationships, so that you are better able to act effectively in box 5 and better able to engage people in box 2 than you may have been the first time round.

Ways you might do this include:

- Participative reflection, in other words several people reflecting together on processes, behaviours and feelings;
- One-to-one discussions that are not tied to performance management;
- Open, questioning, learning behaviours and thinking processes;
- Deutero learning, explicitly asking 'What prevented us from thinking this as we went along?'

If this is going to be done formally (and some of it may be done informally in the pub or coffee shop) then some kind of external facilitation is often a good idea. This allows everyone, including you as the service leader, to be honest and genuinely reflective, in the knowledge that the facilitator will not allow behaviours of blame or vindictiveness that would inhibit the discussion.

Managing in box 9

This can be the box that receives most attention in this row, although again not enough and usually with a particular agenda. When done well this box allows people to feel they are part of a journey, one that they approve of and can see is being successfully engaged upon. This is important for most of us: we don't want to feel we are part of random events, we want to see some sort of direction and progress. However, while we will want to see hope for the future, Karl Weick reminds us that 'Remembering and looking back are a primary source of meaning'.[17] We may not know the full meaning of a story until after we have told it to ourselves and others, perhaps several times, shaping it in the process so that the direction in which true progress lies become clearer to those involved. So in this box you will want to:

- Weave a story that accords with people's experience, that takes into account many but not necessarily all of the facts;
- Help people to see they are part of a longer narrative that is worth-while, not just for the career of the service leader but for their patients and their aspirations for the service;
- Give a sense of direction and purpose and ongoing movement;
- Not deny contrary views or facts but build them into a sense of perspective.

Again all three boxes must be made to happen and it will be important to combine a rigorous look at relevant evidence with 'softer' approaches that allow people to express feelings. The overriding message about this row, how-ever, is that it should happen at all because it so rarely does, and the results should be used to influence how you approach change in the future.

We have seen how to approach prompts number 4, 5, 6, 7, 8 and 9, and now we will look at specific issues that arise when addressing the others. We start with number 1.

When something goes wrong

Does the following sound familiar to you?

A critical incident occurs, a review takes place, someone is found not to have done something that turned out to be significant. So new policies are written, and new training is required. They are added to the existing stack of policies and statutory training requirements. Not long afterwards another very similar type of critical incident takes place, usually in a different part of the system but sometimes even in the same one.

Of course, when something goes wrong we need to investigate to see why. But we need to ensure that the changes we make prevent it happening again by tackling the underlying causes. So often we tackle the superficial symptoms of a problem instead, and often we just write a new policy. One way of encouraging a look at these deeper seated causes is to choose to use, in box 1, a very simple analytical tool called Five whys, so-called because it asks the question 'Why did this happen?' on five successive occasions to get nearer to the real causes of an event. To identify the changes to be made, answers to all the levels of the Whys are considered. You will find an example in Table 5.8.

From Table 5.8, you can see that if you were to make changes to address this complaint, the changes you would make might include:

- Ensuring that clinical issues raised by clinical staff are taken to a designated clinical forum and appropriately addressed;
- Offering training to the physio staff involved in how to address concerns to their medical colleagues;
- Encouraging the relevant medical staff to respond to expressions of concerns from other professionals;
- Encouraging nursing staff to discuss the issue with the physiotherapy team so that the issue is addressed as a team rather than avoided or blamed on one individual;
- Allocating responsibility for the training of locum staff to a single named individual, perhaps rotated every six months.

These will be far more effective than chastising the locum physiotherapist against whom the complaint has been made. (See Case study 1, page 215, for a further discussion of managerial issues raised when clinicians differ radically over the course of treatment for a particular patient group.)

So if you want to introduce change in response to something going wrong you could identify your change agenda using the five whys, and then use the thinking of the other boxes in much the same way as above.

Table 5.8 Five whys

Problem situation: a ward sister complains that a physiotherapist has been unhelpful and is failing to administer adequate treatment to an elderly, terminally ill patient (for a possible context for this, see Case study 1, page 215)

1	*Why did the physiotherapist fail to administer the regime?*		The physiotherapist is a locum who believes she is following the correct procedure for administering physiotherapy to elderly patients.	
2	*Why did the locum misinterpret the procedure?*		The procedure that more active treatment is the norm in this ward had not been fully explained.	
3	*Why has this not been fully explained?*	Several senior physios believe the regime prescribed is over-vigorous for very frail elderly patients. Some medical consultants believe that a short period of discomfort yields lifesaving results. These differences of view mean that physios are unhappy explaining the procedure to locums.	*Why had the procedure not been fully explained?*	The induction training for locums had fallen into disuse.
4	*Why have these differences of view persisted?*	There is no mechanism for these differences to be discussed at a system, rather than individual patients, level.	*Why had the induction training for locums fallen into disuse?*	Shortage of staff meant there were so many locums that senior staff had become disheartened at repeating the training so often.
5	*Why is there no mechanism for considering these issues?*	Expressions of concern from the physios have not been heeded by their (non-clinical) managers. The physios alone are carrying their unease.	*Why had senior staff allowed the training to become less routine?*	It was a shared responsibility and no one was held to account for it.

Testing new ideas

If you are keeping up with journals and conferences and the world around you, you will undoubtedly come across all sorts of ideas that you think might be useful. Here you might find it useful to take this (introducing this new practice) as your change agenda (box 1) and use the other boxes of the matrix to think through how you would be able to introduce it successfully. However some of the ideas you come across are likely to be 'process ideas', ideas that are not so much about clinical procedures themselves, but about how you review services and ensure they are constantly developing and improving. Sometimes these ideas become 'flavour of the month' and you may find yourself being pressed to use, for example, process mapping, quality circles or PDSA cycles. Many of these process ideas are genuinely useful, some less so. Some are useful for some things but not others. The matrix can help you to make judgements about how to use them.

If we look at process mapping, for example, we can see that it is a tool that allows an analysis (box 1) of a particular patient pathway in such a way that all those involved are engaged with the analysis (box 2) and it looks at what really happens as opposed to what should happen (box 3). When the process is redesigned (box 1 again) all the people who will be part of the new pathway are engaged so that when the new pathway is implemented (box 4), they will understand the reasons for the changes, behave appropriately (we hope) and if problems arise find ways of sort them out that are in the spirit of what was agreed (box 5). They may also spot other opportunities to improve the process (box 6). When reviewing progress the same process of involving all the stakeholders in face-to-face discussion could allow reflection in all of boxes 7, 8 and 9. And the new pathway could form the major part of the story that is told about the whole affair. Thus we might conclude that process mapping, conducted in this manner and with sufficient support in the wider organization, is likely to be a useful means of enabling services to meet real needs in a relatively effective and efficient way.

If you work your way through the matrix, applying this to PDSA cycles and quality circles, for example, I think you will find they can also be useful, for the same reason: they address many of the activities described within many of the boxes.

There are other ideas you may come across in management texts that are excellent in addressing some boxes but not others. One example that comes to mind is that of John Kotter, whose book *A Force for Change: How Leadership Differs from Management* (1990) describes a model of change he finds helpful.[18] When compared with the matrix it can be seen that his prescriptions are almost all in the left hand column, and we can suggest that they may well be helpful in informing us how to approach those boxes (1, 4, 7) better, but this is not the whole story and we must find additional ways of addressing the others.

The matrix gives us a means of conceptualizing where a particular change management idea, whether new or old, might fit within a management approach and at which stage(s) of an initiative it might be more or less useful. This is not to say that an idea that fits all the boxes is 'better' than one that fits only one or a few, only to indicate the extent to which a new idea may fit a particular purpose.

Now let's look at prompt number 3 on the list that opened this chapter.

Exploiting a good opportunity

Exploiting opportunities is a box 6 activity. In an ideal world opportunities would present in enough time for you to analyse the situation thoroughly and generally do all the work advocated in boxes 1, 2 and 3. But often they present without warning and need speedy reaction. The lesson of the matrix is that your decisions will be better if you can use the other boxes in the row at the same time, so how might that encourage you to behave differently? Box 4 would require you to take account of previous analysis of your strategic fit, and the plans you made to increase it. The opportunity should therefore be tested against those plans. While it does not have to dovetail precisely with those, if it takes you in a completely different direction you should at least understand how the opportunity is going to deliver a similar (or greater) degree of success to that gained by sticking to the plan.

Box 5 requires you to engage with other stakeholders and allow this inter-action to shape your response, so to honour this box you would discuss the opportunity with others who will be involved (and not only those within your service). Once taken, the decision and its consequences will need to be reviewed using boxes 7, 8 and 9 as before.

Prompt 10 causes a great deal of frustration so we could usefully think about that now.

Implementing a mandated change

This is when someone else or some other organization insists that you make particular changes, including some that you may have reservations about or disagree with. Many service leaders, and indeed organizational managers, become infuriated when they are told what changes they are to make. Recent examples in the NHS in England include being told to meet certain targets for waiting times for particular services. You may see this, using the matrix, as politicians giving you your agenda for change (which should be the end result of box 1) and telling you to start implementing it (box 4). Naturally this is irritating, especially when box 7 will be used for review, and your career may depend on achieving the mandated result. It will be even more irritating if you believe that the people insisting on these changes do not understand your system and are pursuing their own advantage (getting re-elected perhaps).

However, this isn't the only and certainly isn't the most empowering way of seeing the situation. If you have done your own analysis of what your service should be doing (having used boxes 1, 2 and 3) then you will have a change agenda of your own. As part of your analysis you will take account of the trends in 'consumer accountability' and so on that are what the government is often responding to when it announces this kind of target, and you may well already have decided to make changes that will move you towards that. Even if you haven't and the targets arrive as a surprise you will have a direction of travel already in place within which to accommodate these new objectives. In other words, meeting the targets becomes one of your objectives rather than the sole focus. Of course they will require a good amount of attention, but not all of it. Already (I think you will find) they will begin to seem less infuriating *per se* if viewed in this light, more a potential source of energy in support of achieving something you and the service would like to deliver.

You may feel, however, that you are on the receiving end of ill thought out policies, none of which 'join up', and which are purely for political advantage. That would indeed be enraging, so let's look at this issue of political ends and means further.

The NHS, as perhaps the highest profile public service in the UK, will inevitably attract a high level of involvement from politicians, both those in government and those who would like to be. We could consider that the primary role of the public services is to deliver the agenda of a democratically elected government with good will, honesty and integrity. On the whole, politicians are people who like to act to resolve problems, and as ministers are bound to introduce initiatives and be impatient with the pace of change, they will also be impatient with people they perceive to be obstructing change, and intolerant of what they perceive to be excuses. They care about the levels of service both personally and politically, so they want to see good things happening, and for them to be seen to be happening. They will all (regardless of party) want to increase, or at least justify, the productivity of a government-run service, and the quality of its outcomes. The corollary of this is that bad news about the service will cause them immediate and great concern, and the level of concern will depend on the amount of political capital at risk rather than the size or significance of the incident itself. Elected representatives are given a lot of advice from many directions, and they often have little direct knowledge of services themselves. They develop a 'big picture' of the service they want to see, and deliver the broad brush strokes in the form of policies, relying on the service to undertake the detailed paintwork. They will seldom be aware of how all their policies interact, because these interactions occur at the more detailed level, and if we 'zoom out' to the level of detail at which they are viewing the situation they don't see them (and also because, as we have seen, the expectation that these interactions are fully possible to predict is flawed[19]).

We should therefore expect that there will be many policy initiatives that do not all support each other, and that there will be a pressure for evidence of efficiency and quality. We can also expect that any organization creating 'noise' can expect a high level of direct interference, with the level of noise determining how much interference, and not the severity or significance of the incident that prompted it. These are all an inevitable part of our democratic process and a government-run service. If this is not what you want then you really have to think about working in another setting. So let's think more positively about the change that is imposed upon us, and use the matrix to design our own change agendas that deliver these imposed changes in the context of genuine improvements of the kind we ourselves can take pride in.

Of course, if we find that after a competent and genuine effort to achieve these kind of targets we cannot, or at least only if we skew priorities so that other elements of the service suffer, then we need to make this known. After all, public services have another important responsibility, which is to represent to the government their understanding of the complex realities they are dealing with, thus enabling the government to set an agenda that is appropriate and deliverable. So, while it can, very unfortunately, be difficult for people in the chain of command to express their reservations and experiences, it is entirely appropriate that professional bodies, and others, take steps to ascertain the situation and make this view known. This too is part of the democratic process.

The very fact that it can be difficult for career managers to make their views known can be the result of a lack of trust from the centre. Governments may also dismiss the views of, for example, the professional bodies or other dissident organizations. Rather than bewailing this lack of trust, it can be more useful to consider why it is that the centre finds us less than fully trustworthy. Trustworthiness can be thought to consist of four attributes: honesty, honouring commitments to act, competence in an agreed area of activity and the criteria used for decision-making in that area of activity.[20] For example, you would trust a builder if you found him to be honest, to turn up when he said he would, to build the extension to your design and without it falling down and to buy materials on the basis of quality rather than cost (or vice versa if you prefer). If we think about trust in this way we can see that if we are not trusted then it is either because the people not trusting us are mistaken in their assessment (and we need to think about how we can influence that) or because we are not behaving in a trustworthy manner – and those four headings give us a checklist to investigate. Is it that we cannot be believed because we have not always represented the situation accurately in the past? Or cannot be trusted to deliver because we have not always honoured commitments we made? Or because we have not demonstrated our competence? Or because we are taking on a different job from the one they want us to? Or because we are bringing to it different criteria for making choices? We can influence the levels of trust other people place in us, and we need to do so.

All in all, when we groan at yet another set of initiatives arriving in our in-tray, we need to see them as legitimate, as helpful and as something that has a valid claim on our time and attention. Once we have made a sincere and competent attempt to implement them we may also want to make our experiences known in a constructive manner so that all concerned can learn from this.

Concluding thoughts

The thought processes necessary when considering intervening in a service or organization are comparable with those when intervening clinically with a patient, and require similar evaluation of condition, prognosis, options, costs, benefits and risks. Just as *primum non nocere* (above all do no harm) is an important instruction in medicine and the clinical professions, so it is when managing health care organizations or services. It must never be forgotten that all interventions in organizations incur costs and risks and the anticipated benefits should always outweigh them.

Received wisdom has it that with any change there are winners and losers. When that change involves a restructuring of the organization, there are people or departments who end up with more or less positional power than they had before. As a result, restructuring has become an easy option for inef-fectual managers to deal with staff they find difficult – by making them redun-dant rather than developing them or sacking them (both of which require more effort and integrity).

The idea that there have to be winners and losers, however, is a dangerous one, in that it can lead to a callous shrugging of the shoulders over the fate of individuals or services. While it is unlikely that everyone will 'win' by the same amount, it is certainly feasible and desirable to aim for everyone to win some-thing.[21] This cannot be positional power for everyone but, as we saw in Chap-ter 1, not everyone wants that – and even those who do want it have other goals as well.

Max de Pree describes the role of the leader as 'liberating people to do what is required of them in the most effective and humane way possible' If your change programme does not liberate your staff to do what is required of them, effectively and humanely, then please reconsider it. The fact that people have different goals ensures that the means to liberate them differ. This allows you to design a change programme in which everyone gains.

Your staff may gain greater clarity about their role, more systematic and valuable feedback, the opportunity to develop a particular interest and the ability to influence service levels from an interdependent department; and have their views heard elsewhere in the organization. This is not bribery, this is a careful analysis of your staff and their interests (part of your Seven Ss scrutiny) and an honest and creative attempt to liberate them. I say 'honest' because it is all too easy to meet the needs of people we like at the expense of those we do not; an honest attempt will preclude this.

You may like to consider that if, as a result of your change programme, anyone genuinely feels they have been a loser, then you have failed: failed to construct a programme that takes account of their needs, failed to persuade them of the benefits or failed to develop them to a point on the maturity continuum where they can recognize the benefits. At the same time, they must take responsibility for their own reactions and consider whether they have enabled you to meet their needs. A culture in which blame is routinely taken in this way, rather than given, would be novel (and enormously helpful) in health care.

It can never be said that a change is 'for the best', simply because there is no 'best' in this field of human endeavour, except with the wisdom of hindsight. Let me introduce a distinction first coined by Russell Ackoff in 1971. A puzzle has one right answer and if you search hard and wide and long enough you may find it. A problem has no answer. A problem is so multidimensional that it can be addressed in a number of different ways.[22] None of them will be right or wrong, none will be the 'best', but some will be more or less appropriate in the prevailing circumstances. In other words, some will be better, or worse, for now. At different times and in different circumstances, the same problem will be addressed in different ways. This leads to talk of pendulums and swings.

In any situation, we tend to spot the problems with the existing structure, people, systems and so on, and ignore all the features that are working well. We then implement a change programme designed to solve the problems and only then realize that in doing so we have created a number of new ones. Our successive attempts to remove these end up with us introducing a system very similar to the one we were so keen to change, and so it goes on. The more we can remember that there is no perfect solution, that all solutions will be found wanting, that the situation we inherit was devised by people as committed and as able as ourselves, then the more easily we can avoid three temptations: first, to change everything immediately; second, to blame and scapegoat our predecessor and assume the clock only started when we came into post; third, to compare the disadvantages with the structures and systems that we are keen to change with the advantages of the ones we want to bring in, rather than keeping in mind that there are always advantages and disadvantages of everything.

As a result of a certain lack of skill and integrity in this area, in many of the changes that take place in health care today there are winners and losers, and sometimes more of the latter. Unfortunately, whether you and your team will be a winner or loser does not often depend on intrinsic merit. It does not depend on how great your contribution could have been. In addition to sheer luck (which does play some part), what it does depend on is your ability to analyse the situation, determine your goals, identify the obstacles and assisters to those goals and deploy your resources tactically as a result. Whether the organization (and its clients) is a winner or a loser depends on the merit of the people who do that. Thus, if your view is important, if your service has a valuable contribution to make, it is essential that you develop the skills discussed in this chapter to analyse, to engage, to sense patterns and weave stories, to relate robustly with others involved, to reflect and to learn, in other words to really manage change.

Notes

1 This may seem like splitting hairs. Does it matter what words we use to describe the kinds of activity intended to lead to improvement? Only inasmuch as there is a rich literature about change management that can valuably inform our thinking in this area and if we dismiss the terms 'change' and 'change management' or use alternative terms we may miss it altogether.

2 This is also called the deliberate approach and I sometimes call it the classical approach because it has its roots in military strategy in the classical era, and because it is the model classically taught in business schools and implicitly espoused by politicians and senior policy-makers.

3 Ansoff, I. (1965) *Corporate Stategy: An Analytic Approach to Business Policy for Growth and Expansion* (New York: McGraw-Hill).

4 Since then different waves of analysis have arrived, been found useful and then (often) wanting, and have made way for another set. For example, it has in turn been fashionable to analyse the attractiveness of an industry (Michael Porter), the market share within an industry (Boston Consulting Group) and the share of tomorrow's market (opportunity share) (Hamel and Prahalad). All of these can be helpful, but none is the whole answer.

5 And its distinction from 'deliberate' (also a Mintzberg term).

6 For a discussion of the uses and limitations of evidence in this field see Iles and Sutherland (2001) (see Introduction, note 3).

7 It was first envisaged by Gordon Best (formerly Director of the Kings Fund College and founder of OD Partnerships Network), developed further with a think tank on strategy in complex organizations sponsored by Nigel Edwards of the NHS Confederation and then explored in much greater depth with and made much more practical by a learning set of NHS strategy practitioners: Beverley Slater, Helen Cameron, Paul Gray and Pamela Coen. For further thinking from this learning set please see the website www.reallylearning.com.

8 These are the boxes that tend to dominate where change is being devised and implemented by a team that understands and values all three of these schools. Where people have a strong preference for one school, or a lack of understanding or lack of sympathy for another school the boxes that dominate will fall within one column.

9 This is a fairly typical combination, but you would use the same process if addressing only one of these.

10 Some people care passionately about what terms to use and define taxonomies of vision, mission, goals, objectives etc. I choose to use the word mission to cover several of these, because it captures, for me, a sense of zeal and action, as well as more cerebral purpose.

11 For an example of this see Iles and Cranfield (2004), Case 1 'Leading a service through change' (see Further reading).

12 Waterman, R., Peters, T.J. and Phillips, J.R. (1980) 'Structure is not organiza-tion', *Business Horizons*, June, 14–26. The Seven S framework first appeared in Pascale, R. and Athos, A. (1981) *The Art of Japanese Management* (Harmonds-worth: Penguin) and had arisen out of joint discussions in the late 1970s between the authors and Tom Peters and Robert Waterman, who later went on to use the same framework in *In Search of Excellence* (1982, New York: Harper and Row). The model was later taken up by the management consultancy firm McKinsey, and is also sometimes known as the McKinsey 7S model.

13 The skills a service needs can usefully be thought of in four categories: clinical or technical skills; interpersonal or behavioural skills; managerial skills (those to do with deploying resources including your own time); and research/evalu-ation/reflection skills. We look at these again in Chapters 6 and 7.

14 The word has roots in the ancient Greek *techne*, meaning 'art, craft, trade or skill'. Aristotle went a step further by arguing that *techne* was the systematic use of knowledge for intelligent human action.

15 Iles and Cranfield (2004) (see Further reading).

16 For examples of critical paths visit the Mind Tools website (www.mindtools. com/critpath.html).

17 Weick, K. (2001) *Making Sense of the Organization* (Oxford: Blackwell), p. 11.

18 New York: Free Press. Kotter proposes an eight-phase change model: (1) estab-lish a sense of urgency; (2) create a coalition; (3) develop a clear vision; (4) share the vision; (5) empower people to clear obstacles; (6) secure short-term wins; (7) consolidate and keep moving; (8) anchor the change.

19 And is based on linear thinking of the kind we see in boxes 1, 4 and 7 of the matrix, ignoring thinking from the other two columns.

20 This is explored further in a report on the Really Learning website (www. reallylearning.com).

21 This is covered in Covey (1990); see Chapter 3, note 4. Covey uses the terms 'win' and 'lose'. Two psychologists, Kenneth Thomas and Ralph Kilmann, have devised a questionnaire, The Thomas–Kilmann Conflict Mode Instru-ment (XICOM, New York, 1992), to help to assess individuals' preferred con-flict mode, and use the terms 'competing', 'accommodating' etc.

22 Russell Ackoff takes this distinction further and talks of 'problems' and 'messes'. A group of changing problems that interact with each other is a mess. Ackoff suggests that most managers most of the time are dealing with 'messes'. Quoted in Schön, D.A. (1983) *The Reflective Practitioner* (London: Temple Smith).

6 Really managing yourself

Many of the service leaders I meet are unhappy. GPs with their own practice, consultants who lead specialist teams, therapists who manage a range of therapy services: wherever they are, people report feelings of frustration. Do any of the following apply to you?

- Are you surrounded by people who prevent you from achieving all you could?
- Are you often disappointed in the performance of your juniors?
- Are the managers in your organization ill-informed, remote, prone to imposing diktats without seeking your opinion?
- Do some of your patients have unrealistic expectations of the NHS?
- Are there more and more demands on your time?
- Do colleagues in other professions or disciplines seem not to understand the pressures you are under?
- Are other professionals trying to take over some of your role?
- Are politicians trying to wreck the NHS?
- Is a lot of the information you provide misused?
- Have you had change, change and more change imposed on you?
- Is it impossible for you to achieve any more without greater resources?

If this is the case, then naturally you are unhappy, frustrated and dissatisfied. You are possibly wondering whether you made the right career choice, whether you shouldn't retire early or discourage your children or friends from following in your career footsteps. You are being buffeted around by forces around you and are not in control. This chapter is about putting you back in control.

The topics most often suggested by service leaders when we discuss what they would like to cover in a programme about 'managing yourself' are managing their time, increasing their confidence and managing stress levels. So in this chapter we will look at those topics in such a way that we see how to deal with the frustrations identified above.

Managing time

We talk about managing time, but there are only ever 24 hours in a day whatever we do, so we will look instead at making the best use of time, or managing *priorities*.

I am sure that you have a list of 'things to do today', and you may even write one for the week. These are helpful in reminding us of what needs to be done and give us the satisfaction of ticking items off as they are completed. But all too often we find that some tasks stay on the list for days because we just haven't found the time or inclination to take them on. The problem is that our list doesn't reflect what we really care about, so if we can generate one that does we shall find it much more satisfying to complete, and feel much more satisfied with what we are doing. How can we do that, when we are surrounded by people asking or requiring us to do things we care little about? Many people I have worked with find the method described by Stephen Covey in *The Seven Habits of Highly Effective People*[1] allows them to do just this. Let me describe it briefly.

First, you draw up a list of all the different roles you play in your life. You might start by thinking of your work, home and perhaps community roles: so, for example, nurse, mother (and daughter, sister and so on) and choir member. But think too about the roles you play *within* each of those; these are the ones to write down. As an HCP, you have the roles of assessor and provider of care to individual patients. You are also an educator, a supervisor, a researcher or evaluator, a colleague, a member of your professional body, a member of a health care organization. As a parent you are a provider, a nurturer, a developer of skills and more. You will have your own way of characterizing these roles, but you will probably come up with a dozen or so altogether. And in each of these roles, you will want to achieve something or make some kind of contribution. So now you write a short description of the contribution you want to make for each one. This is not something that you can start and finish satisfactorily in one short session. If it is to make a difference, really to help to put you back in control, you may need to contemplate these roles and contributions over a period of weeks. When you feel that the roles and contributions you have envisaged accurately depict what you want your life to be about, then write them down.

Taking the roles in turn, you can now formulate a set of objectives or goals for each. Again it is worth writing these down, so you now have a list of titles (mother and so on) and under each of those a list of roles, and under each of those a set of goals. I find it useful to keep a notebook for this purpose with these listed at the front. Now you have what you need to plan your priorities for the week ahead, because you are ready to think through, for each of the goals, what are the most important actions you need to take this week if you are going to make progress towards it. This is your 'to do' list for the week and looking at your diary for the week ahead you can see what opportunities you will have to complete it. If you have identified your roles perceptively, then every appointment during the week will give you a chance to work towards at least one of your objectives. If it does not, then you have either omitted a role that is important in some way or you have a diary that is still full of engagements you made before you started managing your priorities. You will find there are some activities you can cancel, but, especially to start with, you may well find it hard to fit everything on your list into your diary. It is worth writing them in anyway, even if you feel it unlikely you will manage to get them done, because many people find it surprising how much more they can fit in, and how much more ruthless they can be at refusing additional tasks or avoiding waste of time, once they have in front of them a list of things they know (and feel) are important.

Many people report that the positive results of such an exercise are apparent almost immediately. The small but significant tasks that otherwise tend to be left and to form part of an overall feeling of pressure (a phone call to arrange to meet, sending a document requested, retrieving said document from its file, drafting a memo about leave arrangements or a student visit) will now all be scheduled and tackled. When aware of just how many other commitments they have in a day, and the precise nature of those commitments, most people report a reduction in the time they spend in pleasant but unproductive activities: gossip, speculation, complaining about (but not to) and so on. Being able to tick off activities as they are completed, activities that are seen as important or necessary, gives a satisfaction that is lost when the pressures are perceived as an amorphous and irreducible mass.

In working with clinicians of various sorts over the past 25 years, I have observed that it is often the most highly intelligent, the most incisive and decisive who are the most disorganized. They feel under enormous pressure but fail to recognize that it is greatly increased by their profligate use of their greatest resource: their own time. So the more you think that this approach may be fine in theory but that you do not have the time to put it into practice, the more you are irritated at my naivety and lack of understanding of your service and the pressures you are under, the more strongly I recommend that you try it. I notice too that people often pass this on as a suggestion, perhaps to a disorganized junior member of their team, and that is very helpful – but it is even more so if you try it out yourself first.

If you find that this method does not relieve the pressure on your diary, this is probably because you have been insufficiently rigorous in restricting your goals to the activities that are *critical* to the successful achievement of your mission. It is easy to get bogged down in 'process' rather than 'outcome' tasks, to get trapped in a cycle of meetings when there are other, more time-effective ways of achieving the same aim. If, after further reflection, you still cannot fit all your goals into your schedule, you must reconsider your goals. You are probably asking too much of yourself, setting yourself up to fail, making feelings of stress, anger and helplessness inevitable. Occasionally people find that they are not in the right position to achieve their goals, and this can explain why they are so frustrated. If there is no way of reconciling the two then one or other will have to change.

This is far the most effective way I have found of managing your time, but there are some useful tricks that can help and these are listed in Box 6.1.[2]

Increasing confidence

In Chapter 3 we noted that the role of a *real* manager is to develop the maturity of an organization by increasing the confidence of its members. Engendering confidence in others requires us to have confidence in ourselves, and nurturing this self-confidence is an important part of managing yourself, an aspect that deserves explicit attention.

Box 6.1 Managing your time

- Say no, only make commitments you know you can keep.
- Keep them.
- Do the worst first. Your list for today will include several things you enjoy and some you don't. Do the latter first.
- 'Grab 15'. If there is something you really don't want to get on with, perhaps a paper to be written, don't wait until you have time to do it properly, give yourself permission to give it just 15 minutes of your time today. Mostly you will find the difficult part was getting started and you can go on to finish it, but if that doesn't happen you can stop after 15 minutes and find another 15 minutes tomorrow.
- Do it now. That e-mail that's just come in and wants an answer, don't leave it, do it now.
- Just do it. Don't agonize over it, just do it.
- No temporary parking places. Every piece of paper should be in place or in use (no urgent and non-urgent piles on your desk – you're either dealing with it or it's put away straightaway).
- Handle each piece of paper (or e-mail) only once. Don't open your mail until you have time to deal with it, and then do it.

Confidence results when the demands made of us are within our competence, and when our competences are steadily growing. We have a confidence problem whenever what our intellect tells us we can do, or what our ambition tells us we ought to do, is not in harmony with what we believe we are able to do. Other people have a problem with our confidence when what they think we can achieve is less than we believe it to be. Whichever confidence problem we have (and most of us experience both from time to time), self-awareness is the route to its solution. We need a realistic assessment of our abilities and a sensitive awareness of our feelings.

When we are assessing our skills, there are four types of skill we can usefully consider. Clinical or technical skills are those associated with our core HCP role; behavioural and interpersonal skills are those we employ when reacting to events and relating to other people; managerial skills are those associated with deploying resources; and evaluative skills are those that enable us to reflect and to research. When we bring them to bear, we do so as a package, with each set of skills supporting the others, and it is how this package allows us to make progress towards our goals that we must consider. Comparing our own skill levels honestly with those of others allows us to identify areas of relative strength or weakness and thus opportunities to offer assistance or seek development. Sometimes we dishearten ourselves by using as a comparator a paragon of virtue in this field, and sometimes we do so by comparing individual skills rather than the package as a whole. We will always find others whose prowess exceeds our own on one of the dimensions; but it is the four together that enable us to make our distinctive contribution. Referring back to our personal goals will allow us to see the kind of skills package we need. If your aim is to make a difference to the lives of a particular group of patients, then you will need a skills package that differs from that required if you wish to take a high-profile national role.

Sometimes, far from disheartening us, this comparison leaves us with a fiery glow of satisfaction, and then we again have some checking to do. Have we sought any more objective appraisal of our competences and qualities than our own analysis? Are we confusing the ability to acquire a competence with its acquisition? I have met lots of clinicians who believe that because they can describe a skill they have it. The intelligence to understand how to undertake certain roles is important, but only as a prerequisite for developing the necessary skills and using them.

Knowing whether we have the skills is only part of the problem of confidence, of course. Sometimes it isn't the skill we feel we are lacking but the authority to exercise it. Authority is something that is delegated to us from people above us in a hierarchy, but it is also something that must be sanctioned by the people 'below', those over whom we are to have authority. And it also needs to come from within us. There is a view that full authority is always a myth, that what is needed might be called 'full-enough' authority,[3] in which we check to see whether we have *enough* authority from above, and below, and within, to do what we want to do. There will be occasions when we find we do not, or that we have authority to go so far and no further. Attempting to exert authority in this situation would be miserable, and would sap your confidence further, so it is well worth not trying to be heroic. But if we want to build our competences we must also operate, at least some of the time, right at the edge (or outside) of our comfort zone. There is a book called *Feel the Fear and Do It Anyway*,[4] which challenges us to overcome some of the limitations we impose on ourselves. In it Susan Jeffers points out that every time we increase our skills and become able to tackle comfortably one set of tasks that initially frightened us we will find another new set, at a higher skill level, or operating on a larger scale, that will frighten us again. If we feel the fear but do it anyway, we can develop ways of dealing with that fear and making it manageable.

There is one simple way to increase the level of confidence we feel in ourselves that involves little or no fear, and it is based on this thought: whenever we behave in a way that differs from the behaviour of the person we would like to be we damage our confidence. That suggests that when we adopt behaviours of which we approve our confidence increases. And since we can choose our behaviours (even if we can't choose our feelings), the level of confidence we feel is something we can increase because of the things we do. So if we think it is a good thing to be up at 7 a.m., staying in bed until 8 a.m. will encourage us to view ourselves less positively than if we emerge promptly as the alarm goes off. If I tell someone I will do something then I will feel more confident about myself as a whole if I do it than if I don't. If I see myself as the kind of person who keeps their word, eats sensibly and exercises regularly (and these will differ for all of us), and I like that person, I will be more confident than if I see myself as someone I don't like who can't get up in the morning, can't switch the TV off and hasn't cleaned the fridge out for months. And the great thing about this is that none of these actions involves any courage at all, only discipline. Is there evidence for this? I don't know, but I have tried it myself and passed it on a lot since I came across it. I can only report what I and others have found, so why not try it for yourself?

We can also sabotage ourselves by mistaking what our contribution could be. Suppose you are invited, by someone you rate who is more senior than you perhaps, to be a member of a task group. You are keen but a little diffident. You are not sure you are up to it. It is worth thinking through carefully what your contribution to this could be, what it is that you have to offer. You won't have been asked unless you have something, so what is it that you have that others don't? Other people may be more experienced in this field but unavailable. Your availability is important. Others may have a higher level of technical expertise but not be able to get on with colleagues. Your interpersonal skills are your asset. You may be more junior than others, but your knowledge of operational detail may be just what is needed. If you assess correctly what your contribution could be, then you can ensure that you make it. You won't then be tempted to limit your availability by going on holiday, or to beef up on technical detail when you are needed for your ability to build a team, or to try to join in the debate on strategic issues when you would be more useful thinking about the impact at service level.

One of the occasions when confidence can fly out of the window is when we are confronted with someone angry with us, or hostile in some way. Again, there is a way of maintaining your composure and nerve, and it is based on another thought: that all our negative or upsetting emotions (anger, jealousy, resentment, depression) represent some form of fear; that it is our own fear that leads us to respond negatively; that it is other people's fear that leads them to behave in a hostile fashion. This idea allows two helpful thought processes. First, if you can identify the cause of your fear, the reason you become angry, resentful or frustrated, you can often tackle that cause and achieve longstanding release from those negative feelings. For example, if a colleague uses some of your ideas in a paper and fails to attribute them to you, you may well feel angry. What is the fear behind the anger? The fear may be that others will not credit you with those ideas, that they will not think as highly of you as they might. Is your reputation really as fragile as that? If it is and there is a promotion round coming up, then you must address it, but in many cases you will realize that it is not. Sometimes it can be helpful to think through the worst possible consequences. Often the very worst that can happen is something you can live with. Analysing fear in this way leads, in many cases, to people finding that when they have done so once, they can be relieved of the feeling of anger not only then but on many similar occasions.

Second, you can choose to see everyone as either behaving generously or behaving fearfully and jealously. Approached in this way, a colleague who behaves in a hostile or predatory fashion can be thought of as fearful, as needing your help to overcome that fear. If you can identify the source of their fear, then again you will find it easier to respond constructively, to lose your anger and replace it with concern or compassion. This does not turn you into a doormat. If your colleague's behaviour threatens your ability to achieve your personal goals, then you must defend yourself. Compassion does not equate with overtolerance. However, if attack is in order you attack their arguments or their behaviour, not them personally. You use logic and reason to defend yourself, not uncontrolled emotion.

Very often our fear is of how other people will respond to us. We want them to think well of us. If we can fully appreciate that how others think of us depends less on our own merits than on their feelings about themselves, then we are ready to take one of the biggest steps to becoming a *real* manager. This is the step when we stop worrying about how other people see us and instead devote that energy to considering what we think of them. Are they genuinely confident enough to respond generously to our ideas, to our initiatives, to our mistakes? Or will they be critical of our ideas, resistant to our initiatives and jealously triumphant about our mistakes? Forging a network of people who are both generous and disciplined, with whom you can enter into open, honest relationships based on confidence and trust, is the way that you will increase your influence and achieve your goals. Trying to impress the unimpressible is not. You will need to engage with these but must not allow your self-image to be determined by them.

Nevertheless, we can, and should, *help* people to respond favourably to us by exploiting the 'halo effect'. If we like certain things about a person – the way she looks, the way she sounds – then the 'halo effect' predisposes us to like other aspects, her arguments, for example. Paying attention to how we present ourselves – voice and posture, colour and style of clothing – can help us to influence others and achieve our goals. Professional advice in these areas is well worth seeking.[5] However, although these aspects are a valuable aid in getting a message across, they do not replace the need for a valid message. Without this change of outlook, without a determination to concentrate our attention on others rather than on ourselves, to become a 'go-giver' rather than a 'go-getter',[6] then no matter how classy our presentation (including self-presentation) skills, our effectiveness will be severely limited.

Approaches for dealing with stress

What do we mean by stress? In this section we are going to consider the kind of emotional, cognitive and behavioural responses you make to an event or situation, and think about ways of enabling these to be positive rather than negative.

Many philosophers and psychologists have noted that we become stressed not so much because of the events that happen to us or actions that we directly observe, but because of the feelings, thoughts or behaviours that they prompt in us. Nor is this a recent discovery. Epictetus, a Greek-born philosopher in the first century AD, is reported as having said 'Men are disturbed not by things but by their views of things.' Similar insights, of course, have been at the core of Hindu, Buddhist and Confucian philosophies. And as Hamlet says, 'There is nothing either good or bad, but thinking makes it so.' In what follows, I want to introduce you to two modern ways of thinking that in some respects build upon this common insight and that you may find helpful in relieving yourself of stress. The first is the underlying principle of rational emotive behavioural therapy (REBT), which I introduce below, and the second is one of which you will probably have heard, called transactional analysis (TA).

REBT

REBT was developed by the clinical psychologist Albert Lewis, who had become disillusioned at what he saw as the inefficiency of conventional psychotherapy. It was inefficient in that it took a long time for people to discover underlying problems and even longer to address them. He identified two major categories of human psychological problems: *ego disturbance* and *discomfort disturbance*. Ego disturbance happens when we make unrealistic demands upon ourselves and give ourselves negative ratings when we fail to live up to these; and discomfort disturbance involves making dogmatic requirements that we *should* feel comfortable and not experience any discomfort. He suggested that the healthy alternative to ego disturbance is a fundamental attitude of self-acceptance, in which we accept ourselves as human beings to whom it is not possible to award a single global rating. So we should not think of ourselves as bad or unworthy, we should recognize that we are too complex to be described using any simple measurement scale. The healthy alternative to discomfort disturbance is a philosophy of tolerance to discomfort – accepted not for its own sake but as a means of overcoming obstacles to the pursuit of our goals.[7]

At the heart of REBT practice is the *ABC framework*. A is the *activating event*, which can be either an external event (something that actually happens) or our interpretation of the event. When A happens we bring to that event our *beliefs* or constructed views of the world: B. These beliefs are either rigid or flexible, and extreme or non-extreme. Rigid beliefs are often expressed in terms of 'musts, absolute shoulds, have tos, got tos' and so on. They are irrational in the following sense. Rational beliefs help us to achieve our basic goals and purposes. Irrational beliefs prevent us from achieving those goals and purposes. There are four ways in which beliefs can be rational or irrational. Rational beliefs are: (a) flexible and non-extreme; (b) pragmatic; (c) logical; and (d) empirically consistent with reality. We will see what these mean in a moment.

Irrational beliefs lead to irrational conclusions (irrational in that they are extreme), which generally take one of three forms:

1   Awfulizing. I, or someone else, or this situation is awful, the worst possible, worse than it absolutely should be.
2   Low frustration tolerance. I can't bear it if this situation exists.
3   Depreciation. I really don't like or rate myself, or others, or life conditions.

Rational beliefs are much more flexible and contain desires and preferences that we don't transform into dogmatic musts and shoulds, such as 'I would like to be valued by my work colleagues, but I don't absolutely have to be'. The conclusions we draw from these healthy beliefs are:

1   Anti-awfulizing. It's bad but not terrible.
2   High frustration tolerance. I don't like it but I can bear it.
3   Acceptance. I accept myself and others as fallible human beings who cannot legitimately be given a single global rating, and the world as complex, as having good and bad and neutral elements that can't be given a global rating.

C stands for the emotional, behavioural and thinking *consequences*. When a negative activating event (A) takes place, we can bring rational beliefs (B) to it and the result will be healthy negative consequences. If, instead, we bring to it irrational beliefs the result is unhealthy negative consequences. The fact that we are bringing more rational beliefs to the event does not prevent it from having a negative impact, but it does render the impact proportionate and leave us able to deal with it effectively. The contrast between healthy and unhealthy emotional consequences can be seen in Table 6.1.

REBT suggests that the only long-term way of overcoming these disturbances, these unhealthy negative consequences, which we might think of as stress, is to work against our irrational beliefs and our tendency to think irrationally and dysfunctionally.

The irrational beliefs that we bring to the events around us are often one of three basic musts:

1   Demands about self. 'I must do well, be approved by significant others and if I'm not then it's awful, I can't stand it. When I'm not loved or don't do well then I deserve to be punished.' The emotional consequences are often anxiety, depression, shame or guilt.
2   Demands about others: 'You must treat me well and justly, and when you don't it's awful and I can't bear it. When you don't treat me well you deserve to be punished.' Emotional consequences can include unhealthy anger or rage.
3   Demands about world or life conditions: 'Life conditions under which I live absolutely must be the way I want them to be and if they are not it is terrible, I can't stand it, poor me.' Emotional consequences here can include self-pity, hurt and problems of self-discipline, e.g. procrastination.

A lot of the time we turn a rational belief into an irrational one by adding an irrational element to it. For example, 'I would like X to like me' (rational) becomes irrational if we add 'and if she doesn't it is terrible and I couldn't bear it'. The rational way to finish that would be 'but there's no law saying she has to, and if she doesn't then that's a pity but it's not terrible'. It is also worth noticing that we tend to perpetuate our disturbance in the following ways:

- we insist on a philosophy of low frustration tolerance, we refuse to become uncomfortable now in order to become comfortable later;
- we can also make ourselves disturbed about our original disturbance and beat ourselves up for having irrational beliefs;
- we often employ defences to ward off threats to our ego and to our level of comfort, and we prefer to blame others or our circumstances;
- we sometimes receive a pay-off for thinking in this way, e.g. attention and sympathy from others;
- we can make self-fulfilling prophecies, where our own actions lead to an outcome we fear but predict.

Table 6.1 Healthy and unhealthy emotions

Healthy negative emotions	Unhealthy negative emotions
Concern I hope X doesn't happen, but there is no reason why it must not happen, and if it did it would be unfortunate but not terrible.	*Anxiety* X must not happen and it would be awful if it did.
Sadness It is unfortunate that I have experienced this loss, but there is no reason why it should not have happened, it's bad but it's not terrible.	*Depression* This loss should not have happened to me, it's terrible that it did.
Remorse I prefer not to behave badly but I'm not immune from doing so. If I do it's bad but I can accept myself as a fallible human being who has done the wrong thing.	*Guilt* I must not act badly and if I do it's awful and I'm a terrible person.
Disappointment When I act stupidly in public I am disappointed in the actions I choose, but accept that I am fallible and can make mistakes. I prefer that I behave well but I do not demand it of myself.	*Shame* I condemn myself for acting in a way I absolutely should not have done. (This is often based on the belief that I absolutely need the approval of others.)
Healthy anger I wish X had not done that and I don't like what they did, but it does not follow that they must not break my rule.	*Unhealthy anger* X absolutely should not have done that and is completely wrong.

To work against these irrational beliefs we first have to identify them, and the usual way is to think of a problem you have recently experienced – a time when you are aware you became stressed or disturbed – and see if you can identify the activating event and the irrational beliefs you applied to it. It is then possible to think through in turn why each of those beliefs is irrational (illogical, inconsistent with reality, non-pragmatic in that it will give poor results in the long term) and frame a realistic alternative that is logical and consistent with reality and will give better results. It is then necessary to challenge your irrational beliefs by testing them against reality, so that you reduce your conviction in those and increase it in the rational alternatives. The aim of REBT counselling is a cognitive change in which you:

- give up making demands on yourself, others and the world;
- refrain from making extreme ratings of yourself, others and the world;
- accept yourself and others as fallible human beings;
- accept the world as too complex to merit a simple global rating;
- tolerate discomfort when it is in your best interests to do so.

If you can accept the validity of any of these aims then you may find you can use that thinking to reduce considerably your stress levels. Depending on how stressed you feel generally, the change in the way you see yourself and those about you may be more or less far reaching.

TA

TA (transactional analysis) is a theory about how people interact with each other that was developed by Eric Berne in the 1960s.[8] Again it is a theory, and I am not going to argue that it is the only way of analysing interactions, or necessarily the best. I include it here because I and many of the people I work with find it helpful. They find that it is a concept they can hold on to when dealing with tense situations, and that it is particularly useful when interacting with members of different professions.

The basis of TA is the observation that as adults we do not always behave rationally, bringing all our skills to bear on a problem that we are trying to solve here and now. Instead, we sometimes adopt feelings and behaviours that we either experienced as children or observed in our parents or other authority figures when we were children. This means that at any time we could be feeling and behaving in any one of three 'ego states': parent, adult or child. Indeed, in our lives we need to be able to move between all three ego states: *adult* for problem solving, *parent* for fitting comfortably into society and *child* for spontaneity and creativity. Notice, however, that when we are in the parent or child ego states we feel and behave in ways rooted in the past. Only in adult mode are we dealing wholly with the present.

Two of the ego states (parent and child) are each further subdivided into two: adapted child and natural child; controlling parent and nurturing parent. Furthermore, each of these four parent and child ego states can result in either positive or negative behaviours. The possible ego states are set out in Box 6.2.[9]

Berne observed that any communication between two people is made up of a series of transactions. A transaction is a 'stimulus' from one person and a 'response' from the other. He suggested that each transaction can be one of two kinds: *complementary* or *crossed*. In complementary transactions the

---

Box 6.2 Ego states

1   Controlling parent

Enables the other to act effectively, promoting survival.
Examples of language:
'Do your homework'
'Don't play with matches'
'You're doing very well'
Positive: Aimed at protection, at influencing the behaviour of other person, for the good of that person.
Negative: Tries to put other person down, to control behaviour of someone else for the good of the 'parent'.

2   Nurturing parent

Enables the other to grow and develop.
Examples of language:
'Let me help you with that'
'Let's do something nice'
Positive: Empowering, acting out of a genuine concern for the other.
Negative: Disempowering, 'I know best', keeps other person in inferior position.

3   Adult

Solves here-and-now problems rationally, using all available skills.

4   Adapted child

Modifies behaviour under parental influence.
Positive: Heeds the demands, e.g. being law-abiding, polite, courteous.
Negative: Rebels against the demands, e.g. sulking to get attention.

5   Natural child

Is unaware, or independent, of pressures from 'parents'.
Fun-loving, free, pleasure-seeking.
Positive: Acts within safe boundaries.
Negative: Takes risks with own safety and that of others.

transactional vectors (the lines drawn between the ego states involved on a diagram of the sort shown in Figure 6.1) are parallel, and the ego state addressed is the one that responds. The ego states involved could be, for example, adult to adult, controlling parent to adapted child (or vice versa), natural child to nurturing parent (or vice versa).

When a transaction is crossed then the ego state that is addressed is not the one that responds (see Figure 6.2). A natural child may address a nurturing parent and the controlling parent responds. An adult stimulus may receive a parental, or child, response. When this happens the communication is uncomfortable for both parties and either the communication breaks, or one (or both) individuals must shift to another ego state for it to continue.

It was Beme's view that as long as transactions remain complementary communication can continue between these two ego states indefinitely. He suggested that if you want to change these ego states you must introduce a new topic of conversation, establish a different relationship when talking about that and only then reintroduce the conversation you were having before, in the new ego states you have established.

Sometimes the transaction is straightforward and the words used accurately convey what is meant (by the stimulus) and what is interpreted (by the

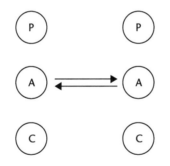

Figure 6.1   A complementary transaction.

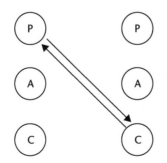

Figure 6.2   A complementary transaction.

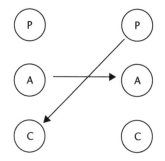

Figure 6.3   A transaction that is crossed.

respondent). At other times there is an ulterior meaning being conveyed, where the words suggest one thing but the tone another. Or the comment may refer back to a previous conversation when different ego states were included. One flat-mate might say to another, for example, 'Where are the coffee mugs?' Ostensibly an adult–adult question, it may really mean 'Haven't you done the washing up yet?', a controlling parent–adapted child transaction.

It is important to remember that none of these transactions is good or bad, productive or unproductive, in itself. In any situation one particular combination may be more useful than others and you can choose to move into that ego state, or not. You may, however, find yourself in a complementary transaction that you feel is inappropriate, but, because it *is* complementary, realize it is difficult to change.

Consider the following vignette.

When you first joined your new department three months ago you were very appreciative of the support and guidance given to you by a colleague. But now you have become familiar with the people, with the ways of working and with the job itself, and you do not want your colleague to advise you any more. Indeed, you find that you disagree with her on certain issues but that you cannot discuss these sensibly because she always tells you that you are too new to understand them properly. You value your colleague's expertise and would like to feel able to collaborate on certain clinical cases where your combination of skills would allow better decisions to be made than either of you can reach alone, but here, too, she automatically assumes the superior role. You try to discuss issues as an equal colleague but somehow always end up feeling that you have not been taken seriously enough, or that your colleague is offended.

If we analyse the ego states involved here we can see that you may have welcomed support and guidance from a colleague when you joined the department and entered into an appropriate parent–child set of transactions. Indeed, we can go further and suggest that these ego states were positive controlling parent and positive adapted child. But now you have found your feet you want to re-establish the relationship as adult–adult. You find that when you switch into the adult ego state there is a feeling of discomfort, and your invitation to your colleague to move into adult has, so far, not been accepted. Berne observed that it is often easier to *cross* a transaction with a change of subject; so in this example you may find it easy to establish the adult–adult communication by discussing something outside work first, and only then introducing work subjects. Of course, because this whole process will feel uncomfortable you will find it easier to slide into a complementary role, and if your colleague is in controlling parent state you may find yourself slipping from the positive adapted child state into a negative one. In this state you may start to gossip about her with other team members, many of whom are probably already in that state themselves – after all, consider why this colleague sought you out on your arrival. This is a critical point for you: you can exacerbate a major relationship problem within the department; or you can challenge it by being thoughtful and careful about which ego state you operate from.

Diagnosing the ego states involved can explain the dynamics between individuals and you can use this insight to perpetuate productive behaviours and relationships, and to *cross* and make uncomfortable the unproductive ones. Choosing your own ego state will invite someone else into a complementary one and give you a way of encouraging a productive relationship. Of course, you cannot guarantee it, only encourage it.

Recognizing the various ego states is important here, and there are primarily two ways of doing this. The first is a behavioural diagnosis, in which you observe the words, tones, gestures, postures and facial expressions adopted. In the child ego states the behaviours used will be the ones that the real child adopted many years ago, and so will vary from person to person. Similarly, the gestures used in the parent ego states will be those of the actual parent and again will differ. However, some behaviours are typical of children in general and of most parents, and these give clues.

Second, a social diagnosis notes the behaviours of people around: if they are in child state then the person concerned is probably in parent state, and so on. In my experience this is the method people find the most helpful, particularly if they are able to note the ego state they are in themselves. If you can identify that you are feeling and behaving like a 'sulky child' you can be fairly sure there is a critical parent somewhere around (or someone you perceive in that role). Similarly, if you find yourself wanting to shake your finger or bash two people's heads together, you may realize you are feeling like a critical parent and that the people you are engaging with are in sulky child state. Once you are aware of this you can try to think how you could frame your questions, statements and body language in such a way that they indicate a *positive* ego state (whether parent, adult or child) and so invite a response from complementary positive state of theirs.

A further development of TA theory is the well-known 'drama triangle', first described by Stephen Karpman.[10] He suggested that in any given situation the people involved very often unwittingly fall into one of three roles: persecutor, rescuer or victim. He represented these in a triangle (see Figure 6.4).

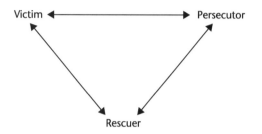

Figure 6.4 Drama triangle.

Consider the following vignette.[11]

James needs a repeat prescription and calls in at the surgery to ask for one. When he finds out that he will have to wait for four working days before he can collect it he becomes worried that he will run out, and the conversation goes like this:

James: But I need to have this medication and I've nearly run out. It can't possibly take four days to write a prescription. I absolutely must have it earlier than that.

Sally: That's what our system is, it says so on that sign over there.

James: But I just can't wait that long. I didn't know it would take that long. No one has ever told me. How could I be expected to know? It just isn't reasonable for it to take that long. Tell the doctor I need to have it quicker than that. I'm sure she'll write one for me. She'll understand even if you don't.

Sally: There's nothing I can do about it, the system is that it takes four days.

James: This is simply not good enough, I insist on seeing a doctor or the manager.

Dr X: I hear you are about to run out of your medication. Obviously it's important that you don't. I'll write you a prescription but please remember another time that we do need four days' notice.

James: Thank you. I knew you would appreciate how important it is. Your receptionist just didn't understand.

I'm sure you will identify Sally as a victim and James as persecutor (although, and this is often the case when we move into persecutor role, he himself feels a victim). You are probably less convinced that Dr X is a rescuer, or rather that this is a negative role to play. My own observation is that as HCPs we very easily fall into this role. It is what the American self-improvement literature might call 'a trip and a trap' – it feels so good to be able to rescue that we do it again and again. When we do, however, we don't build the ability of the victim to be able to handle things without our help, and we reward the bad behaviour of the persecutor, so we can expect that behaviour to be repeated. Because it comes so naturally to us we do it, even though we sometimes regret it later (or even as we are doing it), and then it is not unusual (in the scenario acted out above) for patients to be sent a letter threatening them with removal from the GP list if they behave in this way again.

Am I saying this is not a good way to proceed? I am suggesting that if it can be handled from positive ego states then everyone leaves the encounter feeling that it was handled fairly. You know yourself that when you feel aggrieved the situation can quickly become heated or be defused. Imagine you have turned up with a group of friends to a restaurant for which you have booked a table only to find that no one knows about your reservation and that the restaurant is full. You are very easily swept into the persecutor role, angrily demanding they find you a table. However, because you are a decent person, if the waiter or waitress behaves well, understands your situation, offers some kind of recompense, you quickly deflate from your puffed-up anger and engage with them rationally and sensibly. Because the other person has stayed in a positive ego state, ignoring your invitation to join you in a negative one, you have joined them in turn and, while the situation is still not perfect, it is as good as it can be.

Keeping in a positive ego state is the key message I invite you to take away from this discussion. And although there are occasions when any of the positive states will be useful, there are some when the adult one will work better than any of the others. There are some people who are very effective at dealing with high-status professionals who are behaving emotionally rather than rationally, and others who are not. I observe that the people who are most effective are those who calmly take everything that is said to them at face value and deal with it rationally. So, for example, if a consultant does not like a particular set of actions the manager has taken, he or she might issue an emotional threat that 'this will mean that the staff time taken up by this will result in the closure of a clinic'. The effective manager will ignore the emotion associated with it and deal with the content of what is said. They will address that seriously as a problem that can be explored and resolved. Their first response may be a set of suggestions about who needs to be told of this closure, and how, and a proposal about who will take responsibility for doing so.

Depending on the nature of the action that precipitated this reaction, there may be a proposal that credible information about its impact is sought, so that it can be reviewed if necessary, or there may be some further explanation of the problem that made it necessary and an invitation for the other person to suggest another satisfactory way of resolving it. As the transaction will be crossed (between adult and sulky child) it will feel uncomfortable to both parties, but if you can stay in the adult state, or at the very least another positive one, then you may succeed in encouraging the other person into a more positive state. Indulging in a self-righteous negative controlling parent would simply inflame affairs and lead you both into a situation you will find it difficult to retreat from.

Developing awareness

While I am not advocating the use of these principles without some further exploration of them on your part, I do suggest that a familiarity with these ideas enables us to be aware of our responses to situations and of how we contribute to the difficulties we find ourselves in. If we can stay aware of what we are doing, how we are feeling, what impact we are having on others, and if we can shift flexibly to other ways of behaving, then we not only become more effective but we feel better about it too. It is the NLP[12] practitioners who say that 'doing more of what you are doing will give you more of what you have' and they are surely right. If the way we customarily behave isn't achieving the results we want, then it is up to us to think about changing that. As we have seen above, that will probably mean changing the way we think and the way we feel.

It may be worth drawing parallels with a school of practice called the Alexander Technique, in which its practitioners aim to re-educate their minds and bodies into a much more graceful and efficient 'use of the self'. Their underlying principles of inhibition and direction may be helpful to us when we are thinking about how to use our managerial self. Inhibition requires us to become aware of what we are habitually doing – what we are thinking and feeling, how we are holding ourselves – and stop doing it. We aim for an aware but non-doing state, one that is not simply a state of relaxation either, but a readiness for action, like a cat that is lying on a mat but is able to spring into action instantly. Then we can issue directions about how we are going to proceed. The directions are not about where we are going but how we are going to get there. So we are focusing not on what it is we are trying to do, or achieve, but only on 'the means whereby', some simple directions that will guide our behaviour – whatever it is we are trying to do.

F. M. Alexander developed a set of directions (or rules) over a lifetime of observation, and those I am going to suggest as managerial equivalents have not been subject to such lengthy scrutiny. I put them forward as candidates, and welcome any observations of yours.

The rules or directions I suggest come under two headings: discipline and generosity. The first is a set developed by M. Scott Peck, whose work we have come across before. I suggest that these are directions for us to use generally during our approach to everyday life. The second is a set I have developed from observation and from some of the theory in this book, and these I think are useful as directions for occasions when we are interacting with other people.

Discipline

Peck describes discipline as having four component behaviours: (a) the delaying of gratification; (b) acceptance of responsibility; (c) dedication to reality; and (d) balancing.[13]

Delaying of gratification

Delaying gratification is a 'process of scheduling the pain and pleasure of life in such a way as to enhance the pleasure by meeting and experiencing the pain first and getting it over with. It is the only decent way to live.'[14] In practice, this means that if your scheduled tasks for the day include two you will dislike, eight you feel neutral about and three you will enjoy, then you tackle them in that order – delay gratification and start with those activities you like least. This does not mean that you rush through those displeasing activities. Indeed, because you are dealing with them when you are at your freshest, you will handle them better. The impact on your feelings for the rest of the day will be immense. There is a great release of pressure when you have given someone the bad news, have written that report, have telephoned to make a complaint or (worse still) have apologized. We all know we should live this way, but we very easily find reasons not to.

Acceptance of responsibility

If you have a problem, then *you* have a problem. It is your problem and you must try to resolve it. It doesn't matter if the problem is caused by other people; you cannot leave it to them to solve because *you* have the problem.

If managers are making your life difficult because they do not understand the impact of their requirements or decisions on you and your team, then you have a problem. Complaining to colleagues about the remoteness of management will not solve the problem. Waiting for management to come to you and ask you if you have a problem will not solve it. The only way to solve it is to get them to see how much better you and your team can perform if they change their policy. You could try telling them in no uncertain terms about how difficult they are making things for you. You could try to secure a vote of no confidence. Or you could explain to them calmly the problem their actions have caused, find out the reasons behind their decisions and work with them to find a solution to meet both sets of needs. I am sure you can see that only the latter is 'accepting responsibility'.

Similarly, if you are disappointed in the performance of some of your staff, then you have a problem: the problem of having to be available to them more often than you would like, or of exposing your patients to greater risk. Blaming them does nothing to solve your problem. Making sure that they have clear instructions, guidelines, access to training and support, and proper feedback will all help. So will reviewing your recruitment procedures to see whether you can avoid creating problems for yourself in the future.

Whenever you are experiencing discomfort, *you* have a problem and it is up to *you* to solve it. Often when working with HCPs I hear a list of their woes. It is interesting that almost every time I ask them what they can do to improve their situation, what they give me is a lengthy list of all the things they *cannot* do. Only when I point out to them what they have just done and ask them again what they *can* do, do some of them start to accept responsibility and recognize their own role in the creation of the difficulty.

Dedication to reality

'The more clearly we see the reality of the world, the better equipped we are to deal with the world.'[15] We all know that the way we see the world changes with our life stages, the circumstances we are in, the information we gain. At no stage can we know everything about everything, so our view of the world is, of necessity, a model of it – a simplified version of it. The closer our model approximates reality, the more effective we can be in our interactions with the world. We come across individuals whose model is a very jaundiced one, others whose model is an over-rosy, optimistic one, so we can see when the models of other people are faulty, but can we recognize the flaws in our own?

Dedication to reality, according to Peck, requires 'continuous and never-ending stringent self-examination'. In practice, this has two essential elements: an openness to challenge from others and a preparedness to challenge ourselves. If we are able to take criticism from our children, spouse, colleagues, staff, students, and are able to accept its validity, then we are enabled to increase our effectiveness by making some changes to the ways we operate. If we reject it as ill-informed, prejudiced or non-valid, then we cut ourselves off from that opportunity.

We all make mistakes. If a meeting has gone badly, we can blame the other party and protect our self-image, or we can challenge ourselves. How could I have been more persuasive? What was I doing when the meeting cooled? If we recognize that we have made a mistake, we can work to avoid making it again. We need not blame ourselves, just learn from the experience. If we deny the mistake, then again we deny ourselves the chance of increasing our abilities, of becoming better at interacting with the world. Often we trap ourselves in what Chris Argyris describes as 'defensive routines', habitual reactions to situations that we perceive as threatening or painful, but that could be, if we behaved differently and were prepared to challenge the mental model we have of it, opportunities for us to learn. Argyris describes this process if unchallenged as leading to 'skilled incompetence'.[16] We become better and better at not learning because we become better and better at avoiding looking at reality.[17]

Are the people around you, the ones who prevent you from achieving more, actively setting out to do so? In some cases, they may believe they are doing the opposite: helping you. Others are simply not aware of how, in seeking to achieve their own goals, they impinge on yours. In a few cases, they may be feeling punitive towards you. Why? How could they be interpreting your actions as hostile? In situations involving people (i.e. at the higher levels of the hierarchy of natural descriptions discussed in Chapter 2), there is rarely a single cause resulting in a particular effect. Here linear thinking needs to give way to systems thinking, to an appreciation that we ourselves are part of an open system and that we constantly influence other components of it.

Balancing

Balancing, according to Peck, is 'the capacity to flexibly strike and continually restrike a delicate balance between conflicting needs, goals, duties, responsibilities, directions etc.' At almost every instant of the day we have choices to make about the way we behave or approach things. Most of the time we make these choices on autopilot, scarcely noticing that we had an alternative option, often governed by emotions and beliefs that are not altogether open to our scrutiny. An important aspect of balancing is to become aware of these choices, to become aware of our habitual responses to those choices and to test them for logic and pragmatism. When we do so we will find that the menu of choices open to us contains several unhelpful options and also several that are all 'good' in some way or another. For example, we have said that delaying gratification is important, but it is also essential to enjoy ourselves and be able to act spontaneously. When we balance we are not only choosing between good and bad approaches, we are often deciding between one justifiable action and another.

If discipline is what we bring to life in general, generosity is a linked set of principles that usefully inform our interactions with others.

Generosity

There are five elements to generosity and we have come across most of them already in this book.

Choosing to care

In Chapter 2 we defined care as engaging in acts of work and/or courage to nurture another's growth. This means that we can choose to care, that care is not a feeling that arrives from nowhere, or can only be directed to people we like or feel are somehow worthy of it. Using this definition we can care for anyone. I suggest that if we routinely try to care for the person we are interacting with we will be observing a 'direction' that will help us, almost whatever the reason we are engaging with them.

Choosing to meet hostility, aggression and self-congratulation with compassion rather than fear

We saw earlier in this chapter that we can think about many of the negative emotions as being rooted in fear, and that if we do so we can see people behaving badly towards us as being frightened of something. It is then easier for us to feel compassion and to lose our own fear of them. We can also choose more effective strategies for dealing with them, by trying to find approaches that do not exacerbate and may even abate their fears.

Choosing to include and value rather than exclude and compare

We saw in Chapter 2 that all groups are prone to 'hard-heartedness' to people the members perceive as outside the group. Actively encouraging ourselves to do the opposite, to try to include others and look for contributions of value they can make, will allow fruitful collaboration instead of mean-spirited competition. Of course, I do not dismiss the benefits of competition in sharpening ideas and practices, and if you are dealing with someone who cannot do anything other than compete then you will have to choose judiciously what you will do, but so often our automatic response is to exclude and compare, and if we can just give ourselves a choice about whether to include and value we will be doing well.

Choosing to expect the best

You know that when you work with people who expect you to behave well you really do try to live up to those expectations, yet so often we do the opposite for other people. We expect people to behave in ways that are going to cause us problems. Of course, we cannot sensibly expect everyone to behave as a paragon of virtue, and sometimes the best we can expect from them is not very wonderful, but if we use some of the tools in this book for analysing what we can expect and then let them realize that we do expect it, we will be helping them to behave well, and in the process helping ourselves.

Choosing not to allow self-image to be shaped by the ungenerous

A lot of the people we are working with will not be generous, and we can think of them as ungenerous, perhaps even as mean-spirited. Their ability to perceive our potential and make reliable judgements of our performance must be suspect, and we would be foolish to rely on it for a major input to our own self-image, yet we tend to. The way we see ourselves needs to accord with reality and not with a mean-spirited assessment, nor with an overgenerous one for that matter. The more we can assess our progress and performance for ourselves the more we can make changes when we need to and not when we don't. Assessing that takes regular attention, and in the next section we look at patterns for doing this.

Preparation

Work on feelings, generosity and discipline was for centuries the province of religion, and there is much benefit to be gained from some of the patterns of preparation and reflection that are to be found in the major world religions. Many of these include a daily period of reflection and preparation, a weekly review and an annual period of more serious questioning and reaffirming of goals.

We have already considered an important function of the annual and weekly reviews. Identifying your roles and the goals you want to achieve within them is something worth revisiting about once a year, as both of these do change over time. The scheduling process described at the beginning of this chapter is a weekly one and often takes about an hour. Both of these are highly productive uses of time, as they allow you to align what you are doing with what you think is important and give you a realistic sense of progress that can be difficult to retain in the hurly burly of everyday interactions and deadlines. Daily review is also worthwhile and can be used for two important functions: learning from the day completed; and preparing for the day ahead. It needn't take long – many people find ten minutes is about right – and can become something you find indispensable.

As you think back over the day, your first recollections will probably be those that engendered strong emotions, emotions you are perhaps still experiencing. You may still be furious at the behaviour someone used in a meeting with you, guilty at the way you responded or regretful that you didn't perform better when you gave a presentation. You may, equally, be ecstatic at the way the presentation was received, or pleased at the way you handled a conversation you had been worried about. Each of these is an opportunity to learn. As Benjamin Franklin put it, 'That which hurts instructs'. So, while we cannot lose the hurt we can make sure we try to learn from every painful experience. We can learn too from when we have done well, noting what we achieved and how we did so.

If you recognize any of the emotions you feel as those described as unhealthy in the chart on page 162 you could consider whether you have been bringing to the situation any of the irrational beliefs on page 160. Similarly, if you remember that despite your intention to behave in a rational, considered manner, you found yourself feeling and acting like a sulky child, or a critical parent, you can think about whether you accepted an invitation into a complementary ego state, and what alternatives you could have chosen. You may also notice how you chose to apply more rational thinking or to resist the invitation, and reinforce to yourself the ways in which you did so.

You will also be able to see how many of your priority tasks you finished, think about whether any need to be rescheduled and identify what it was that prevented you from completing them today.

You may well find that there are several things you want to do on a regular basis, even every day: having some quiet time with each child, eating five portions of fruit and veg, exercise and so on. I find it helpful to draw these up as a chart at the top of each page of a notebook kept for this purpose. Ticking them off, or not, gives me a good sense of how disciplined I am being, and indeed helps to increase that discipline. The rest of the page can then be divided into two under the headings 'What have I learned?' and 'Have I added anything of value?' The kind of lessons I have just described can be noted under the former, and looking back on these from time to time is very helpful. The latter can be enlightening. We may find that we have done something well, something we were asked to do, or chose to do, and we may even be able to learn from it that our choices of behaviour were effective and can be used again, yet we may not be able to see that we have added anything of value. Personally, in a work setting, I try to undertake only assignments or tasks in which I think I can add value and/or learn something new. I think you would find this so satisfying that you felt you were, as the title of this chapter suggests, really managing yourself.

The second purpose of the session is preparation for the day ahead. This is an opportunity to consider your agenda and how you feel about what lies ahead of you; an opportunity to see if you are taking a disciplined approach to it. Will you do the worst first? Are you accepting all your responsibilities and owning all your problems, or are you trying to offload them on to others? Are you seeing the situation as widely as it merits? Are there needs that require balancing?

It is an opportunity too to use the tools in Chapters 1 and 2 in your meetings with other people. A chance to think through what you know of the other people involved, what kind of arguments they may respond to, what behaviours they will appreciate and they will dislike, and how they will perceive their status in relation to others and to you. With this in mind, you can prepare your arguments, think about your behaviours and prepare to ensure that status is used appropriately. When you know how you want to behave you can run through the meeting in your mind, imagining yourself behaving in that way. Although that sounds unnecessary, it is something that elite sports people are reputed to find helpful, and we can see it as a kind of exercising of the emotional muscles, something that will enable us to fall more easily into our desired behaviours because we have prepared a pathway for our emotional responses instead of leaving them to use automatically another well-worn and less productive path. To be most effective we need to imagine the situation as realistically as possible, including our own feelings and the way these change as people play out the roles we fear they might. As they say something that might anger us, we can practise losing that anger and remaining calm, or we might imagine becoming fearful of a particular response and practise overcoming that fear, perhaps not completely but at least to the point where we remain effective.

Perhaps there is a session when you have to give someone some bad news – to a patient, say, or a junior member of your team who needs to improve their performance. When you have imagined your feelings of discomfort, embarrassment or self-consciousness, imagine replacing those with feelings of concern for the other; imagine forgetting about yourself and concentrating entirely on the needs of the other. The more vividly you can imagine these new feelings, the more easily will you experience them when the time comes.

Sometimes it is difficult to challenge ourselves; we are either too gentle or too condemnatory. For that reason, some people seek additional challenge in other ways. Some find action learning sets[18] a valuable resource, others look for a mentor (either formally or informally), some book regular 'supervision' sessions with an individual outside the workplace, whereas others have a particularly open, honest and challenging relationship with their spouse or a friend. The time spent on such support must, of course, be productive. Its purpose is to help people to be more effective, not just to understand why they are not. In my experience a few individuals appear to derive so much support from their set or their mentor that this makes them forget about the value of trying to change their behaviour in their work setting. So if you find that your support mechanisms are marvellous for off-loading but are not enabling you to change anything at work, you may want to review them. Your annual reflection on roles and goals is also a good time to reflect on the methods you use for support and challenge, and an opportunity to consider any need for skills development.

In this chapter we have looked at a number of ways in which you can change the way you feel about situations and people, about time, about yourself, but we have not looked at those circumstances you really cannot control.

Circumstances beyond our control

You may be thinking that none of this will help when the pressures are societal, or at such a macro level that you can have no influence. Patients, for instance, have expectations that you cannot possibly meet. Politicians, driven by a political and ideological agenda, are trying to destroy the very system to which you chose to devote your career. Nothing we have said so far will resolve these, surely? But, here again we can choose to respond generously or jealously to the individuals exerting these pressures. Donald Berwick phrased it very neatly when he said about patients that 'behind every unreasonable demand there is a reasonable expectation'.[19]

Certainly there are people whose expectations are unrealistic, often because they do not appreciate the complexity of the system that is required to meet what, to them, appears a simple need. A few others, unfortunately, have an aggressive expectation of poor service and, by their demeanour, contribute to the fact that they receive it. Some are thoughtless about their use of services and some are overanxious. Many are worried and not as accommodating as they might be when dealing with other services. But, on the whole, patients simply expect to be treated in the way they are in other service settings. What is more, they exhibit great tolerance of poor service and sympathy for its providers, and complain far less often than they might. The generous response, when a patient expects something of your service that you cannot provide, is to let that expectation challenge your thinking. Could we provide this? Should we provide this? How could we organize things differently in order to do so? Would doing so be more in harmony with my goals than not doing so? As HCPs we have the ability to devise systems that meet most expectations, or at the very least to influence those expectations to a level we can meet. When we become self-absorbed, or precious, or a victim perceiving them as a persecutor, we lose that ability.

Somehow we have come to expect stability. We have come to believe that if we pass through the life stages of dependency, development and education, then eventually we shall reach a point when we have learned all we need to know in order to meet a fairly predictable set of demands. This is a new belief that has accompanied the massive increase in life expectancy and the absence for 60 years, in the UK anyway, of a major destabilizing factor such as war. We have no right to such an expectation. Until relatively recently, as a visit to any graveyard reminds us, early death was commonplace. Family life and individual well-being were very far from predictable. Advances in knowledge have granted, to populations able to exploit them, longevity and predictability undreamed of by our ancestors. But with those advances have come others, and the tremendous developments in technology have led to changes in systems and structures – and also in opportunities – that affect us all. Over 30 years ago Alvin Toffler wrote *Future Shock*, a book about the (then) rate of change;[20] some of us are now experiencing 'present shock'. Yet we must learn to deal with change, because not only is it here to stay but its rate is accelerating. Generally in the UK there has been much less change in the health care system than there has been in other sectors, where new technology has reduced workforces by 50 or even 70 per cent in some cases. We must expect more and more change, arriving faster and faster. Our ability to respond to change is a critical area to develop – in ourselves and, even more crucially, in the next generations.

Given the changes in technology and increases in longevity, politicians (of whatever flavour) do what you or I would do in their place. They aim to contain the explosion in funding that could take place, while requiring accountability for the way current monies are spent. We can quibble with their choice of methods, or the way they choose to sell it to the electorate, but not with the task. Our ability to respond is diminished when we personalize issues and attribute blame to individuals and parties instead of recognizing that our world is changing and that we cannot expect anything else.

There is an old Christian prayer, a version of which is used by Alcoholics Anonymous, that asks, 'Lord, grant me the courage to change the things I can change, the grace to accept those I cannot and the wisdom to know the difference'. As running into a brick wall, either literally or metaphorically, is both painful and damaging, it is worth trying to recognize a brick wall when we see one. Covey suggests drawing two circles (Figure 6.5).[21] The first should include all the issues, events and people you care about (this is your circle of concern). The second encompasses all the issues, events and people you can influence in some way (your circle of influence). Most people have circles of concern and influence that have much in common, but find there are many things they are concerned about but cannot influence. Thus their circle of concern includes, but is greater than, their circle of influence.

Spending time and energy in our circle of concern, outside our circle of influence, where we can achieve nothing, is counterproductive. It diminishes our ability to work within our circle of influence, where we can and will have an impact. Thus when we come across a situation that angers or saddens us, the effective response is to determine whether it lies within our circle of concern or our circle of influence. If it falls within the latter, we should take appropriate action; if the former, we should not dwell there for long. We do not improve that state of affairs by indulging in unproductive anger. Sometimes there are actions we can take that may contribute to a solution; for example, writing to an MP or forming a lobby group. These actions and the research they require are now part of our circle of influence, but the rest of the

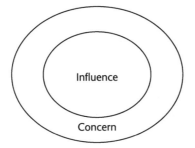

Figure 6.5   The circles of concern and influence.

issue remains in the outer circle of concern. Again we must focus on what we can do rather than on what we cannot if we are to contribute without burning out.

We will always be surrounded by events we cannot influence, but we can control how we respond to them. To do so requires work. Many of us will not invest in the work required and will remain unable to control the course of an event. But that is our choice. We should not (although we will try very hard to) blame anyone else.

Notes

1 Covey (1990); see Chapter 3, note 4.
2 Several of these tips are taken from two texts in the Fifty Minute Book series (Menlo Park, CA: Crisp Publications): Lloyd, S. R. and Berthelot, T. (1992) *Self-Empowerment: Getting What You Want from Life*; and Scott, D. (1992) *Stress that Motivates: Self-Talk Secrets for Success*.
3 Obholzer, A. and Roberts, V. Z. (eds) (1994) *The Unconscious at Work: Individual and Organisational Stress in the Human Services* (London: Tavistock Publications). 'Full enough' authority is a term derived from Winnicott's concept of 'good enough' mothering. Winnicott, D. W. (1971) *Therapeutic Consultations in Child Psychiatry* (London: Hogarth Press).
4 Jeffers, S. (1987, New York: Ebury Press).
5 For many people, and women in particular, the advice of a good colour consultant can be very liberating, as well as fun. Feeling confident that you look your best means that you never have to think about it and you can concentrate on the task at hand. House of Colour and Colour Me Beautiful are both reputable companies.
6 See Batten (1991); see Introduction, note 2.
7 Lewis' work is well described in: Dryden W, *Rational Emotive Behavioural Counselling in Action*. 2nd Edition. Sage. London, 1999. I found this text very helpful, and used it as the basis of my description here.
8 Berne, E. (1964) *Games People Play* (Harmondsworth: Penguin).
9 These are well described in Stewart I, Joines V, *T. A. Today*. Lifespace Publishing, Nottingham 1987. This is a very accessible introduction to this field.
10 Karpman, S. (1968) *TA Bulletin*, 7 April, 39–43.
11 You can see another example on the website www.reallylearning.com
12 Neuro-linguistic programming. There are many introductory texts to interacting effectively with other people, e.g. O'Connor, J. and Seymour, J. (2003) *Introducing NLP* (New York: HarperCollins).
13 Taken from Peck (1979); see Chapter 2, note 12.
14 Argyris, C. and Schön, D. (1996) *Organizational Learning II: Theory, Method and Practice* (Reading, MA: Addison Wesley).

15 Ibid.

16 See Chapter 4, Note 7.

17 See Wind, J. and Crook, C. (2004) *The Power of Impossible Thinking: Transform the Business of Your Life and the Life of Your Business* (London: Prentice Hall). The authors describe vividly how we imagine ourselves driven by data when actually we are driven by hypotheses. We don't just see facts, we see facts and then interpret them in the form of a hypothesis. The process of developing that hypothesis is invisible to us. Senge, P. *et al.* (1994) *The Fifth Discipline Field Book* (New York: Doubleday) describes this same process in terms of leaping up the 'ladder of inference'.

18 There are different forms of action learning sets available and they can easily turn into much less helpful discussion groups, so it is worth looking for those with a coherent and disciplined approach. Look out for facilitators who talk of Reg Revans, Roger Gaunt and Ian McGill as influences.

19 This view was expressed by Berwick at a conference on 'quality management' run by the British Medical Association in 1993.

20 Toffler, A. (1973) *Future Shock* (London: Pan).

21 See Covey (1990); see Chapter 3, note 4.

7 Really managing organizations

Health care at the heart

First, a clarification. This chapter is about really managing health care organizations. It is about the role and behaviours we need managers to fulfil if heath care professionals are to meet the needs of their clients. Some of those roles and behaviours are also needed in other organizations, but rather than starting with the needs of a standard organization and amending that for the particular dynamics of health care we will look first at the distinctive needs of organizations meeting health care needs through their professional staff.

It is easy to picture a health care organization (HCO) as a single large entity with an executive management team and a board, lots of buildings, staff, structures and systems, to think of it as a whole. When we do, we tend to lose sight of the care that is at its heart. It is a common observation, for example, that in their focus on strategic decisions, organization structures and governance processes, discussions at board meetings rarely mention patients.

So let us think about HCOs from the inside out, so to speak. Let us start with the interaction between clinician and client and think about the nature of the organization and the managers required to ensure that this interaction is effective. The staff in any HCO include some of the most able and committed in society. That is why it is so regrettable that in most of these organizations there is negative synergy, where the whole is very much *less* than the sum of these parts. If we derive the nature of the organization from its core task then we may discover how to change that for the better.

Roles of the real manager

If we think outwards from the client–clinician interaction and we apply the concepts introduced in preceding chapters in this book we find that there are many roles that clients and HCPs need someone to play. If we can derive a job description for managers from this central core we will have defined the role of the real manager – someone fundamentally necessary to the effective delivery of the essential purpose. If we develop people to take on these real management roles then HCPs and the public will stop seeing managers as an unneccessary burden and start to value their contribution.

Looking back over the contents of previous chapters we can identify a number of behaviours and beliefs we can expect of HCPs, because they are individual human beings, because they are professionals and because they are members of groups. We can also see behaviours and attitudes we need them to adopt if the quality of the interaction with their clients is to be optimal and if they are to make the most of their resources. These are all summarized in the left hand column of Table 7.1. In the right hand column I have listed the kinds of activity that we need a manager (a real manager) to play, in relation to these behaviours, if the best interests of the patient are to be served. Please have a look at this table, on pages 184–188 now.

What I am suggesting is that, if the left hand column accurately describes the ways that we, as HCPs, can be expected to behave just because we are human, then the role of the real manager needs to include all of the right hand column. If this role looks daunting then it is not because it is not necessary to the task, it just means that this isn't how, traditionally, we have come to view the managerial role in health care. And if the role is different then the behaviours, too, need to be different. And if both of these are different, then we will develop (and require) different organizational cultures. Many of the roles and tasks listed in the right hand column will be familiar to you because we have already explained them in earlier chapters. There are a few we have not yet considered and these I have indicated in italics. So in this chapter we consider the aspects of the role in the right hand column that we have not yet looked at (those in *italics*), at the behaviours the role requires of real managers, at organizational cultures and how to change them, and at the implications of all this for the board of a HCO.

Additional roles of the real manager

Encourage trust between professionals by increasing trustworthiness

It is often said, and sometimes in an accusatory way, that things would be much better if levels of trust were higher. But it is worth thinking about trust before we make such a sweeping assertion. As we saw in Chapter 5, trust is something we place according to our assessment of someone's trustworthiness. Someone is trustworthy if they have a fairly reliable tendency to behave in ways we value. And we limit our assessment of their trustworthiness to a particular area of activity – so we trust a plumber to fix a boiler, for example, but not to manage our pension. And within that area of activity they are

Table 7.1 Deriving the roles of the real manager from the needs of clients and HCPs

Because HCPs are people we can expect them to	In the best interests of patients someone (a real manager) needs to
Need to know the role they are fulfilling in this particular setting, the resources available to them, support they can expect, and whether their performance is matching expectations.	Implement the three rules so that all HCPs know what is expected of them, are confident they have the skills and resources to achieve that, and receive feedback on whether they are doing so.
Respond in different ways to different arguments and events.	Present arguments in ways that recognize the interests and preferences of the individuals concerned.
Be reactive rather than proactive quite a lot of the time.	Consistently, though gracefully, rephrase reactive comments as proactive alternatives. Give examples of evidence that disconfirms negative assessments of a situation. Not collude with this mindset by blaming others.
Behave emotionally rather than rationally on occasions.	Deal with the *content* of statements. Be aware of the emotion but not get sucked into it.
Have more productive relationships with some people than with others.	Increase the ability of HCPs to deal constructively with difference. Observe where relationships are not productive and intervene where necessary.

Because HCPs are professionals we can expect to	In the best interests of patients a real manager needs to
Have a body of professional knowledge and practice they need to maintain.	Ensure decisions made for other reasons do not prevent maintenance of this knowledge and practice base.
See themselves as possessing positive characteristics of professionalism, including altruism. Have a valuable self-belief, and also a certain self-righteousness about this.	Encourage the positive professional behaviours and the self-belief, while not blindly accepting assurances about, for example, altruism. Gently challenge self-righteousness.
Hold a status conferred by society, including themselves and other members of the organization. Use this status unawarely, even where it is not appropriate.	Ensure that decisions are informed by expertise of the sort required, and not that of the highest status profession present.

Undervalue members of several other professions or specialties.	Ensure that members of lower status professions are supported in their dealings with higher status ones. *Encourage trust between professionals by increasing trustworthiness.*
React defensively and angrily if actions are taken that threaten their status. (This reaction may include withdrawing positive behaviours associated with professionalism, e.g. altruism.[a])	Be familiar with the sources of status. Enter into decisions that threaten this only in full awareness of the understandable reaction.
Tend to focus on the particular area of ill health they specialize in.	Help to put people back in touch with why they came into health care in the first place.
Lose touch with the underlying purpose of the consultation: the health and autonomy of the client.	Keep this purpose fresh in people's minds, partly by taking an interest in clients as people and not just cases.
Tend not to communicate effectively with members of other professions as they will often be referring to different aspects of the problem and using different vocabulary.	Not blame individuals when this happens, and *design systems that do not rely on people doing something unnatural to them*. Encourage ways to increase awareness of the different vocabularies and the need for confirmation that people have understood. *Ensure everyone receives the information they need.*
See the public sector as morally superior to other sectors.	Be familiar with other sectors, with people in other sectors. Be able to challenge any untrue and unhelpful generalizations.
Value people for their personal power and their membership of a high status professional group rather than their position power. (This means that the organizational opinion formers will tend to be found among high status HCPs).	Understand the dynamics. Listen to and discuss with everyone, so that there is credible evidence about the impact of a decision on all concerned (and not just the opinion-formers). Pay particular attention to explaining these decisions to opinion-formers, framing arguments in terms they will value.

Continued overleaf

Table 7.1   continued

Because HCPs are members of groups we can expect them to	In the best interests of patients a real manager needs to
Be 'soft headed' and 'hard hearted'. Not challenge thinking sufficiently within their own cozy group. Stereotype as unhelpful any challenge from outside the group.	Gracefully challenge both soft-headedness and hard-heartedness. Provide credible evidence that supports reality.

Because HCPs have had little training in management or about organizations we can expect them to	In the best interests of patients a real manager needs to
Know little about the organization or wider system beyond their service.	*Increase their organizational literacy. Encourage creative thinking about systems for the funding and delivery of health care.*
Have few skills in analysing their service to identify key issues that need to be addressed.	Support them with expertise and information about the world outside their service, including future trends.
See organizational responses to changing circumstances as 'change, change and more change' with little point to them.	Develop with HCPs a narrative that explains previous decisions, shows the direction of travel and indicates where people and services are now.
See managers as a burden. Believe the system would be better off with fewer of them.	Develop relationships that are robust, that allow frankness on both sides. *Add value to each service.* Encourage HCPs to become managers and/or take on corporate responsibilities.

If we care about the quality of the client–clinician interaction we want to ensure that HCPs	So we need a real manager to
Want to improve services for their patients.	Challenge any complacency about how good services are or about how little can be done to improve them within available resources.
Understand the whole experience of the patient, including services provided by other HCPs.	Encourage 'whole system' exercises, e.g. process mapping, use of patients' narratives.
Are exacting customers and obliging suppliers in their triple role within the process of care.	Introduce these concepts and encourage them to become real by using them to structure questions, comments. *Demonstrate these behaviours in action.*

Measure the quality of services they are offering.	Demonstrate the value to patients and the service of doing so, supporting and advising and making sure the measurement is used wisely.
Understand variation in the system's performance.	Understand variation and help others to.
See incidents as due to systems not individuals, processes not events.	See incidents as due to systems not individuals, processes not events, and use this awareness constantly
Engage with other service stakeholders to understand and influence their perspectives.	Encourage engagement. Support with facilitation skills.
Feel in charge of their own destiny (within acceptable limits).	Encourage the ability to weave narratives that encompass positive outcomes and successful processes. Keep negative ones in perspective.
Learn from experiences of managing change as much as they learn from experiences of managing patients.	Support and encourage evaluation, reflection and learning on both personal and service levels.

If HCPs are to be able to make the most of their resources they need to:	**So we need a real manager to:**
Understand where resources come from, and how theirs fit into a wider picture.	Tell them, keep referring to these processes and the sums involved and don't assume they know. Include in this not just ££ but also, e.g., labour markets – so HCPs see themselves as part of a dynamic bigger picture.
Know where their money goes. Know how changes in activity or mix will affect their costs.	Ensure they understand their costs: fixed – variable direct – indirect relevant – irrelevant opportunity – sunk And understand how to use these to appraise service options. Use this vocabulary with them. Make this a standard vocabulary of decision making.
Understand their budget and monitor their performance against it.	Support services in negotiating their budget, teach them about variances and how to monitor their financial performance, encourage them to keep their figures themselves. Ensure every service knows the impact of any overspend on other services Establish a means for service leaders to account to all other service leaders for any such overspend.

Table 7.1   continued

If HCPs are to be able to make the most of their resources they need to:	Someone needs to:
Appraise different service options against financial as well as quality criteria.	Gracefully challenge any proposals which do not include a full range of criteria.
Take an interest in unit costs, and take pride in reducing them – while maintaining quality.	Use this terminology when agreeing service objectives, when discussing the service, when comparing with other units.

[a] Is this confusing? At one point I seem to be saying that HCPs aren't altruistic and at another that they are. What I am suggesting is that HCPs do indeed display altruism, and their good will towards patients and HCOs is very valuable, and that this may be jeopardized when they perceive their professionalism to be under attack. However, they are also not as altruistic as they think they are. (Are any of us?)
[b] Account, as before, means explain the reasoning behind it. Thus service leaders may still be able to make decisions that have adverse effects on their financial performance if they believe other service leaders will back that decision.

trustworthy if they are technically competent and share our values or criteria about decisions they may make on our behalf.

This way of thinking about trust has two implications. First, for trust to be useful in an organization it must be wisely and well placed; otherwise we will have people being trusted when they are not trustworthy and this is much more dangerous than realistic levels of scepticism. So if we want to increase trust we need to help people to make competent judgements about others' trustworthiness, being neither credulous and gullible nor cynical and suspicious. Second, if we want to increase levels of trust from other people, we need to work on our own trustworthiness.

Respect is another word often used in multiprofessional settings; not because there is too much of it, but because people perceive it to be lacking. We have talked, in Chapter 2, about the issue of status and how difficult it is to define and describe properly, and this is another example of an area where it is relevant but in ways that are incompletely understood. We can see, though, looking around us, that it is difficult for groups of higher status to respect those of lower, or defer to them, and we shouldn't berate them for that, we should look for something more achievable. For this reason alone I would suggest that respect is a concept too indefinable and impractical to be advocated, and liable to become confused with false deference; but if we add to that the fact that our ability to respect others is so governed by our own 'inner worlds', the way we see ourselves and others, then that fuels my suggestion that simply calling for more of it is a waste of time. More useful would be an emphasis on increasing trust between individuals and between groups, by encouraging them to enhance their ability to make assessments of the trustworthiness of others, and by increasing their own trustworthiness. Once people know they can place greater reliance on others then, especially if they become more adept at framing persuasive arguments (using their ability to diagnose individual preferences and group behavioural norms), and find that others become more cooperative as a result, then we may even end up with something looking remarkably like respect – without trying to do so.

Design systems that recognize human nature

Systems should work with and not against human nature. In other words, it must be easier to comply with a required system than not to do so. If systems are not designed to take human nature into account in this way, then when something goes wrong it is the system (and its architects) that must shoulder the blame. Designing such systems requires us to understand quite a bit about human nature so we will need to take into account relevant factors from both psychology and sociology, several of which are mentioned in Chapters 1 and 2. One important example is that systems must be designed with the implications of the hierarchy of clinical descriptions in mind. As we saw in Chapter 2, different professions and disciplines will operate at different levels of the hierarchy. We also saw that it is very difficult (if not impossible) to focus on more than one level at a time. Clearly, therefore, someone doing valiant battle at electrolyte level (a senior house officer in accident and emergency department, for example) is not simultaneously considering the needs of the patient and their family for a 'good death'. If a complaint from relatives is forthcoming, instead of blaming the individuals concerned, the real manager will redesign their systems (or rather, prompt the HCPs most closely involved to redesign them) so that there is no longer a reliance on people undertaking the impossible (or even the very difficult). My personal view is that ensuring that every level in the hierarchy receives the attention it requires is one of the greatest challenges for HCOs and their real managers.

Ensure everyone receives the information they need .

Health care is a 'know how' industry in that every aspect of the health care process involves the use and/or transfer of information.[1] If health care is going to be delivered effectively then everyone in a HCO must have in front of them the information they need, when they need it. In many ways we can suggest that information and responsibility run hand in hand: unless people have information they cannot take responsibility, and once they have information they have a responsibility to act on it. So if HCOs are going to be able to be responsible for, and held accountable for, clinical outcomes and the use of resources, then taking an interest in how people receive and use information is a vital part of the managerial role.

Many organizations have realized that the knowledge held in the heads of their staff is a huge asset, and that a significant factor in their organizational performance is how well this knowledge is used and shared. Knowledge management has become a subject of study. Since knowledge is such a broad term it is worth giving it a context: the link between data, information and knowledge. Information has been described as 'data with meaning attached', so we can think of the three terms in the following way:

> If someone asks you to collect it, it is data. If the data is of use to you, it is information. If the information enables you to do something, it is knowledge.

Information is needed for both operational and strategic purposes. It supports and arises out of the same events – patients being treated by staff – yet historically information collected for operational purposes has been kept completely separate from that used for strategy formulation. Strategic decisions do not require information at the same level of detail as do frontline clinical decision-makers; however, they rely on that detail being faithfully aggregated in the reports that go to top levels in the organization. Where the link between strategic and operational information is unsound, the organization is quickly in trouble. One means of ensuring the link between operational and strategic information is the development of robust relationships between HCPs and managers. It is, indeed, the destruction of this link that guarantees the underperformance of the organization with low quality relationships.

Ensuring that all the members of a large, complex organization receive the information they need, without having to waste time wading through lots of it that they do not, calls for an overview of just what information is needed, generated and transferred. We could think of this as an IMT (information management and technology) strategy or, thinking more broadly, as knowledge management.

If we use our previous rationale of letting the needs of service providers determine the shape of the organization then we need to define what information or knowledge is needed by whom if patients and HCPs are to interact effectively. As this is done so rarely I suggest a means of doing so in Box 7.1.

Any effective information and communication strategy needs to be service-led and it also requires a large amount of work at a detailed level. The temptation to offload this on to information (or even computing) specialists is very strong and really needs to be resisted. Managing information flows is at the heart of management and the personal involvement of senior managers in IMT and knowledge management strategies is crucial. If they have the robust relationships described on the previous page real managers will find this easier and these relationships will be one of the ways in which information flows through the organization. I believe it is not too strong a statement to say that any organization that has neither robust relationships throughout nor a

---

Box 7.1 A service-led approach to knowledge management

Step one. First we identify *who* may require information and so we[2] list all the people or agencies who are involved in any way with that service. Usually these 'stakeholders' fall into one or more of seven groupings: (a) clients and carers; (b) service team members (both clinical and support staff); (c) referrers; (d) referees (a slightly confusing use of this word to mean people or agencies to whom the service team refers); (e) managers (i.e. anyone who can make resource allocation decisions that affect the team; it is helpful to include commissioners here); (f) professional advisers; and (g) suppliers.

Step two. Next, we need to identify *when* information is required. As we saw in Chapter 5, every service can be thought of as a series of stages through which the client progresses. If we list these stages, most services find that they fall into the pattern shown in Figure 4.5, page 100. We can also add management (e.g. service planning and performance monitoring) and commissioning processes.

Step three. The stakeholders can now be linked to the stages, thus clearly identifying everyone who is involved at each stage. Some are involved in several stages, some in only one and some (e.g. the client and the service team) in all of them. If anyone is involved in none of the stages, then he or she is not a stakeholder. Clear thinking is necessary here: typically the first attempt by a community-based service nominates the GP at every single stage, while their acute services colleagues deny the GP a role in any. As neither of these reflects reality, service members need to be challenged to think again.

Step four. We can now look in detail at the information required by these stakeholders if each stage is to be completed effectively and efficiently. We can also specify the standards and objectives we mentioned in Chapter 4 in order to measure the service quality, to make sure we include the information needed to monitor them.

Step five. It is once this process has been completed within a range of services in an organization that it becomes most useful. First, the requirements can be aggregated to form a set that, while it does not cover all the requirements for every service, does include most of them; and is a set that we can use to think about how that information is best provided across the organization as a whole. Second, we can put together portfolios of information requirements for groups and individuals who have a stake in more than one service. For example, we can generate a list of the information that is needed by the chief executive, or by, say, GPs, if the organization is to be able to provide its services well. Similarly, a list of information required *from* the chief executive or GPs can be gathered. This is exciting because we are now in a position where we can tell people what information they need, rather than having to rely on what they think they want.

detailed service-led information and communication strategy owned by the chief executive is simply not being managed.

Increase organizational literacy

When I work with GPs I quite often find that they are unhappy because, they feel, they can't spend enough of their time being a doctor. Instead they are having to deal with all sorts of other things. Interestingly, though, I find it isn't working out ways of removing all their other commitments that increases their satisfaction; that only happens when they come to the realization that they are *owners* of their practice as well as doctors. As owners they have the right, but also the responsibility, to determine the direction of the whole practice, to deploy its resources and to influence its culture. By doing this, by consciously and actively running their practices, they can be so much more influential in the lives of their patients that it is intrinsically much more satisfying for people who chose their career on this basis.

The NHS National Staff Survey in 2002 found that all the professional groups except managers expressed levels of job dissatisfaction, and if we look at the aspirations of young people entering health care professions, and consider that those professions are being deprofessionalized, with the best of intentions, by managers at all levels, then we can see why. As there can be no putting back of the clock, and clinical guidelines and protocols are, rightly, here to stay, we need to find ways of using the talents and refreshing the enthusiasm of the people without whom health care would be impossible. We need to involve them very much more in *running* health care organizations. Many HCPs feel they are being 'done to', that systems which will affect their working lives significantly are designed without their input, that decisions about the care they offer are made by people distant from that care and that they fight to provide services despite the efforts of their organization to make it difficult for them to do so. At the same time, managers, while talking of the importance of clinical engagement, complain that clinicians do not make useful contributions to discussions. And that is often true. If clinicians will not look wider than their own interests, if they will not see unnecessary care as waste, and as something that must be tackled, if they make unsupported assertions about the superiority of one form of organization over another, or of one way of doing things that just happens to be the way they have always done them, then there is little of value they can add to a decision. And yet it is the people on the front line who know most about what will work in practice, where the duplication and gaps exist and what patients tell them about their wishes and frustrations. This knowledge is critical to organizational decisions. What we need is for HCPs to become much more literate about organizations, about the way things work, about the inherent tensions within organizations that deliver health care, so that they can, and want to, be much more influential in their design and operation. To become, in other words, real managers or, in the term used by Kaiser Permanente,[3] 'thought leaders'.

This is so important. It is difficult to see how it will ever be possible to debate meaningfully all sorts of critical tensions within health care without the active involvement of HCPs, yet we are not developing them (and they are not developing themselves) to be able to discuss creatively and constructively, for example:

- how to balance safeguards and standards with experimentation and innovation;
- how to align the interests of HCPs, patients and populations;
- *meaningful* accountability to local populations;
- how to involve patients in decision-making (really involved, about real decisions);
- who should make decisions about rationing, and how.

It will be when HCPs start to insist that their managers add value to their services and to take on these roles themselves that this will begin to happen, and then the organization will be able to become greater than the sum of its parts. Unless it does happen then health care will go on being a source of frustration and dissatisfaction for so many of the brightest and most socially committed people in the country.

Encourage creative thinking about economic systems that improve public health

Many of the tensions highlighted in the previous section are relevant not only for HCOs and other organizations but for the country. So we need HCPs to become literate in the ways of organizing society. As HCPs we need to take an interest in what makes societies tick. If we open our minds to the fascinating world of human interactions with goods and services, we find they are often described through economic language. The language of economists tends to give precedence to concepts such as competition, rational self-interest and markets; and there is a need for people who believe that ethical considerations are important, that a sense of obligation is as inherently human as is competition, that motivations for (for instance) relationships and self-esteem are as relevant as those for material advantage, to be able to contribute to the debate.

Instead, as HCPs we tend to have closed minds about economies. Many 'hate' the private sector, they say, attributing to their colleagues working in it only financial motives, failing to give any credence to the possibility that they may have moved into it to be able to offer care better than they could in the NHS.[4]

HCPs are not alone, of course. There is something known as the British disease, a 'fatal combination of excessive government intervention and anti-business snobbery',[5] and Jane Jacobs would have no difficulty in recognizing this as a regulatory cast of mind.[6] But just because this is the case we need to ensure that the debate about the shape of our society is not left to the only people who are taking it seriously, the economists. We need to be in there, bringing to it values and experiences that are otherwise mute. Of course, we cannot expect to be taken seriously unless we are well informed, and we will not be able to challenge other views unless we have considered them carefully. So we need to be aware of different schools of thinking about welfare policy,[7] and to have seriously considered how to gain benefit from human instincts for competition *and* for cooperation. We need to be able to accept that companies have brought the world great benefits, as well as express our worries that there may now be a need for a check on corporate power. We need to think seriously, rather than lazily, about how to make accountability meaningful, to think about the related but distinct roles of consumer choice, citizen participation and democratic accountability. We need to take an interest in both societal and individual drivers of health. More specifically, we need to think seriously about the role of the voluntary sector, and how we can encourage altruistic activism without the unaccountable arbitrariness this can sometimes degenerate into.

As much as anything else we need to know about 'creative destruction', as it was called by Austrian economist Joseph Schumpeter in the 1940s,[8] and 'satisficing', the term used by Herbert Simon a couple of decades later.[9] As Simon put it, modern societies are primarily not market but organizational economies. Most of their value is created not by individuals transacting autonomously in the market (as economists tend to encourage us to believe) but by companies where people act collectively, shielded from the market, inventing and creating and developing new goods and services, in line with their own and their organization's sense of purpose. Once they are delivered to the market then that will tend to compete away the very inefficiencies that allowed the creativity in the first place. So companies and markets have a symbiotic coexistence and jointly drive the process of creative destruction. This, according to Sumantra Ghoshal,[10] means we need a model of management for organizations that concentrates not only on driving costs down but also on enabling that collective creative activity that takes society on to new levels of productivity through the development of whole new technologies. Once we understand and can debate these arguments we could play a role in encouraging this across the national economy.

As HCPs we should have a special interest in how economies impact on health but again we rarely, credibly, enter the debate. For example, we rarely look seriously at how society can remove the barriers that disable some of our citizens more than does their state of health.[11] When we do consider how the 'neglected diseases' of the world do not attract the drug research and development that might maintain or transform the lives of millions of the poorest people on the planet, we lazily blame pharmaceutical companies instead of considering how in a democratic country we allow that to happen, and how we would need to change the system to enable it to improve. The past thirty years have seen the disparity between income levels of the richest and poorest in our own society increase (to an extent that would have seemed inconceivable in the 1970s) and this is having profound impacts on health, social mobility and social cohesiveness. Yet there has been little challenge (or informed and credible challenge, at least) to the prevailing dogma that globalization and markets lead inevitably to this. There are many models of markets and many means of regulating global trade, and it would certainly be possible to establish international bodies with different values from those that currently exist. In this way the health of societies could be protected as much as is the health of corporations. In order to influence the course of the debate here, able and committed individuals like HCPs need to take an interest in the economic system in which we live and its international regulatory frameworks. An open minded, intelligent interest. Encouraging this kind of interest is, I suggest, another important role for real managers.

Add value to each service

Economists, looking at mergers and acquisitions of commercial companies, have long pointed out that any such activity must add to the value of the total enterprise and not just involve a change of ownership, and that without this added value there is no rationale (no justification) for the ownership to change. Strategy researchers Michael Goold and Andrew Campbell[12] have explored further the role of the parent company in relation to subsidiary businesses in companies with this structure. They suggest that the purpose of any corporate parent is to add value to the businesses within their portfolio, net of any costs that are associated with belonging to the portfolio. In other words, the businesses should perform better in aggregate than they would as independent companies, and ideally the parent should add so much value that the businesses perform better than they would in the ownership of any alternative parent.

However, adding value is not easy, and value can be diminished if the corporate parent imposes undue burdens on the subsidiaries. Added value can only occur when two conditions are met: the subsidiary must present a parenting opportunity; and the parent must possess the relevant characteristics, capabilities or resources to exploit this opportunity.[13] Corporate parents also have governance and compliance roles: they must ensure on behalf of stakeholders that proper processes are in place and are being applied. These are clearly necessary but because they do not add or create value they need to be implemented in such a way that they minimize value destruction.

Many companies consist of more than one tier of corporate management, and this gives rise to what Goold and Campbell call 'intermediate parenting'. They suggest that intermediate parents can play one of two roles: they can add value to the units they manage: or they can be 'span breakers', managing the units on behalf of the corporate parent, implementing just the decisions that this senior parent makes, monitoring performance against criteria they set and no more. They observe that there is a particular danger of value destruction when intermediate parents develop views or monitoring procedures that duplicate or contradict each other, so it is necessary for the additional tiers to act in a complementary way. Of course, in organizations that are complex and where the sub-units are interdependent[14] the role of the corporate parent is also more complex; however, the underlying principle of adding value is still relevant.

Does this idea apply to HCOs, and does it apply to the NHS? We could suggest that in any large HCO offering a range of services, the top levels are corporate parents to those services. If that is the case then the organization should be adding value to the services within it, as well as fulfilling all the statutory governance roles required. We can also consider that other organizational tiers within the NHS, or, rather, other NHS organizations that have a policy implementation and performance management role, are parents of one sort or another. They too must either add value or break the span for a more senior parent, or perhaps have sections that do each of these.

Of course there are also differences. The 'customers' of the NHS do not have as much scope for finding competitors to turn to as do customers in other sectors, and the governance role may be more important and complex in health than it is in private business, but we may still discover some useful insights if we explore it as an idea.

Let us think for a moment about the way in which strategy could be developed in a HCO in which the top levels see themselves as corporate parents, intent on adding value to the services within their remit. The senior managers would prompt service leaders to develop their own service strategy, by asking (even requiring) them to do so. They would then support them in that activity, perhaps by offering training and by providing, for example, information about current realities, trends into the future, and scenarios that may come to fruition, so that the service and its leaders can build these in to their strategic analysis (using the approaches described in Chapter 5). They would then find ways for service leaders to present their strategies to each other, so that all the services are able to build the intentions of other departments into their own thinking. In all these ways managers would be ensuring that the strategies developed by their services are more robust than if developed in isolation.

The executive management team (and board) would also need to develop or review their own strategy. If they are to add value then this cannot be merely an amalgamation of the service strategies. It cannot, either, include a set of decisions in relation to those services that do not take into account the strategies those services have developed, since that would almost certainly destroy value. The strategy for the top of the organization needs to be about how to undertake its own role. It needs to use the principles of strategic analysis (similar to the way the services have undertaken theirs) to reflect on what it needs to do to improve its own performance in running the organization. To do so it needs first to clarify its role: value added parenting, ensuring it is the most appropriate parent for a particular service (and if not, helping the service decide who is), compliance and governance. It will then look at the resources it has available to achieve that, and the environment in which it is doing so.

Thus the strategy of a large HCO is made up of a set of strategies – those of the board, of the services, of the support departments – all interacting with each other, and all created through a process of interaction. This is a dynamic and ongoing process and not at all static and fixed. At times it will need to be captured in a document, and perhaps in other imaginative ways, so that it can be presented to others and to the organization itself, but that will reflect only the thinking of that time and will need to be amended as events occur, unforeseen opportunities are taken and reactions emerge. At every level in the organization the matrix of the approaches to change that we considered in Chapter 5 will be being enacted.

Just as we see that the strategy for a HCO as a whole is arrived at by a set of dynamic interactions between strategies at all levels, so too must the strategy of the NHS. The role of HCO boards is to ensure that their own organizational strategy is developed through this interactive process, and to contribute to a similar process with other organizations in their health economy and local NHS.

Changing roles, changing behaviours

I hope I have convinced you that the role of the real manager in health care is rather different from that which we have allowed to develop over the past twenty years. And if the role is different then so too are the behaviours that we need.[15] HCOs need managers of deep commitment and conviction, people who are personally involved with the essence of the organization. If we think about these terms more deeply we can see that:

- Commitment accompanies an intimacy with the core of the organization – that is, clinical care.
- Conviction springs from a deep understanding of the people who comprise the organization and a real belief in their potential contribution. This belief is accompanied by a realistic assessment of the

personal factors preventing them from realizing that potential and a preparedness to develop skills, attitudes and awareness where these are lacking.

- Personal involvement is manifest through the robust relationships that are the key to really managing an organization.

Let us look at these in turn.

Commitment

In many parts of our lives we can see that commitment accompanies intimacy, and it is the same in the part of our life that is managing a HCO: intimacy with the core of the organization. It is this that allows a real manager, a chief executive, for example, to have a sense of the organization as an organic, dynamic system; as a set of relationships that are constantly changing in detail, although contributing to something recognizably the same. Understanding those dynamics requires an insight into motivations and behaviours, the way people perceive others and work with them. In many industries managers who do not regularly spend time on the frontline lose this awareness (or never gain it), and without it they lose both the credibility that accompanies a sound grasp of operational detail and the ability to predict trouble – to know almost intuitively when things are going wrong. Without these they cannot engage in one of their most important functions, that of selling problems, and they will be tempted instead to try to solve them. Instead of calling upon the skills and insights of the people who understand the complexities of the factors that contribute to the problem, an ineffective chief executive, advised by others equally removed from the frontline, imposes a course of action that solves part of the problem but creates many more problems in the process. Time-consuming though it undoubtedly is, *selling* problems to the people who are most affected by them will be far more successful than taking decisions without them.

Real managers benefit their organizations by building and demonstrating their commitment by spending enough time on the frontline and throughout the organization to gain a familiarity with the factors that influence care and shape organizational performance. The real manager's interests when spending time in this way will include:

- Exactly what is required of these staff?
- Are they adequately skilled and resourced?
- Do the organizational systems support them?
- Do those systems work with or against human nature?
- Are staff learning from their mistakes?
- Are there systems for the organization and myself to learn from those mistakes?

- Are individuals in positions where they can play to their strengths?
- How can they be liberated to achieve what is required of them?

It can be a useful mental experiment for executive management teams to consider that they themselves do not generate any income for their organization, that it is the provider departments, the front line, that do so. In this scenario, it is not managers who dispense resources to departments and services, but the other way around. Departments and services pay a 'management tax' to pay for certain common support services, for the statutory responsibilities of the organization to be undertaken, for ensuring that interdependency is achieved and for any value that managers add to their service. The bulk of their income, however, remains their own. With this mindset it is clear that chief executives, with no spare financial resources of their own, have no choice but to engage fully with their frontline, gaining their support for any initiatives, or any changes, and having to persuade these departments to bankroll them.

Chief executives intimate with the business at the heart of their organization and fully committed to optimal clinical outcomes are likely to take an interest in relevant research, new developments and approaches. Moreover, they will be perceived as a resource by clinicians, not for their clinical knowledge but for their clarity of thought, enthusiasm and concern. However, if they are to be seen in this way, then they need to be aware of the boundary between decisions that are clinical and those that are managerial. Confusion over where this boundary lies has allowed individuals and groups either to over- or to understep it, with the former causing resentment, and the latter an absence of accountability. This is the province of clinical governance and that has a large literature of its own that I won't attempt to summarize here. But it is possible to explore this boundary by applying a widely known systems science concept to health care. This is that every system has a structure, a process and an outcome. In the 1970s, Avedis Donabedian applied it to medical care in the USA as follows:[16]

- *Structure*: the relatively stable characteristics of the providers of care, of the tools and resources at their disposal, and of the physical and organisational settings in which they work
- *Process*: the set of activities that go on between clinicians and clients
- *Outcome*: any change in current and future health status that can be attributed to antecedent health care.

To make this relevant beyond medical care in the USA in the 1970s we need to: (a) widen the application to health, rather than solely medical, care; (b) include the consumer perspective; and (c) include the organizational systems of which HCPs are a part. When we do so, as in Table 7.2, we will see that the structure, process and outcome differ for managers, clinicians and clients.[17]

Table 7.2 Structure, process and outcome

For the manager
Structure:Policy requirements, money, people, equipment, materials, premises, activity requirements etc.
Process:Developing and maintaining all aspects of the organization.
Outcome:HCPs have skills, resources and motivation to diagnose and meet the needs of their clients.
For the clinician
Structure:Policy requirements, Including performance and financial targets; the tools and resources they have at their disposal; and the physical and organizational settings in which they work.
Process:The set of activities that go on between clinicians and clients.
Outcome:Client is informed, and supported in decisions, about treatment.
For the client
Structure:Consultation with HCP, information about clinical condition and treatment options.
Process:Programme of treatment.
Outcome:Change in current and future health status that can be attributed to antecedent health care.

A number of interesting points arise from this. First, the 'outcome' for one stakeholder is the 'structure' for another. This means that none of these three stakeholders can, alone, ensure an optimum final outcome. Second, a manager (even a real manager) has no role in the interaction between an autonomous, fully trained clinician and an individual patient – this is the realm of clinical; judgement. And this is true even when the manager is a clinician; for example, when a GP employs a physiotherapist or when a number of consultants form a directorate managed by a clinical director. Where patients can be grouped together, however, for example by diagnosis, particular clinical features, age, ethnicity, or clinician, then there will be a managerial role. There will be issues of system design; for example, means of enhancing the application of research evidence, of ensuring clinical competence, of enabling patients to have access to an interpreter, of re-enthusing a clinical carer who is no longer caring. The actual design of such systems is best carried out by the people most closely involved or affected, but the responsibility for ensuring they are in place rests with the manager.

Third, just as there is a need to observe the boundary between clinical and managerial decisions, that between clinician and client responsibilities must be borne in mind. If patients are not given all the information they need on which to base a decision, if that information is meaningless to them or if they are not accorded the respect and the time that allows them to take decisions, then there has been trespass over that boundary. Another role of the real manager when spending time with clinicians is to challenge systems (and individuals) that lead to that trespass.

Many of the health care professions appear to continue to equate the outcome as perceived by the clinician with that of the client, so this boundary is also worthy of further consideration. As many clinicians, philosophers and policy-makers have observed, health is very much more than the absence of disease. Health status can be thought of as the outcome of the interaction of two highly complex systems: the individual human and their environment. Both of these systems have a large number of component elements and influencing one or more of these elements in either system may alter the health status. In complex, dynamic, non-linear systems, the nature of the outcome of an intervention cannot always be predicted, nor indeed can any system malfunction always be correctly pinned down to the behaviour of one particular element. The nature of clinical decision-making has to reflect the lack of certainty inherent here, a point not always appreciated by the public, the media or lay managers. And if managers are to achieve an intimacy with the clinical task, then they need to have an understanding of this uncertainty.

The complexity of both of these systems (the individual and their environment) requires the involvement of a number of different specialists if the health status is to be maximized. Unfortunately, specialists, as we saw in Chapter 2, are prone to take responsibility only for their specialist task and not for the overall outcome. In other words, members of health care professions can become desensitized to the *health* needs of clients in their efforts to rid them of disease. One of the roles of the real manager is to keep the attention of their specialists focused on that overall outcome, health. Seedhouse suggests that the role of the clinician is to create, maintain and respect the autonomy of the patients.[18] Real managers enable them to do so. They do this by encouraging reflective practice and freshening up reactions that have become jaded and by challenging attitudes whenever they come across an approach to care they would not wish to receive themselves.

Conviction

Conviction springs from a deep understanding of the people who comprise the organization and a real belief in their potential contribution. This is not the same as wishful thinking about people: it requires an ability, and a preparedness, to make judgements about performance, judgements about the reliability of individuals in performing what is asked of them. If, knowing that certain people are unreliable, you continue to rely on them, then the responsibility for any failure lies with you. Judgements like this can only happen with time, with exposure to the kinds of people being managed, and by making mistakes.

If we are to make judgements it is helpful to be clear what it is we are making them about. We have seen in previous chapters that the skills needed in HCOs fall into four categories. They are: (a) clinical or technical; (b) behavioural; (c) managerial; and (d) research and reflection. The demarcation between them is fuzzy because the application of clinical and research skills requires behavioural and managerial skills, and the personal maturity that underpins behavioural and managerial skills often develops from a competence (and hence confidence) in clinical, technical or research arenas. However, to distinguish between areas in which further development is needed and those where performance is reliably unproblematic, the classification is useful. Certainly within the organization there must be systems for appraising all four kinds of skills.

All four? Does a lay manager really have the right to make judgements about *clinical* skills?[19] For a number of reasons they do. Really managing an organization means taking responsibility for its outputs. In HCOs this means managing clinical risk. To manage risk requires a knowledge of the size and nature of the risk. This cannot be acquired without an appreciation of the clinical skills of staff. Really managing an organization also involves ensuring its viability, which requires the ability, as an organization, to persuade commissioners and patients of the benefits of using this service, this organization rather than another. Understanding the clinical quality and how it compares with that of others is an essential part of strategic decision-making.

When it comes to research and reflection skills, real managers probably need to take an active interest in research and understand different research methods and their appropriateness in different situations. If they are serious about developing a culture of reflective practice they must also believe (and demonstrate this belief) that mistakes made are opportunities for people to learn and progress, and that complaints are valuable sources of the feedback that we all need in order to improve our performance. Encouraging a culture of ongoing review also requires real managers to reflect regularly on their own performance.

It is people whose behavioural and managerial skill levels are high who are likely to be the real managers of the organization, its leaders, its opinion-formers, especially where they are members of high status professions or specialties. Most often, these real managers will be termed or think of themselves not as managers, but as clinicians. Identifying these real managers is one of the keys to really managing an organization. Failing to do so is one of the reasons why organization charts are often not taken seriously by people at the front-line, because they do not accord with these realities, the people who genuinely carry influence. For credibility as well as effectiveness it is important to find out who these people are.

The easiest way of assessing leadership abilities is to examine the people who are following. De Pree puts it thus: 'Signs of outstanding leadership appear primarily among the followers. Are the followers reaching their potential? Are they learning? serving? Do they achieve the required results? Do they change with grace? Manage conflict?'[20] Real managers are perceived by their teams and departments as a resource, a means of helping them to contribute, not as a police officer constantly looking over their shoulder to see that they are obeying the letter of the law. Real managers, in the words of W.E. Deming, whom we met in Chapter 4, 'drive out fear', so they engender confidence and faith in others.[21]

Fear is a big enemy of real management. Fear can be the root cause of immaturity in individuals and in organizations. Recognizing, gracefully acknowledging and learning from mistakes; respecting, crediting and assisting colleagues; supporting, motivating and developing staff; these are all behaviours only consistently contributed by the individual who is not afraid, or who recognises his or her fear and consciously works to overcome it. In looking for real managers we should therefore look for signs of generosity, of open, honest relationships, of individuals and teams prepared to risk making themselves vulnerable by relying on others. Alongside this there will be evidence of discipline – no scapegoating, no self-righteousness, no culture of gossip and blame.

Real managers, aware of the sometimes thin line between delegation and 'copping out', will help members of their teams with aspects of their role that they themselves find unpleasant. Most people, for example, do not enjoy dealing with poor performance, or the giving of bad news, or having to choose between two or more equally bad alternatives. The real manager will be a genuine resource here. She or he will physically accompany members of staff, if appropriate, to meetings where there may be flak flying, and will never send other people in to fight battles she or he would not want to fight personally. It is worth remembering that good managers are not necessarily those who naturally and easily handle these situations well. Paraphrasing only slightly, 'Those who can, do. It takes those who can't to teach.' Good managers are both confident in their strengths and aware of (and comfortable with) the areas they find more difficult. They do not feel the need to hide these, or fear exposure of them. They use their insight into their own feelings and reactions to assist others through situations where they will feel the same.

Another pointer to the identification of real managers is that we will find them listening. Listening rather than talking. In particular, they listen to information moving up an organization. Imagine an organization in which at every level of the hierarchy each individual has ten people accountable to them. Even if we assume that information moving up the organization has the same value as that moving down (and for many reasons we could suggest it was worth more), then every manager would need to listen to information coming from below ten times as often as to that coming from above. As they listen they will also challenge and by doing so they will encourage their staff to accept their proper responsibilities, to interact effectively with others, to avoid group-think, to act rather than complain.

In *The Fifth Discipline*, Senge suggests that 'the hallmark of a great organization is how quickly bad news travels upwards'.[22] We can see why this is by considering the previous two paragraphs. For news to travel quickly upwards, the organization must have managers who listen to information coming from the frontline. For *bad* news to travel, then, these managers must feel sufficiently confident of their abilities and, even more important, open about their weaknesses not to fear exposure.

Personal involvement

Managing a HCO requires intimacy with its core business, a deep understanding of its members and a genuine belief in their potential to contribute. When individual members are not realizing that potential, then real managers must ensure that they have opportunities to develop the ability to do so.

Individuals or groups stuck in reactive mode (as described in Chapter 3) will not realize their potential until they can be moved along the maturity continuum. Because they are dangerous in leadership positions, personal maturity must be one of the chief executive's (CE's) criteria when she or he makes senior appointments. In some cases, we may not find in one individual both the clinical skills needed for a particular role and this level of maturity, and we will have to help someone to develop it. It is possible, although sometimes time consuming and emotionally draining, to do this, and when successful it is immensely rewarding for both of the individuals involved and for their organization. Some people, however, are so deeply reactive that the time spent moving them forward will deprive others of the CE's assistance. She must therefore select individuals who appear able to respond to this kind of input. Belief in the latent capabilities of staff is not enough on its own; the real manager also makes an assessment of the input required of her and others if these are to be released.

People are sometimes trapped in dependency behaviours because they are trapped in a dependency system. As Peters says, 'People want to be in control of their worlds.'[23] If your system does not allow them to be so, then you can expect resentful, immature behaviour. Where you observe this, it is worth investigating further. Is there anything outside the control of a team that is impeding their delivery of a good service? Would a dedicated lift change the mindset of a surgical team? A dedicated porter for the laboratories? Equipment budgets for each community nursing team? Your gut reaction may be to balk at the cost, but often there is little additional cost, more a redeployment, a different way of thinking about things, and it is worth encouraging the team to see how it could be done. Real managers build systems of interdependency rather than dependency.

Moving people along the maturity continuum is easier said than done and requires the overcoming of the defensive routines people adopt to protect themselves from the pain of acknowledging that they have learning needs. This is not an area that can be tackled by theorizing; it requires example and the modelling of the desired behaviour. It demands the disclosure of feelings and acknowledgement of insecurities to people who may believe this signifies weakness. The courage that this will require can only be found where there is intense personal involvement and a passionate desire for the organization and its members to succeed.

It is not enough, of course, for CEs to identify the real managers in their organizations, they must now develop robust relationships with them, relationships in which each can challenge the thinking, the behaviour and the self-image of the other, and be open to such challenges in return. These relationships will not always be comfortable, often the reverse, and developing and maintaining such relationships requires time, effort, courage and integrity. Above all, integrity is needed, because executives must *model* the behaviours they wish to see in others.

A robust relationship contains no sycophancy, nor does it require that the parties like each other. They must trust and value one another but if a manager is always liked by their staff, the chances are that that person is neither valued nor trusted. We have seen from the research work of Argyris and Schön that, in practice, managers are often neither liked nor trusted despite the fact that those managers espouse values of caring for those around them. This is because they are perceived as tending to adopt behaviours in which they advocate their own views very strongly, pay lip service to those of other people and try to find a third party to blame when they turn down their ideas, all the while telling them how much they value them. Instead, Argyris and Schön describe an alternative style of interaction in which we spend as much time enquiring into the reasoning of the other person as we do making our own case, where we respect the other person enough to be able to handle our frank and honest views and where we do not try to hide behind third parties. This is the kind of exchange that will allow robust relationships to flourish.

Developing these robust relationships is not an optional extra for the real manager; not something to be done when time permits. These relationships and those established by her team, and throughout the organization, are the means by which she manages, really manages. These relationships are her way of ensuring the organisation is in control, achieving its potential, its vision. What vision? Or, rather, whose vision? Management orthodoxy has it that it is the chief executive who defines the vision of an organization. Indeed, many of the mission statements produced by health care trusts over recent years are clearly the work of the top management team. Certainly a really managed service will be one *with* a vision, where people know the direction in which they are heading and are enthusiastic about travelling there. But the vision will not have come from the top. The role of the chief executive (or any real manager) is not to create a vision but to find it – find it held by the people they are managing. According to Gary Hamel, a leading business strategist, companies the world over are now saying that 'the last thing we want is a vision', that all too often 'a company vision statement is indistinguishable from the delusions of the chief executive'.[24] While delusions must be avoided, so too must allowing externally imposed targets to masquerade as the organizational purpose. The vision, the purpose, is in the commitment and enthusiasm of staff. Meeting waiting list targets or financial limits is merely a 'table stake', something you have to do to be in the game, but not the game itself and certainly not the prize.

Thus real managers as CEs will be 'middle-up-down' managers in the terminology of Ikugiro Nonaka.[25] The middle-up-down management hierarchy is one in which the people at the top tend to lay down values (through their behaviour) and policies (arising from the constraints of the environment in which the organisation operates). They then synthesize the innovative actions that flow up from those beneath. These managers spend most of their time listening, responding, nurturing and formulating policy from ideas and practices that have emerged from below.

As Senge points out, unless a shared vision is made up of personal visions, we can expect only compliance from our staff, not commitment. Sometimes HCPs lose their vision and look back with frustration or embarrassment at the naive ideals that drew them in to health care. If they can be put back in touch with their vision, with those ideals then anyone can benefit. Since helplessness or powerlessness is one of the reasons they have lost sight of those ideals, they will need tangible encouragement – evidence that if they make a reasonable case for something they want to do, perhaps a service they want to develop, then they will receive a helpful response. If managers are to support them in this way they will need to be prepared to invest both time and emotional energy.

The real manager manages his or her organization by putting people back in touch with their vision, with the reasons they came into health care, and removing the obstacles preventing them achieving it: poorly designed systems and antagonistic relationships. She or he develops and fosters robust, high quality, challenging relationships throughout the organization. This isn't complicated, it's simple. Simple but very hard.

Changing cultures

Along with different management roles and behaviours, what I have described in this chapter are HCOs with very different cultures from the ones being lived out at the moment. Is this realistic? Since management theorists have told us that cultures are longstanding and slow to change, isn't this a pipe dream? Let us look further at what management academics have actually said about how to facilitate change at the cultural level.

Ed Schein[26] suggests that 'Organizational Culture is the pattern of basic assumptions which a given group has invented, discovered or developed in learning to cope with its problems of external adaptation and internal integration.' He describes three levels at which culture operates:

- *Surface level*: artefacts and creations, e.g. a mobile phone.
- *Middle level*: values, e.g. 'it's good to talk'.
- *Deepest level*: basic assumptions, e.g. life depends on intercommunication.

This description accords with our observation of culture, and leads to the view that cultures are indeed deep-seated and take a long time to change. However, it is not the only way of thinking about culture.

Jamshid Gharajedaghi, a writer in the field of systems theory, suggests that culture is one of three elements involved when we make decisions, the other two being reason and emotion, and that 'culture results in *default decision making*'.[27] This conveys a sense of culture forming a framework through which we look at the world, which is invisible to us. This allows us to imagine that if we could make the framework visible, or if we can replace it with another, then we have a means of changing culture, perhaps more quickly than the Schein description suggests.

Paul Bate[28] (drawing on Karl Weick and others) contrasts a 'scientific' with an 'anthropological' view of organizations. He suggests that in the scientific view culture is seen as a thing, in its own right, something that is part of a bigger thing – the organization. This leads us to think we can change culture separately from, or as a way of influencing, other aspects of the organization. He advocates instead an anthropological view in which societies don't *have* cultures, they *are* cultures. He describes culture as a particular way of thinking about an organization – a *paradigm* for interpreting organization life processes, a *perspective*.[29] In other words, rather than thinking *about* cultures it is more helpful to see people (including ourselves) as thinking *culturally*. This means envisaging organizations in a non-concrete, non-objective way, as social creations and constructions that 'emerge from actors making sense out of ongoing streams of actions and interactions'. Another way of expressing this is that culture is a web of stories all interacting with each other, that people weave from incidents and events they observe, a narrative[30] they (i.e. we) develop to make sense of what they see. Since these stories are not reality, but models of it we have created ourselves; they can be seen as fiction. Furthermore some of these stories will be helpful to us and to others and some will not.

If we approach organizational cultures in this way, then if we want to change a culture (i.e. the way people are thinking, the stories they are weaving) then we first have to identify what stories are being woven. We can then distinguish between those that can usefully be developed, because they are basically helpful, and those that need to be transformed into something different. Thus we would support some stories, perhaps with confirmatory evidence, or perhaps with behaviours that endorse them. We would also challenge others with the aim of replacing them with stories that are helpful. To do this we might provide evidence that disconfirms, or we might ourselves provide a narrative that uses all the 'facts' included in the unhelpful one, and takes account of the personalities and motivations of the people involved, but reads differently. Thus Bate describes managers as fiction writers. This should not be seen negatively: no one can coerce anyone else into weaving a new story or into changing the way they see things, they can merely offer an opportunity to do so. The opportunities Bate himself offers to key clinicians and other decision-makers include hearing first-hand accounts of patient experiences.

This diagnostic stage, Bate suggests, is usually given little attention. This is a pity because, in my experience, the diagnostic stage can be revelatory. People who have previously railed against a culture that is causing them problems realize that they themselves are weaving stories about others that are unhelpful and are unsupported by evidence, and that their behaviours are contributing to negative stories being woven by others.

Bate's suggestion is that we can change small patterns of behaviour (cultural practices) and eventually have a profound impact on the culture of the organization as a whole. This allows us to be optimistic that real managers will be able within a reasonable time frame to foster the kind of cultures, the kind of narratives, that will enable everyone in the organization to contribute more effectively and recognize that they are doing so.

Generosity and discipline

Is there a type of culture (a genre of stories) we should try to foster? I would like to suggest the concepts I used in Chapter 6: generosity and discipline. Cultures in which the stories that are woven describe people choosing to care, choosing to meet hostility, aggression and self-congratulation with compassion rather than fear, choosing to include and value rather than exclude and compare, choosing to expect the best of others and choosing not to allow their self-image to be shaped by ungenerous colleagues. Cultures in which people delay gratification, accept responsibility for problems that are theirs, sincerely seek to check their model of the world against reality, are aware of the number of times in a day they have a choice to make and are careful to balance those choices.

These contrast so strongly with the backbiting, backstabbing, criticism and blame that describe the cultures of many HCOs that it is worth a look at how these cultures develop. Culture of defensiveness and gossip often result from individuals who feel sufficiently insecure to find relief in disparaging others. This insecurity would be surprising, given the intellectual abilities of those individuals, if it were not for what we know about the educational, formative and socialization processes required for entry into the health care professions. In medicine, 'education by humiliation' has still not been completely eliminated, and the still common 'see one, do one, teach one' approach in the training years does nothing to instil the sense of security needed if individuals are to relate productively with others. The other professions, in the course of educating and registering their members, engender a deep-seated perception of a hierarchy among the health care 'tribes'. Medicine holds unchallenged the first tier, with most of the others jockeying for a place on the second, often by disparaging the competition (i.e. other professions). Clearly, this does nothing to enhance the confidence and self-respect of individuals or the fruitful working relationships that spring from it.

Manifesting an interest in the education taking place in and for their organization will enable real managers to provide role models who are themselves deeply secure, and also to decommission practices that inhibit the development of the confidence and maturity of junior staff.

It is worth stressing that constructive cultures do not in any way require conformity. Real managers can usefully remember that in their clinical staff they have some of the most specialized people in society. It can take more than 20 years to develop the skills that society requires of some of its clinicians. The rewards for this level of skill and degree of specialization are often not financial. Even consultants with substantial private practices might have made more money had they pursued a different career path. These individuals are more likely to be motivated by autonomy and the opportunity to continue being innovative and creative. If as a society we are to encourage the development of skills we need, we must cater for the idiosyncratic behaviours of such individuals. As we have seen, unhelpful stories we weave about others are usually reciprocated in the form of negative stories woven about us, and behaviour tends to breed like behaviour. If these individuals are treated with generosity (in the sense I have used here) they are likely to respond similarly, while confining, curtailing or limiting them will result in explosive resentment. Of course, there are organizational requirements of these individuals – for example, budgets, contracts and the training needs of others – and they cannot be given complete autonomy. However, so often the response to any difficulties they raise is for managers to impose a solution, and as we have seen in several other sections, the role of the manager is to *sell* problems, not to solve them.

Gary Hamel[31] draws a distinction between numerator managers and denominator managers. The numerator and denominator in question are those in the following equation:

$$\text{return on investment} = \frac{\text{net return}}{\text{investment (or headcount)}}$$

A denominator manager is one who increases productivity by reducing manpower, impoverishing skill mix and downsizing. A numerator manager similarly increases productivity but by increasing the volume and/or value of goods and services produced. Numerator managers see highly qualified staff as assets that can provide more services of greater quality. Denominator managers see such staff as expensive, as the focus of skill mix reviews, whose departure will reduce unit costs. The difference between numerator and denominator managers appears to be cultural. The Japanese have managed numerators for decades, while in the UK and USA we have managed denominators. Incidentally, Hamel points out that stock market investors are suspicious of denominator managers, and that they require greater short-term returns (dividends) from them than they do from the numerator managers. If the stock market prefers numerator to denominator managers, should not the investors in the NHS: the taxpayers? We could suggest, then, that the role of the real manager is to enable skilled specialists to flourish and become more productive.

Where does this leave the board?

The people with the formal responsibility for ensuring that organizations are really managed are the members of the board. It is at this level in the organization that requirements from outside and from inside are synthesized into a local programme of action that should have as its focus ensuring that sound processes are in place for the organization to support the care process. By listening to information travelling upwards, by prompting and engaging with the strategy development processes of the services, by generally taking an interest in services, staff and clients, board members will develop a sense of what is required to ensure that the HCO delivers the kind of care their staff wish to provide. They must combine this knowledge with pressures coming from outside the organization. Obvious examples of these pressures include government policy, legislative or regulatory requirements and the needs of partner organizations. If they are to be able to develop a genuine synthesis of these two sets of agendas, rather than a 'trumping' of one set by another, there will need to be considerable constructive and creative discussion. They will need to encourage a spirit of continuous improvement throughout the organization, up to and including the board. If they are to do this then they need to work collectively as a board and not as two teams: executive and non-executive directors (NEDs). Board members will also, individually and collectively, need to model the kinds of behaviours that need to be reflected at all levels of the organization; after all, if they cannot cooperate effectively and openly, how are they going to expect others ever to do so?

If boards are to work in this way then they will have to observe the three rules of Chapter 1. They must agree what it is they are aiming to achieve, they must ensure that between them they have the skills and resources they need to do so and they must devise ways of receiving feedback on their performance as a board. Sometimes chairs and boards find it difficult to distinguish between *their* role, *their* resources and *their* performance and those of their organization. If they are to be effective they need to consider what is *distinctive* about the contribution made by a board, and then ensure that they are equipped to make it and receive feedback on whether they are doing so. As part of this discussion they will agree what is *not* the business of the board and they will agree areas of, and limits to, authority that they delegate to the management team. Naturally they should not then interfere further with these, unless the regular reporting (arrangements for which are agreed at the time of delegation) suggests there is a problem.

And if boards are to work in this way then members may need to clarify the roles of the executive directors and the NEDs. Some research in the USA (by Gerald Davis and Michael Useem)[32] has confirmed my own perception: that NEDs can often act in ways that defend the interests of service users, but that they are less likely to challenge or dismiss underperforming executives and less prone to contribute to really useful strategic guidance. This can often lead to the view that NEDs are there as a rubber stamp, and that meetings of board members are a means of 'bringing them up to speed'. This is a waste of the valuable experience and talent that NEDs bring, and where this attitude exists it should be seen as dysfunctional, and perhaps even as a symptom of a dysfunctional organization. If the board is to develop a programme of action that is a genuine synthesis of the priorities mentioned above then NEDs need to ask questions about the processes that are being used to identify service priorities, questions that will test the coherence of the thinking of those making a case for a particular course of action. It is not up to them to provide answers, they are *non*-executive. They must contribute to finding answers, to recognizing answers when they see them, but they should not feel abashed at asking questions that demonstrate that a course of action is suboptimal simply because they cannot themselves suggest a better alternative. At the same time, their executive colleagues also need to behave as board members, to leave their executive 'hats' behind them and to engage with colleagues not as director of finance or of operations, but as co-understander of a problem and co-creator of a solution.

The role of the board is to ensure that people and processes are in place that allow HCPs to be supported in their provision of care to clients, care that is continuously improving, care that meets the needs of clients and of populations, care that is determined by all the providers along the care pathway. This involves ensuring that the organization is full of real managers, a good number of whom probably see themselves as clinicians and not managers, fulfilling the roles identified at the beginning of this chapter. This role for the board looks rather different from the conventional one: members will be working together, concentrating on whether their organization is flourishing. Here they are all equals: while EDs will know more about the detail of their services, organizational flourishing is something many NEDs are very knowledgeable about.

Concluding thoughts

Really managing an organization is an intellectual challenge; however, it is also much more. It calls for commitment, conviction, personal involvement and an unremitting concern for the care process. Above all, it requires an ability and a willingness to engage actively with HCPs on their own ground. Whether these qualities are to be found in a chief executive can be judged by examining not reports, not papers, not even contracts or financial statements (although these are important), but the attitudes, behaviours and day-to-day decisions of frontline staff.

My observation is that we don't have enough people who do this, and that is not because there are not excellent people running organizations. It is because that is what they are doing, concentrating on running an organization. They are not defining their role as providing the organizational support that is required if the client–clinician interaction is to be effective. One way of encouraging a change of perspective in this direction is for HCPs of all kinds to aspire to these top management roles.

When we have organizations full of real managers, including at the very top, we will see health care flourish, and since that is what HCPs care about why is it that relatively few of you take up this challenge? In part, I believe, it is something to do with the issue of status that we considered in Chapter 2. We saw there that the status associated with a particular role depends on the nature of the knowledge base (how definitive and technical it is) and the degree of interpretation that is required to apply it to particular situations. I think it is fair to say that the knowledge base for management is not as definitive as that for, say, medicine, even that taught on a good MBA programme. So management is not perceived by HCPs, especially those of high status themselves, as offering an attractive career option, an interesting role of equivalent status. Management positions tend to attract those HCPs whose status will be enhanced, or at least not diminished, by their taking on that role. While we will want to continue to encourage these people, we also need to encourage the others. And this chapter may give us some clues about how to do so.

If we make sure the role is that of supporting the client–clinician interaction, and we make sure that organizational charts reflect reality, so that the people most influential with HCPs are identified in a formal way, then it will not be a great step for them to take on corporate responsibilities. The status of the corporate roles will then follow that of the people within them and demonstrate to others that there are attractive and worthwhile alternatives to the directly clinical.

I also want to reinforce the point that society needs HCPs – intelligent, able people with a commitment to the welfare of individuals and communities – to take an interest in the wider economy. There are major debates to be had in the coming years about the way trade is organized and regulated, both nationally and internationally, and to date the participants in this debate are largely people from businesses with vested interests, various lobby groups and politicians. We also need people concerned about the health, welfare and well-being of others to engage knowledgeably and constructively in it; not in an antagonistic way from the sidelines, but from a credible knowledge base built from in-depth association with business. We need to make health care a mainstream part of the national economy, and its providers economically and politically literate, so that we all live in a wider system that genuinely enhances health for all.

Notes

1 Information handling is also the essence of management: as soon as we no longer perform a task ourselves but rely on someone else to do so, the two-way transfer of information (or 'communication') becomes essential.

2 By 'we' I mean members of a service, perhaps supported by someone familiar with this approach.

3 Kaiser Permanente is a not-for-profit health care provider organization in the USA that has run programmes designed to train networks of what it calls 'thought leaders' to help to plan health care for the future.

4 I am not at all suggesting that this is always the case, any more than that it is never the case.

5 From Micklethwait, J. and Wooldridge, A. (2003) *The Company: A Short History of a Revolutionary Idea* (London: Weidenfeld and Nicholson). This book charts the invention and development of the limited liability company. The authors suggest that 'The Victorians invented an institution that changed the world. They could not quite invent an institution to change Britain.'

6 Indeed, she gives Britain a special mention in this regard.

7 See, for example, Deacon, A. (2002) *Perspectives on Welfare: Ideas, Ideology and Policy Debates* (Buckingham: Open University Press).

8 In *Capitalism, Socialism and Democracy* (New York: Harper, 1942).

9 See *Models of Bounded Rationality* (1982).

10 See Ghoshal S. and Bartlett C. (1997) *The Individualized Corporation. A Fundamentally New Approach to Management* (London: William Heinemann), Chapter 11.

11 For more information on how we can stop further disabling those people who have disabilities, visit the UK Disability Rights Commission website (www.drc.gov.uk).

12 Of the Ashridge Centre for Strategic Management. For more information, including on publications, visit their website (www.ashridge.org.uk). See also Goold, M., Campbell, A. and Alexander, M. (1994) *Corporate Level Strategy* (New York: Wiley).

13 A parenting opportunity arises where the subsidiary can improve its performance by doing something that can be achieved more readily if the parent is involved; or where it cannot do so on its own because it needs to involve other subsidiaries.

14 So that they have interdependent relationships with each other and not just hierarchical relationships with the corporate parent.

15 Please note that I am not suggesting that past and current managers are not people of commitment, conviction and concern for patients, but that we can usefully explore a different understanding of these terms.

16 Donabedian, A. (1980) *Explorations in Quality Assessment and Monitoring, Volume 2: The Definition of Quality and Approaches to Its Assessment* (Ann Arbor, MI: Health Administration Press).

17 I am not ignorant of all the work on the co-production of health, and the model of clinician and client working together to reach an informed decision about treatment. However, I have deliberately kept this simple (oversimple) here.

18 Seedhouse (1991); see Chapter 2, note 11.

19 Of course, I am suggesting not that they personally assess those clinical skills, but that they take an active interest in the assessments undertaken by others.

20 de Pree (1989); see Chapter 1, note 16.

21 See, for example, Walton, M. (1991) *Deming: Management at Work* (London: Mercury).

22 Senge (1990); see Chapter 6, note 14.

23 This is a quote from one of Tom Peters's videos, entitled *Excellence in the Public Sector* (Melrose, 1989).

24 Hamel expressed this view at a seminar at the London Business School in 1994. See also Hamel, G. and Prahalad, C.K. (1994) *Competing for the Future* (Boston: HBS Press).

25 Hampton Turner, C. and Trompenaars, F. (1994) *The Seven Cultures of Capitalism* (London: Piatkus).

26 Schein, E.H. (1985) *Organizational Culture and Leadership: A Dynamic View* (San Francisco: Jossey-Bass).

27 Gharajedaghi, J. (1991) *Systems Thinking: Managing Chaos and Complexity. A Platform for Designing Business Architecture* (Boston, MA: Butterworth Heinemann).

28 Bate, P. (1994) *Strategies for Cultural Change* (Oxford: Butterworth Heinemann).

29 Sheldon, S. (1980) *Symbolic Interactionism: A Social Structural Version* (Menlo Park, CA: Benjamin/Gummings).

30 A narrative is a relating of actions and events that reveals causal connections between them.

31 Hamel and Prahalad (1994); see note 25 above.

32 Davis, G.F. and Useem, M. (2000) 'Top management, company directors, and corporate control'. In A. Pettigrew, H. Thomas and R. Whittington (eds) *Handbook of Strategy and Management* (London: Sage), pp. 233–59.

8   Case studies

These case studies were originally written as much to introduce the concerns of HCPs in a number of different settings as to illustrate real management concepts; I hope that they do both. They are fictional sequences of events constructed from incidents that are wholly real. The characters in them are also fictional. They are composites built from people I have worked with, observed, met, conversed with or read. No one should recognize themselves, or their organization. Even where I have used a sustained series of events from one organization to provide a framework for the storyline, all the detail will have been drawn from elsewhere, and it will be peopled by individuals and groups who are foreign to it. All the discussion refers to these fictional characters and organizations.

If, as you read, you observe a detail that does not ring true, you could be right: I may have oversimplified in order to move the story along. I have also not worried about using organizational names that are current, on the basis that they will be out of date by the time you read this anyway, and that the dynamics are what is important. They are deliberately written in 'airport fiction' style, a style that, I have noticed in my teaching experience, even those who profess to hate it will actually read.

Hillside Hospital

Ruth Anderson, Chief Executive of Hillside Hospital NHS Trust, parked her car on her return to the hospital and briefly thought back to the meeting she had just left. The Hillside and Donwich Health Board had asked for a meeting to discuss the contract specification for palliative care. Hillside's contracts manager had invited the trust's consultant in palliative care, Dr John Norland, to accompany him, and Ruth had decided to join them.

The board had expressed concern about issues of equality in palliative care. They had observed that the local hospices tended to cater for white, middle-class patients with cancer and wanted to ensure that other cultural and diagnostic groups had access to support towards 'a good death'. Their survey data and feedback from public forums had suggested a level of unhappiness with the services available to patients who were known by their carers to be in the last stages of their lives. This rarely gave rise to formal complaints, yet concern had been expressed about both acute and community services, and the board was keen to promote the application of the philosophical principles of hospice care on a much wider basis.

There were four statistics that had prompted them to question current practices. The first was that recent local figures confirmed that nearly 70 per cent of deaths occurred in hospital. They contrasted this with the second, that several surveys had reported that 60 per cent of the people asked were strongly of the opinion that they wanted to die at home. The third was that a recent analysis had suggested that half of the per capita spend on the NHS was incurred in the last few months of an individual's life. The fourth was that, of all deaths, only a third were due to cancer, yet this was where palliative care was concentrated.

John Norland had reassured them that patients on his palliative care ward did not fall into the white, middle-class category, indeed that his ward, on the fourth floor of a hospital originally built as a Victorian workhouse, provided care for a wide range of people, of whom a current patient, homeless and in the final stages of liver disease, was not unrepresentative. The board had clearly been impressed with John, so she anticipated no problems with the placing of the contract.

Among the incoming post awaiting her when she reached her office was a letter that, with the morning's discussion fresh in her mind, Ruth read with special interest.

Ms Ruth Anderson
The Chief Executive
Hillside Hospital NHS Trust

Dear Ms Anderson

I have never previously complained about any aspect of care in your hospital, or indeed the NHS. However, I do wish to register my concern at the way my aunt was treated in your hospital recently.

My aunt, Mrs Hilda Jones, was 89 years old and was in your hospital (on Mullin Ward) because she had had a bad fall at home and had broken her arm. While in hospital she suffered a stroke and her condition got worse and worse.

After two weeks it was clear to all her family that she was dying. My brother, her nephew, asked for her to be transferred to a hospice and it was agreed that the hospital palliative care team would assess her so that she could move. Before that could be done she died.

My complaint is about the way she was treated in the last few days before she died. She was forced to get out of bed for most of every day in case she caught pneumonia. On the day before she died I was with her when she begged to go back to bed. She was told that she could 'soon', but it was over 90 minutes later when she was put back to bed.

When I protested to the nurse about the delay she said, and I quote, 'Everyone has to wait their turn.' I appreciate that she was trying to be fair and not to be cruel but the result of her actions *was* cruel to my aunt.

While my aunt was in hospital I tried to make sure I was there at lunchtime with her, because if I did not help her she did not eat anything. The meals seemed quite unsuitable, solid bits of meat and lots of vegetables. In the last few days my aunt only ate a bit of the custard.

When I asked a nurse if she could order some milky foods, she said that they had ordered a light diet but that 'the catering staff have a funny idea of a light diet here'.

All in all it seemed to our family that the whole of the ward was geared to those who are going to get well and come out of hospital. They never treated my aunt as someone who was dying.

I have written this letter because I would not want anyone else to suffer as my aunt did.

Yours sincerely,

Elizabeth Smith

When David Young, Director of Corporate Affairs, came to see her a short time later, she showed him the letter and asked what he knew about Mullin Ward and the staff involved. David had worked in the NHS since he left university twelve years before. He had first met Ruth when he was on the management training scheme and he had been a trainee in her department. Since then, he had worked for her on several occasions, even following in her footsteps twice.

Mullin Ward he knew little about. Actually, he knew a lot about it – how the plumbing needed to be upgraded, the walls repainted, the bedside furniture replaced – but, in that, it was very similar to half a dozen other wards. He knew little that was peculiar to Mullin.

Of the Mullin Ward staff he knew similarly little detail, with one exception, the allied health care professionals (AHPs). He had been managing physiotherapy, along with speech and language therapy, occupational therapy, radiography, dietetics and pharmacy, for some six months now. When the trust had last restructured no one had known quite what to do with the AHPs. The professions themselves had been implacably opposed to being split into the clinical directorates, protesting that this would mean a loss in specialist skills and insufficient training opportunities. What they also objected to, and in David's view this was their real concern, was being managed by doctors. All the clinical directors were medically qualified.

When he had asked Ruth if he could manage them, knowing that some clinical management would strengthen his CV, they had been delighted. Their gratitude had not survived the next round of efficiency savings, however, and he was now locked in conflict with them as he tried to get them to consider modernizing their services.

He thought back to the last meeting he had attended of the physiotherapy management team. There had been quite a lot of concern expressed about the way that certain consultants insisted on a very vigorous treatment regime even when the family, the patient and the physiotherapist concerned felt it was inappropriate. He mentioned this to Ruth. She asked what those at the meeting had decided to do about it. He reflected for a moment and replied that in his opinion it wasn't action they had been after, but an opportunity to whinge. Ruth grimaced, slightly comically.

After David had left Ruth re-read the letter from Elizabeth Smith and decided that the proper course of action was to refer it to Anne Jones, Director of Nursing and Quality. This she did, appending a short note asking to be kept personally informed of the outcome. After further thought, she also dropped a line to Jane Chisholm, Medical Director, asking her to investigate the apparent stand-off between medical and physiotherapy staff.

'Yes, the commissioners were being much more constructive these days', she reflected. Perhaps she could suggest to them a few areas where she would find it helpful if they were to require further service improvements. It was always easier to persuade her clinicians to change systems and practices if there was the 'muscle' of the commissioners behind her.

In his office on Nightingale Ward, John Norland reflected on the figures he was incorporating into a paper. They showed that whereas he was achieving a good level of pain management in 95 per cent of patients, on the other Hillside wards the figure was under 50 per cent.

His length of stay figures (average two weeks) and discharge rates (60–70 per cent) had surprised his colleagues in the medical directorate. They had imagined that lengthy peaceful decline characterized his patients, whereas the reality was that he provided respite care, dealt with acute problems and even offered rehabilitation.

He had been trying for some time to interest his colleagues in palliative care. He firmly believed that the principles – holistic assessment of patients and their families, good pain management, an interdisciplinary approach to care – could be applied anywhere, not just in designated wards or hospices. 'It's the care, not the where' was the slogan he tried to keep in mind. They had not shown much interest to date, usually saying 'It's all right for you, you have the staffing levels and the technology', despite the fact that the staffing levels were similar and the technology available to all. When he mentioned his other cardinal rule – 'Never abandon the patient' – many of his acute care colleagues interpreted this as 'Never give up therapeutic hope'. But for a proportion of patients it translated not into ever more invasive procedures to prolong life but providing good quality care and comfort, and relieving distress, of patients and also of families and friends. However, when he broached this, he found he almost invariably got a negative reaction. Privately he thought that many of his colleagues were still not prepared to accept the concept of 'a good death' – seeing death as a failure, and wanting to postpone it for as long as possible. Even, when it was about to arrive, quickly arranging for it to happen somewhere else.

On Mullin Ward, Lesley Wilson, a senior I physiotherapist, was just arriving to see, for the fifth time that day, Mrs Bird, an 80-year-old who had recently had a stroke and required physio input every hour. The staff nurse, Peggy West, greeted Lesley cheerfully and offered her a chocolate. Lesley asked how Mrs Bird seemed to be doing: 'Oh don't talk to me about Nellie Bird,' said Peggy, 'I've had her son on to me all morning. He wants his mother transferred to a hospice. Says she hates it here.'

'Does he? I have been wondering about the physio regime', said Lesley. 'It seems *so* vigorous for someone so frail.'

Peggy shrugged, 'Well that's Dr Kendal for you, he's always been the same. It's his ward round in half an hour, why don't you have a word with him about it?'

Lesley sighed, 'Even when it is obvious that a patient is going to die, he insists on these regular passive movements and nasopharyngeal suction. Having a tube repeatedly stuck up your nose is unpleasant for anyone but must be awful for someone who's so frail and elderly.'

'Why do it then?' said Peggy. 'I thought you were practitioners in your own right and could use your own clinical judgement? I'm sure you've told me that before.'

'Well, we are, but in cases like this we must carry out the consultant's wishes. I will take it up with him during the ward round, though.'

Both of them looked up as Katie Tyler, the Complaints Officer, walked in and asked to speak to Sister. 'Oh no, just what we need, another complaint issue to deal with,' muttered Peggy. When Katie explained that she wanted to find out about a recent patient, Mrs Jones, Peggy knew nothing of her, pointing out that she had only recently returned from leave. She offered to see if her notes were still to hand.

As she walked over to where Mrs Bird was lying in bed, Lesley observed two young doctors poring over a set of notes, with a slightly anxious air. As she watched, a middle-aged man, sitting next to her patient, went over to them. She heard him ask about hospices and how to get his mother admitted to one. Both of them looked rather nonplussed and one said that social services might be able to help; perhaps Mr Bird should visit the hospital social work department. Given directions, Mr Bird disappeared in that direction. Lesley, despite knowing that this was not the best way to get Mrs Bird referred as he wished, did not stop him from going. She knew he would be distressed when she applied the suction and was relieved that he would not be present.

A few minutes later, the source of the junior doctors' anxiety was apparent as Adrian Kendal, Consultant in General Medicine, entered the ward followed by a retinue of assorted white coats. Peggy West emerged, thrust the notes into Katie's hands and quickly joined the group, already at a bedside. Katie realized that she would gain no further information until the ward round had finished and decided she could usefully read the notes she had been given. She noticed they were only the nursing records, and she walked down to the day room at the end of the ward.

In the day room, a group of patients were exchanging views about the nursing staff. One complained that when she arrived on the ward she was scolded for wearing an expensive watch and bringing too much money with her: 'How was I to know what to bring?' she exclaimed. 'I've never been in hospital before, not as a patient anyway. It's all very well giving me a booklet about it when I get here, but why didn't they tell me before I came?'

'Anyway,' another responded, 'they had no right to tell you off like that, we're not children in a school.'

'And what about the way they treat Mr Lawrence?' said another. 'He'll starve to death soon. Every mealtime they plonk his food in front of him and then leave him to it. Sometimes they don't even take the sandwich out of the plastic. I haven't seen him eat anything. His relatives have complained about it but nothing seems to change.'

'Has your call button been fixed yet?' asked the first. 'Mine hasn't.'

'No, but it doesn't matter so much now I can get up', was the response. 'I just hated not being able to call for help when I could only lie there. And I know that new woman, the one who came in last night, the bed next to me, was really upset, when she wet the bed because she couldn't get anyone to bring her a bed pan. They told her she should have called out but she didn't want to, not about that and not in the early hours.'

'That poor Mrs Bird,' said another, 'all that palaver every hour with that tube thing, all that noise behind the curtain, that's why I'm in here, to get away from it. You can tell the old dear hates it. Be kinder to let her die in peace.'

The group turned their attention to an elderly man sitting by himself in the corner. Unlike the others he was dressed in day clothes, including an overcoat. 'Bert's waiting for an ambulance to go to a nursing home, he's been ready since just after breakfast', said one. 'I hope he doesn't have to wait as long as Elsie the other day, they didn't collect her till gone five', responded another.

Katie recognized the problem: it was one that yielded a number of complaints. As the ambulance service was managed separately, Hillside had no direct control over their activities, and was not finding it easy to agree service standards. She did wonder whether Bert really needed to be kept quite so ready to leave, however. Was the overcoat really necessary? She wondered briefly whether to raise this with the ward staff and decided against it. She would be seen as a 'snoop', she had no doubt.

The ward round was coming to an end. The last patient required no physio input, so Lesley left the group and made her way to the nursing office, furious at the way her view had, yet again, been overruled by Adrian Kendal. She had even been unable to persuade the group to await the return of Mrs Bird's son so that all involved could take part in the discussion. Ever since the European Working Time Directive had come in, many of the medical staff had become even more impatient about getting things done on time; well, getting *their* things done. What made it all worse was that she felt so helpless. She had complained so often to her head of service and absolutely nothing changed. Everyone was driven by targets and the push to reduce waiting times and bed stays. Anything that wasn't ultimately about that fell on deaf ears. With the current A&E targets putting even greater pressure on beds, care on the inpatient wards was bound to be compromised.

As she watched from the office, one of the junior doctors peeled off from the group at the side of the last bed in the ward and came over. She had been on the receiving end of a particularly sharp response from Dr Kendle, and Lesley wasn't surprised to see her looking distressed and angry. Peggy joined them in the office and mentioned Katie's recent visit. The young doctor's response was defensive: 'When did you say she died? Three weeks ago? Well that's one thing, at least, that can't be my fault. I hadn't started here then. Oh I'm sorry if I seem rude but I've had so much paperwork to catch up on and in spite of doing my best I always seem to be being wrong-footed.'

Jane Chisholm, the Medical Director, thanked Adrian Kendal for sparing her some time, and reminded him what she wanted to discuss: relationships between medical and physio staff. Adrian responded that he was not aware of any problems and asked if there had been any complaints. 'Oh not formally', Jane replied. 'Apparently David Young mentioned something to Ruth, in passing, and she's asked me to look into it.'

'Oh, another example of managers going the long way round?' said Adrian. 'If he's got issues with clinical decisions he can come and talk to me. If people are unhappy or have questions why don't they speak to me in person instead of complaining behind my back? I know some of the physios aren't always happy with my decisions, and I guess they have been making noises to Ruth saying I overrule their clinical judgement. But they sometimes give up too easily. Just because a patient is elderly doesn't mean they should receive a lesser standard of care. A short period of discomfort may give them an extra ten years. If I deferred to physios as often as they'd like there would be howls of complaints from patients' families, and rightly so.'

'Yes, I thought it was probably another example of "doctors never listen" when the opposite is often the case', said Jane. 'And Lesley Wilson does seem to have a bit of a beef about it. While you're here, have you read John Norland's paper yet? Apparently he's achieving much better pain management on Nightingale Ward than we are elsewhere. Shall I ask him to come and discuss his approach to total pain management at an audit meeting soon?'

She could hardly have achieved a more explosive response if she had lit a fuse. 'Don't talk to me about "total pain"!', scoffed Adrian. 'Nightingale Ward! That's all I ever hear about from the commissioners. If I had Nightingale's staffing and their funding on my wards I'd be able to offer a Rolls Royce treatment too and have all the time in the world to write papers about it!'

Question

How would you advise Ruth Anderson on her priorities if Hillside is to address the concerns of their commissioners over care for the dying?

Discussion

The commissioners' concerns can be summarized as follows: 'People are not dying *where* they want to, or *how* they want to; although good practice is available, it isn't to the majority of patients.' People dying in the wrong way in the wrong place. Although this is simple to express, if we consider that it arises because of a large number of incremental decisions made about patients by different HCPs, then we can see that this is a multidimensional problem that will require changes on many fronts if it is to be resolved. It is a real test of the priorities and the effectiveness of the chief executive and senior clinical staff: front-line attitudes, behaviours and practices always are.

If individuals undergoing one of the most important of life events are to do so well, then Ruth Anderson must ensure that:

1   She and her staff are *really managing* health care, that front-line staff are managed, really managed by people with whom they have a robust relationship that allows any unacceptable behaviours to be challenged.

2   The interdependent specialists who comprise Hillside Hospital take individual responsibility for the total services provided to the patient. While operating primarily within their own professional boundaries, they keep the total 'service package' in mind and intervene across boundaries if they perceive there to be a problem.

3   Her organization as a health care system does not confuse health with the absence of illness.

In the case study, there is much evidence that Hillside is failing in all three respects.

Hillside needs more real managers, people focusing on health care and not the organization

Let us look first at Ruth Anderson herself. She has attended a meeting where she comes across (if she didn't know it already) the suggestion that although 60 per cent of people say they want to die at home, 70 per cent are dying in hospital. So, many people who want to die at home will be dying in her hospital. What would be a real management response to this news? Shock probably – it should bring her up short anyway, and make her think, make her want to investigate further. She has a great resource here in John Norland; he could give her facts and figures if she asked him. He could help her to think through what is needed on wards other than his, for them to be able to discharge people who are dying, and for them to be able to support patients and their families so that the dying individual is not abandoned, but is supported and pain free. She doesn't do this. She doesn't find out enough about what he is doing, what impact he is having on the rest of the care staff, for her to realize that he will need her help if he is going to be successful.

Is this an isolated incident? In a short meeting with David Young she hears him disparage the motivation of some of the people he is managing, the physios, and does nothing to challenge this attitude. Indeed, she appears to collude with it. Let's look further at David's approach to management. He trivializes valid professional concerns expressed by the AHPs as 'not wishing to be managed by doctors', when at the very least he should ask 'Why?'

He does not require the physios to operate right up to the boundary between managerial and clinical decisions. He stays far too far on his own side of the boundary, so that there is a void between them, into which Mrs Bird and others fall. As a manager he does not have any role in the treatment of Mrs Bird as an individual; that is a matter for the judgement of clinicians. However, managers do have a role in the treatment of groups of patients: groups such as the frail elderly prescribed nasopharyngeal suction, or patients over whom there is a dispute between clinicians about the most appropriate care. In either case, the managerial role would be to sell the problem to all the professionals involved, to persuade them to identify the causes of the problem, to challenge constructively their thinking, to resell to them the problem, to cajole them into working together to design a solution, to require them to review and evaluate their solution. David Young has not yet admitted that there is a problem, or not one he will consider selling. He is failing to realize that information and responsibility go hand-in-hand; he isn't responsible only for what is explicitly included in his job description; once he has received information about differences of professional opinion on care regimes then to do nothing about it is irresponsible.

Is Ruth a real manager? Is Hillside really managed?

At one point we see Ruth wanting the commissioners to be more exacting, to provide a bit of additional 'muscle' in her discussions with HCPs about the way they organize care. In all case studies we have to fill in a lot of gaps to help us make sense of them, and here is such a gap. We don't know whether she is using this muscle as a screen to hide behind, so that she can present herself as 'nice' and the commissioners as the 'nasties', which of course we can see is both cowardly and unproductive; or whether she has wisely decided that this is a useful source of extra energy to support a direction in which she is already travelling, and in which she is already engaging her key 'thought leaders'.

Perhaps more tellingly, we see almost no sign in the case of the three rules being enacted – anywhere. Ruth misses the opportunity of the conversation with David to refresh expectations about how to manage the AHPs. Indeed, she sees David very actively *not* caring about care, and gives him no feedback about this. No one appears to be sitting down with John Norland and discussing with him what it is he could be achieving and whether he has the skills and resources to do it. Adrian Kendal's treatment of his junior doctors is appalling, and must be widely known about, yet Jane Chisholm misses an opportunity to express her expectations about how these vitally important people should be being supported and developed. She also avoids the task of giving Adrian feedback about his behaviour, at least in a direct way. We see her trying to influence his care by referring him to John Norland's research, a very indirect approach when we know that Adrian has a very direct style. If she is going to have any impact on his behaviour or his attitude to other HCPs she will have to be much more courageous than this. She will have to stop trying to be 'nice' and tell him, in a well-argued case that addresses his genuine interests and concerns, what it is about his behaviour she believes he needs to change.

We may be tempted to doubt Jane's integrity. She appears to be more of a shop steward than a leader. Instead of giving people constructive feedback about their behaviour and performance Jane focuses on personalities, jumps to conclusions and makes unhelpful value judgements. But incumbents of this kind of hybrid managerial role not infrequently appear uncomfortable, particularly if they are doctors, feeling 'neither fish nor fowl'. As a result, they can be perceived to be 'running with the hare and with the hounds', as they seek to find points of agreement with whichever camp, management or medical, they are at that moment interacting with. This limits their influence considerably. They would be far more effective highlighting issues of *dis*agreement and providing explanations about the other party's reasoning.

The discomfort they experience should not surprise us if we consider that the medical career path rarely requires individuals to experience the feelings associated with a first managerial role. In other health care professions, and most other walks of life, people are promoted to an explicit management role while still in their twenties. The realization that they are no longer 'one of the team', that they cannot be constantly popular *and* effective, that they must often choose between being liked and being respected, is often a painful one, but it is learned early. There are few parallels in the medical professions and it is asking a lot of individuals to experience this 20 years further on. Medical and clinical directors therefore need a lot of support, particularly regular constructive feedback and the opportunity of a credible mentor outside the profession.

Are we asking too much of Jane to expect her to challenge Adrian's behaviour? Certainly we are unless we show her how to do so. The rules for giving feedback could help her, being within an organization where the three rules are widely enacted will help her, but perhaps, as much as anything else, the thinking in Chapter 6 may help. If she can find ways of staying in a positive ego state she will encourage others around her, including Adrian, into one as well. She can also do this indirectly, if in her own interactions with the junior doctors she is always in adult or positive parent states; she will thus encourage them to remain in positive states themselves, and take that set of expectations and behaviours with them when they deal with others. Adrian Kendal gets away with treating people like naughty children partly because they let him.

Unless the three rules are being used throughout the organization, it isn't being really managed. So the answer to the question posed above is no: Ruth Anderson doesn't look like a real manager. And Hillside is not really managed. One other way we can tell? The management chart does not reflect reality (see Figure 8.1). Certainly David Young and Jane Chisholm and are not among the organization's leaders – no one is following.

The parts take responsibility for the whole

How often do you *make* a complaint? How often do you *feel* like complaining? Most of us rarely put pen to paper, pick up the phone or e-mail in our

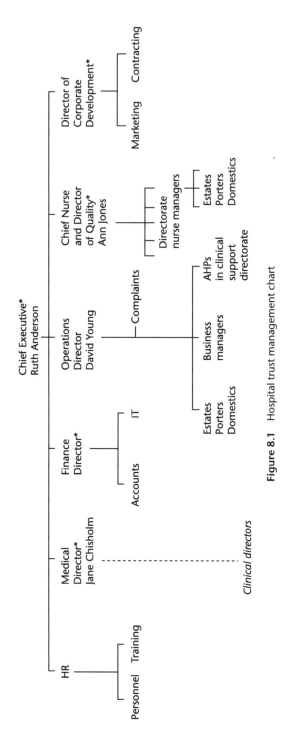

Figure 8.1 Hospital trust management chart

concerns. So when people have taken the trouble actually to do it, their complaints are worth taking seriously, they are a source of very valuable information. At Hillside, staff respond defensively, seeing them only as problems. We saw in Chapter 2 that HCPs need to respond generously to challenge if they are together to ensure good care, so this selfish defensive reaction is an indication of a problem with quality, and with care at the boundary between professions.

Let us look at whether the people in the case are behaving generously across boundaries to ensure a good quality package of care, a good overall service for the patient.

John Norland, while ensuring that his own patients are relieved of pain, is aware that half of the patients in the care of his colleagues are suffering. The publication of papers on the subject is necessary both for his personal credibility and for the advancement of his specialization; however, he does not take opportunities to challenge the practice and the thinking of his peers, only privately concluding that they see death as a failure. More generosity on his part towards his colleagues, as well as honest and open self-reflection with them whenever opportunities arise, would lead him to realize why this is the case and enable him to help to design systems that permitted excellent medical or surgical interventions but within a framework of care with the patient's autonomy as its focus. After all, there are a number of different assumptions in Hillside about what is meant by 'health', 'care' and the roles of HCPs in decision-making (see Chapter 2), but no one is helping to surface these assumptions in a constructive way. As a result they surface negatively, in back-biting, in jostling for resources and professional status and in rubbishing potentially good ideas. A real clinical manager would be able to play a central role in enabling these hidden assumptions to be explored constructively.

Lesley Wilson allows Mr Bird to waste his time finding the social workers because it will make her life easier. She also takes no responsibility for making her remonstrations to Adrian Kendal effective. To exercise real responsibility, she would need to find out his reasons, his concerns, check her own reasoning, address her arguments to his concerns and in a way that takes into account his motivation profile, preferred relationship style and conversational ritual. Taking responsibility always requires a challenge to your own thinking and thorough preparation. If Lesley Wilson cares for her patients, she needs, in this situation, to engage in an act that will involve both work and courage. Unless she does, her care will remain ineffectual emotion.

The ward nursing staff are also failing to take responsibility. When patients cannot eat the meals provided, they blame 'catering'. When patients, not knowing that it is better not to, bring money and valuables with them, staff blame the patients. And when faulty call buttons cause patients distress, they blame both electricians and patients. Of course, the fact that nurses are more numerous than other professions involved and that their involvement with the patient is greater (nurses will be providing care 24 hours a day) mean that the opportunities for failure are more numerous, and we must be careful not to develop a negative view of nursing because there will be numerically more mistakes from this profession than others. But we could also suggest that it is all the more important that nurses, more than any other group, take responsibility for the total service that patients receive, and that we support them in doing so.

If the nursing staff on Mullin Ward had been taking responsibility for the service experienced by their patients, how would they have behaved differently? Food that is inedible is not food. Nurses on Mullin Ward are starving their patients. Their responsibility is to ensure that patients are offered an appropriate diet. Since this requires effective working relationships with the catering service, it is their responsibility to ensure that such a relationship exists. Incidentally, the ownership of the catering service (whether it is run by the trust or by a commercial company) is irrelevant here; taking responsibility means nurses making their experiences heard at top levels, if they themselves cannot achieve a change in service standard. This requires an understanding of decision-making processes. It is therefore a nursing responsibility to know how the organization is managed. Yet to far too many nurses, the organization outside the ward is a non-specific 'they'.

Similar arguments apply to their relationships with both the engineering and patient information functions. In both cases, when other functions are failing, the nurses need to devise short-term solutions. These will probably require greater input from them (a system of checking every patient every half-hour to relieve the anxiety caused by the lack of a working call button, for example), and they may take the decision that such short-term measures jeopardize the chance of a longer-term solution, because the engineers will rely on them doing so. In such cases, which one hopes would not be the norm, they must make sure that the discomfort experienced by patients is made known and loudly. They must use it to ensure that the longer-term solution is realized. This must be a conscious decision, a weighing up of two unacceptable alternatives in the awareness of the negative consequences of each. This is very different from simply sending off a form, making a vituperative phone call or complaining only to each other about it.

Katie Tyler chooses not to question Bert's unnecessary overcoat with the ward staff, believing that it is more important that she is not thought a 'snoop' than that patients receive good care. The junior doctors, not knowing the answer to Mr Bird's question, do not take the responsibility of finding out, or of telling him they do not know, but take a guess and send him off somewhere inappropriate. This ungenerous act is occasioned by their own apprehension – as ungenerous acts usually are.

Last but not least, Adrian Kendal has valid reasons for his clinical views, and his commitment to his patients is not in doubt. However, he allows no challenge to his perception of reality, either from the physios or from John

Norland's paper on palliative care. The lack of this element of discipline makes him difficult to work with or for. In a system of interdependent specialists (indeed in any organization, as opposed to a one-man band), it is everyone's responsibility to engage in productive working relationships. Kendal is probably one of the organization's leaders, one of the opinion-formers. His behaviour exerts a powerful influence on his junior staff, who are of critical importance to the service delivered. So while Ruth Anderson may prefer to spend time with the more amenable Chisholm, she should choose to spend it developing the kind of robust relationship with Kendal that will enable her to challenge his mental models.

Focusing on health rather than illness
In part, this wide failure to accept responsibilities is due to a desensitizing of professionals to the needs of patients. Part of the role of a real manager is to keep reactions fresh.

The letter of complaint, research by the commissioners, concerns of the physios as a group and disparity in practice between the palliative care ward and others all indicate that parts of the trust see their purpose as the treatment of a clinical condition. If they saw it instead as 'the removal of obstacles to the achievement of patients' potentials' (Chapter 2), then they would have to give consideration to what those potentials were. In Mrs Jones's case the potential was for dying a good death.

In some, perhaps many, cases, like Mrs Bird's, where the outcomes are especially unclear, a decision must be made: whether to continue with treatment aimed at the lower levels in the hierarchy of clinical descriptions (see Chapter 2, page 48), which may prolong life and enable the patient to regain potentials at the higher levels, but may not, and will certainly prevent the patient from achieving their potential for a death that is a fitting end to their life.

Here the decision needs to be made by someone, or a group of people, focusing on the potentials of the patient (levels 0, +1 and +2), while understanding levels −1 to −9 sufficiently to be able to assess probabilities of outcome. The clinician responsible for levels −5 to −9 may not be the best person to take this decision, at least not alone. In the case study, Adrian Kendal appears to do just that. What is more, the person with the greatest interest in Mrs Bird at levels 0, +1 and +2 (her son) is dismissed by Peggy West as a problem and is not allowed to contribute to the formal discussion of his mother's treatment because the ward round cannot wait for him to return.

This is such a thorny issue that solutions in different places will differ. The development of palliative care as a specialty is one response to the problem; GP beds in hospitals is another; the increasing interest in End of Life care protocols is another. Chief executives will not know the solutions, but they must persuade their staff to work together and with other agencies to try to develop them.

Hillside Trust has a centre of excellence, Nightingale Ward, yet its philosophy, principles and practices of care are not shared more widely. Why not? There is a respectable volume of management literature analysing the reasons why dissemination of good practice does or does not occur. One of the issues identified is that of 'star-envy', a belief, among peers of the leaders of lauded projects, that 'It is all right for them because they've got extra resources, better people, better premises etc.' What is more, this star-envy increases with the plaudits received, and occurs regardless of whether there are in fact additional resources. Dissemination *has* been successful where other staff have rotated through the project, particularly when project graduates are put in charge of similar initiatives elsewhere.

So Ruth Anderson, Jane Chisholm and John Norland need not berate themselves for the fact that this is happening at Hillside, but they do need to find ways of ensuring that it does not continue to do so. They will need to consider what kind of evidence Adrian Kendal and his colleagues will find credible, what will convince them that there is a problem and that they need to make changes and how they can be convinced that Nightingale Ward can be a resource rather than a threat to them.

Of course, HCPs lose their ability to care when others stop caring for them, and we need to make sure that they are given proper support, not moral support ('I know you're doing a great job'), not slushy sentimental appreciation, but robust support and challenge, in the manner described in this book.

If we do not make efforts to ensure that people facing such a significant, unimaginably awesome, event as their own death do so with support and care, then we are indeed 'abandoning the patient', we are not really managing, we are not really caring, we are not doing our job.

Community mental health services

'We keep hearing about all this new money and yet you're telling us we've got to make cuts, how is that?!' Chris Graham demanded. 'This is preposterous, it's a service that's truly effective and we've got to disband it? I thought things were supposed to be getting better after the trust merger, this is just as bad as ever!'

'Chris, you know it's so that we can begin introducing the Early Intervention Service,'[1] said Trisha.

'For which there is no real evidence whatever!' interrupted Chris. 'Innovative practice, yes, and lots of support from the centre,[2] but proven effectiveness? Hardly. There's plenty of evidence to show that IPS[3] *does* work. And now it has to be cut. You know it's having demonstrable results, and not just here. You'd think that getting people back into work would be seen as a vote-winner, by someone, wouldn't you?'

'Yes I know,' sighed Trisha, 'but we've got to give greater priority to EIS, it's a government target.'

'Yes, but they also want sustainable communities, social inclusion, and to build up "social capital"!' snapped Chris. 'And we could make progress towards all that if they would just leave us to do so, without all these targets. It would be good to give them a target, to abolish targets!'

Trisha laughed. 'Chris I understand how you feel but we've got to do it, let's just work out the best way, so that staff who are affected by the changes don't get demoralized.'

'And clients? Don't they matter?' retorted Chris. 'We've got people on the brink of getting employment, as well as those in jobs for the first time in years, who are dependent on our ongoing support. It will mean them all getting back into the income support trap. They'll be *financially* as well as *therapeutically* worse off, doesn't anyone *care* about this?!'

Trisha did care, she did know how valuable the IPS service had been. She was a sector manager in the new Trust, and Chris was the consultant psychologist attached to her sector. Chris had been a major sponsor of the IPS, which had been operating for over two years now. It had managed to move several clients back into competitive employment – which meant they were much better off both financially and therapeutically, Trisha thought, than in sheltered employment and work placements. Good as these were, clients had never got anything like the going rate for the work they did. It had taken a while for front-line staff to adjust to offering the new service; many had been taken aback by the level of coaching some clients needed, once they were in employment as well as beforehand; but all in all it had been a great success and everyone involved was pleased with the results.

Only a year ago she and Chris had both been employed by Deanside, a Trust that was wholeheartedly enthusiastic about working jointly with colleagues in social services and education, to address social and employment needs of their patients as well as health care. She remembered discussing the merger with Chris when it was first proposed. They hadn't opposed it either, assuming, naively she now thought, that because Deanside was providing services that were more effective than those of North West City, the Trust with which they would merge, Deanside would 'take over' and spread their practice throughout the new, larger Trust. How wrong they were. The chief executive of the combined Trust turned out to be the NWC CE, and he had brought his whole team with him. There had been lip service to the 'impressive culture of engagement in Deanside', but all the management decisions taken since had undermined or directly sabotaged their collaborative approach. Compared with Deanside, the NWC executive team had never had such good relations with their local authority colleagues, and were suspicious that any collaborative ventures led to resources being shifted from the people who needed them most: patients with the most severe mental illnesses. The results of the merger had been characterized by the informal grapevine as a 'back to health' policy, as managers with health backgrounds were appointed to all the key roles.

Trish knew that some people supported the changes. If mental health was to fight the big guns (the large acute sector trusts) for a fair share of resources, it needed management teams of the highest calibre, and certainly the team from NWC seemed to have the support of the Strategic Health Authority, the people who monitored trust performance and made decisions about Trust mergers. But the impact on services, on the lives of their clients, certainly worried her, and many others. The IPS was the latest casualty. Now that Day Care services across the combined Trust had been merged, to achieve efficiency savings, IPS had been chosen as the saving. 'IPS is an excellent idea' the new Day Care Services manager had told Trisha, 'but it's not *cost effective* in today's climate.'

Trisha completely sympathized with Chris's despair, she too felt helpless. She had thought that perhaps the local authority (LA) would jump up and down about it. Failing that, the local strategic partnership (LSP). But so far these had hardly been consulted, and the LA had a devastating financial situation of its own, so they probably weren't in a position to object. She and Chris had been asked to investigate other, less costly employment alternatives to IPS, including work placement and voluntary work, and come up with an alternative proposal, but they knew the answers to that already. They had investigated all of these when the IPS had been set up, and had monitored them since. None of the existing employment schemes could duplicate IPS. Voluntary placements were all well and good, but didn't get people back into gainful employment, and better integrated into the community. Everyone recognized that in the end something like IPS was far more likely to improve people's confidence and self-esteem and keep them in work. All the evidence suggested it led to fewer incidents of relapse, and hence to a lessening of the long-term burden on care services. But somehow this wasn't what people counted when they looked at 'cost effectiveness'.

It had been such a great success, but then she did want to see the Early Intervention Scheme in operation too. 'This would never have happened in the old Trust,' she thought, 'somehow or other we'd have managed both.'

A few hours later, Trisha and Chris were again sitting at the same table, this time with thirteen other colleagues. 'It's like that in mental health,' thought Trisha, 'everyone wears so many hats, you keep meeting the same people at different meetings!' She wondered whether that was why so many of the meetings ended up covering similar ground, and often didn't seem to resolve any issues or agree a way forward. This time it was the 'Children's Mental Health Liaison Group' an opportunity for all those working with children who were in any way affected by a mental health problem (whether their own or their parents') to share information and management strategies. Trisha wasn't a member of it, but had been invited along when she had raised the question of how the new family therapist was working out, and what outcomes she could demonstrate. 'Oh, she's invaluable,' Trisha had been told, 'come to the liaison meeting and you'll see just how much we need her.'

Now here she was and, to her surprise, almost the entire one-and-a-half-hour meeting was devoted to just one case, introduced by a health visitor, of suspected child abuse on the part of a co-habiting couple with a history of problem drug use. It became apparent quite quickly that neither the health visitor, nor anyone else present, had any evidence of the abuse that the health visitor feared was taking place, and the meeting concentrated on the health visitor's feelings of anxiety and how she could deal with them.

When the meeting finished, with no recommendations with regard to the child or family in question but several for the health visitor, one of the senior social workers, Henryk, buttonholed Trisha.

'I've been looking at the service specification for the Early Intervention Service,' said Henryk. 'I notice that yet again there is no social worker input on the cards. But family work and family therapy are considered essential to this kind of intervention, that's just what's missing at present, and very much one of our department's strengths. Why on earth wasn't I invited to comment on staffing and structure?'

'It's all been a bit of a rush, frankly, because of the restructuring' said Trisha. 'There *is* some mention of giving more attention to social models', she added.

'But no talk of incorporating any of the people who embody these models!' Henryk sounded exasperated: 'All the emphasis is on hiring more people from a cognitive-behavioural therapy background. That's good of course, but it's just not rounded enough. Presumably people assume social workers are hostile to assertive outreach on principle. Honestly, we're as enthusiastic about this as the next person!'

'I don't think you've been singled out for exclusion', said Trisha. 'OT seems not to have been consulted either'. 'What a missed opportunity!' Henryk sighed. 'Do the managers and commissioners ever actually ask clients what *they* see as their problems, how *they* would like to function, what kind of professional help *they* need?! Or do they only care now about profile, stars, and management careers!?'

Trisha ignored this and tried to think of something positive to say about the EIS. She knew it was career suicide for a manager in the present Trust to cast serious doubt about its targets or strategic direction. It *could* all be for the best, she thought. Early intervention *might* be as efficacious as people were hoping, but it could just be an example of policy makers, managers and clinicians all jumping the gun. She hoped it wasn't just to help a government get re-elected or research papers published.

'Pity to see the IPS go though', said Henryk.

'Yes', said Trish, 'but if EIS had to take precedence I'll try to ensure that it works.'

'Yes, but will all your clinical colleagues?' asked Henryk.

And Trisha wasn't sure. The clinicians were angry at being told what to do by people they saw as jumping to the tune of those who shouted loudest. She would try and get staff to focus on the positive, but it would be difficult.

'Well at least no-one is being made redundant,' she said in reply, 'that's one good thing at least.'

Fiona White, Edgelee's Medical Director, was wondering what to do about a circular that had just arrived on her desk from the Department of Health, inviting bids for spending £200k on hepatitis C prevention among injecting drug users. But the deadline was the 4th of June, just one week away. A call to Frank Sargent, the consultant responsible for dependency services, seemed unavoidable, much as Fiona would have *liked* to avoid it. It wasn't long since he had been extremely rude to her about plans to introduce service users onto recruitment panels for clinical staff. He hadn't shown the slightest interest in listening to the evidence Fiona had offered, that showed that the new arrangement created none of the headaches he imagined, and had also been positively evaluated by everyone concerned, including the job candidates themselves. Fiona had found this the more irritating as all this had been discussed at a meeting of clinical directors that Frank had attended three months ago. Now he had pretended it had come as a bolt from the blue. She had e-mailed him the papers anyway, but had not heard from him since.

That wasn't the only reason Fiona was sure Frank wouldn't respond well to her request for help with this bid. He wasn't responding well to any requests for assistance at the moment. She knew he was very aggrieved at the discussions over his job plan,[4] protesting strongly that he took on far more than colleagues but that this wasn't being recognised in his P.As. Ever since he had refused to take on anything extra. 'Only if you pay me, Fiona', he had said on several occasions. 'If the government wants to turn us into piece workers then they'll have to pay when they want extra pieces.'

'But Frank, this isn't the government, this is me, this is for your patients', Fiona had thought, but not actually said.

She knew that Frank did care about patients, but she felt helpless in the face of this obduracy. Caught between two obstinate sides: politicians and her colleagues!

Meanwhile, what about the circular? She gritted her teeth and lifted the 'phone.

'Trisha. I want to have a word with you', said Jane Gupta, Head of Counselling Services, as they both made their way to the Sector Management Team meeting. 'I'm getting good reports about Daniella, the family therapist, and I wondered if we could think about giving her some extra hours? The CMHTs are finding it so useful to have someone to refer to.'

'Well, I don't know,' said Trisha, 'with the merger of all the Day Care Services there are other staff who may be available, without us incurring more costs. That could work well if Daniella could be a source of advice and support to them. I think that was what her job description specified, wasn't it?'

'Well, yes it was, but she really doesn't have time to do that,' said Jane, 'you saw how useful she was in that liaison meeting the other day, and her diary is full of meetings like that one.'

'Well, perhaps you could have a word with her about that when you both have your next one-to-one, and get her to refocus?' said Jane. 'Get her to concentrate on what we employed her to do?'

'Trisha, Daniella herself feels this is the best way to use her time, and she's a professional, I think we can assume she is the best judge of that. We just need to give her a few more hours, that's all.' The conversation had ended there, as Trisha had needed to open the meeting.

Thinking about this exchange later, Trisha laughed. Well it was better than crying, she thought. She had investigated the 'health visitor support group' (as she now called it to herself) afterwards, and learned that several of its members seemed to have little or no support or supervision, and so used the meetings for that purpose. Of course, Trisha had no remit for staff belonging to other organizations, but it applied to some of her own sector staff too. Something else for her to get to grips with.

She had tried to persuade her sector management meeting to think afresh about the resources within the sector, so they could see how best to deploy any Day Care Services staff who might become available. To help inform the discussion, she had asked all the heads of the services offered in the sector to give her their most recent activity figures. What a nightmare that had proved to be! Some had made a genuine effort, but several had insisted they couldn't disaggregate them from the figures across the whole Trust. And of those who had, none could answer questions about the impact on them of any changes in staffing. 'So we're making decisions blind'. she thought. 'This is how people can get away with decisions to cut services in the name of efficiency, because we never have any decent information to challenge them with. What an impossible and thankless job this is.

Questions

In many parts of the country, professionals working in mental health feel that their service is desperately underfunded. If this is the case, it is all the more important that resources devoted to people with mental health needs are used wisely, to the very best effect.

1 Are the resources referred to in the case being used wisely?
2 What changes do the Trust management team need to make if the Trust's clients are to receive effective, efficient services?

Discussion
Are the resources being used wisely?
On the contrary, the resources described (mostly people and their time) are being used with great profligacy. For example:

- Too many meetings: the Children's Mental Health Liaison Group meeting wastes over 22 person hours on the discussion of an issue outside its remit. There is an indication too that this kind of poorly chaired, unfocused, multidisciplinary meeting is a regular and frequent occurrence.
- Cuts instead of efficiencies: a service (IPS) that shows evidence of long- term effectiveness and cost savings is being abandoned, and the experience and skills, that are a valuable resource, are being lost with no plans to capture them in any systematic way.
- Repetition: Trisha is going to investigate alternatives to IPS and to write a report, when the information is already in the organization. This will waste not only her time, but that of anyone who reads the repetitive report.
- Lots of 'feel bad' talk: people (e.g. Chris and Trisha) spend a lot of time complaining about a decision, but do not use that energy and time to come up with alternative proposals or effective strategies for challenging the decision.
- More haste less speed: the staffing structure and skill mix of the EIS has been decided without consultation with partner departments and disciplines, resulting in a model that is unchallenged (hence not as robust as it could be) and not supported by people who are potential referrers and who may yet prove to be useful resources.
- Not being ready: when opportunities for new resources arise (e.g. for hepatitis C prevention) the Trust is poorly geared up to take advantage of them and has to think afresh each time how to approach them.
- Ignoring dynamics: an initiative which shows promise, such as the inclusion of patients in staff recruitment, risks being scuppered because its rationale has been poorly presented to a key opinion former.
- Not using information: the skill mix and staying levels in Trisha's sector are potentially inappropriate; no-one knows whether this is the case, and can't find out.

- People not using their time effectively: the family therapist is not observing her job description, and is not being challenged about this. Other staff feel they are not being supervised and take time from other meetings to seek support.

All this waste, and yet the individuals described are all passionately concerned about their work. How does this happen? It is the result of reactivity, when people and organizations are in 'reactive' or 'victim' mode.

In the case study, we see Chris Graham furious with the government at its insistence on introducing a particular form of care, even though it has certainly not insisted that other services should be disbanded. We see Trisha feeling helpless at the decisions of the Trust, believing it to be 'career suicide' to express a contrary view and feeling that 'this would never have happened' under the previous management team. We see her worrying that government priorities and decisions by the Department of Health are being skewed by a few people whose motives she distrusts. Henryk assumes his exclusion from the consultation process is based on a stereotype of social work, and is cynical about management priorities. Fiona feels a victim of Frank's intransigence, and he of hers. Frank is so disgruntled about the discussions over his job plan that he is letting it affect the way he approaches his work. Jane sees the family therapist as a victim of a constraining job description.

As a result of their feelings of helplessness, people miss chances to influence events for the better. Trisha reacts to management requests compliantly, rather than determining what are her own priorities and raising her concerns. She sees herself and her services as a victim of cuts, short-term political gain, and half-hearted support from senior management. Chris doesn't make his evidence about IPS available in a constructive manner, to people who can change the decision, instead he complains about it to someone who can't. Trisha doesn't challenge the people at the liaison meeting about their use of time, instead she stores it in her head as part of a litany of complaints about her 'clinical colleagues'. When Fiona has a chance to shift Frank's mood, by reminding him of his patients, she doesn't do so. And Jane is annoyed at Trisha's suggestion that she manage the family therapist's performance, rather than using this thought to reflect on whether she could achieve what she wants by changing her own management style.

Where there is a culture of reactivity, people feel that decisions are made without consultation and then presented as *faits accomplis*, that there is lack of concern for the care process, that there is little accountability 'downwards' only 'upwards', that they are powerless to alter the course of events. This powerlessness prevents them from seeing what they *can* do. They are not blind, stupid, or uncommitted, just disabled by this helplessness.

Underlying this reactivity is, often, a profound lack of information, and a lack of sufficient analysis of information that *is* available. Decisions are 'taken

blind', as Trisha suggests. Without credible information to endorse it, any decision can be seen cynically as politically motivated or as supporting someone's
career. In the case we see information not being available to support important
decisions about how to reconfigure day care services. Equally, we see good
information (about the inclusion of service users on appointment panels) not
being used effectively. Frank's attendance at a clinical directors' meeting was
mistakenly taken to mean that he supported the new appointments process. If
Fiona believed this initiative to be important, she should have engaged much
more directly with the people who need to endorse it, finding ways of helping
them to hear the evidence that supports her case.

If people were behaving proactively, how would things have been different? Chris and Trisha would have made a strong, well-evidenced case for the
IPS, at the same time demonstrating how the Trust could afford the new EIS.
They may have achieved the latter by enthusing colleagues about the potential of the EIS, and encouraging them to identify people and other resources
they could free up to staff it. They would have asked for ideas and evidence
about the shape of the service and the skills needed, and have knitted together
a proposal from the ideas they gathered. They may have found it useful to
make it clear that the EIS was a requirement and not an option, not in a
manner that fosters resentment and despair, but finding good arguments to
support it (the arguments that convinced policy-makers) and encouraging
people to help design it well, rather than have a less effective design imposed
upon them.

The two of them may also have reflected together on how it was that NCW
made a 'clean sweep' of the executive team in the merged Trust when the
Deanside managers were much more effective at service provision. They could
learn from this that whenever you are dependent on others for resources or
power doing well is not enough. Being seen to do well is also important. The
reputation of the Deanside team was not as good as that of the NCW one with
the people who had the greatest influence – the Strategic Health Authority –
and so their good services suffered as a result. Chris and Trisha may like the
Deanside managers more and applaud their client focus, but should also recognize that they failed in a key management task. This will help both of them
to accept the new team, to understand their emphasis on presenting a positive
front, and to gauge when and how to deal with them.

What changes do the Trust management team need to make if the Trust's clients are to receive effective, efficient services?

It is all too easy to imagine the new executive team despairing of many of the
people we have met here. There will need to be a considerable amount of
generosity and discipline to avoid writing these 'victims' off, especially as the
new team are on the receiving end of considerable hostility. If they are to 'turn'
some of these staff round and revitalize them and, with them, the organization

as a whole, they will need to develop significant personal credibility based on an insightful understanding of the issues, genuine commitment to meeting the needs of clients and empathy for the professionals involved. This does not mean that they have to leave day care services, for example, untouched, but it does mean that they must focus on efficiencies rather than on cuts.

When people are deeply into being a victim, challenges to their thinking and behaviour have to be gentle and, where possible, personalized to the individual concerned. Fiona's response to Frank about his fury at inclusion of service users on appointments panels misjudges his motivations by assuming that what will alter his perception is 'hard evidence'. This may have convinced her but he is feeling a victim, he needs something else as well. Instead of sending him an e-mail, she might have finished the call with something like: 'Why don't we make a time to discuss it, perhaps next week, and I can invite some of our colleagues who have been involved in the pilot. I know you don't have much time, but I think the kinds of problems you raise do need to be discussed and worked through.'

Sometimes reflecting back to people their own arguments can help:

> 'So, Jane, what you are telling me is that you don't know exactly what the family therapist does, and it isn't at all the same as the role we originally employed her to do, but she's well qualified and you like her, you want to increase her hours, costing us more money at a time when we are having to close our IPS service to meet our commitments on early intervention. Can you see this isn't a convincing case? I know you care very much about this service, so why don't we discuss it next week when you have had time to prepare a more convincing one. Yes, I know you are short of time, and that's why you might find it useful to discuss with it Trisha or to look at this case for additional funding that the Board has recently approved. I'm sure we can agree on something that suits us all.'

Keeping calm, staying in a positive ego state, rephrasing angry, helpless, accusatory statements in neutral terms that allow issues to be discussed. All of these are important.

There is always a danger with mergers of increasing the degree of reactivity (of people feeling 'done to') so the merger process always requires great care. This is especially so when designing new organization structures. The *way* the new charts are drawn up, people consulted, information and impressions gathered, thinking shared, will be every bit as important as their content. Indeed, because there are both advantages and disadvantages associated with every possible organizational structure, the actual result, the structure chosen, may be much less important than the manner in which it was decided upon.

Is that true? Are there not 'right' and 'wrong' structures for different circumstances? Let's think about it. An organizational structure is basically a way of representing who is accountable to whom for what. There are fundamentally only three choices to be made about it. One is whether you want a tall, thin organization, or a wide, lean one, and this is determined by how great a span of control you want at every level. In other words, does everyone have seven people reporting to them or seventy? Another is whether you want to centralize all your decision-making, so that important decisions are made by the people in head office and not by people on the shop floor (which you might if you were running, say, a burger chain), or decentralize it so that decisions are made by the people closest to the actions the decisions are about. The other is whether you cluster people together according to their specialization or function (accountants reporting to accountants, nurses reporting to nurses) or whether you do so around a product or a market, perhaps a geographical one (e.g. a locality team), or a particular client group (elderly care, cancer patients) or a particular kind of service (e.g. day case surgery).

None of these alternatives is good or bad, they are just better or worse at doing particular things. So a tall, thin organization is very useful in circumstances where you want to employ people for a long period and want to motivate them by being able to promote them regularly. It is good, too, at developing specialist skills because people receive good supervision. It is bad at transmitting information from the front line to the top management (because it has to go through so many levels to do so), so it isn't very useful in turbulent times and changing markets. A wide, lean organization is, of course, just the opposite. Great for moving information from bottom to top speedily, not good for supporting individuals when they need it. A 'functional' structure where people are managed within professional specialties is excellent at nurturing state-of-the-art specialist expertise, but not good at allowing communication between individual professionals (because formally any request for a change in practice would have to travel all the way up one professional line until it reached the point at which it joined that of the other profession and then all the way down that one). Divisional structures around care groups or localities allow good front-line communication but can sacrifice specialist expertise.

There are advantages and disadvantages of centralizing and decentralizing. Factors that tend to favour centralization are the need for speed and the ability to concentrate in one place the decision-makers and the resources that can support them. A desire to have decisions informed by local concerns and priorities and to make sure the organization and its front-line staff are engaged on the same purpose (especially where the staff concerned are specialists and professionals) will tend to favour decentralization.

It is very common for managers of organizations, particularly when they are newly in post, to observe all the disadvantages of the current structure, and to perceive all the advantages of an alternative. But they must think carefully and clearly, and compare the advantages and the disadvantages of each, and present both of these to the people involved. Of course, no organization is ever a 'pure' type, and most organizations work because there are enough of the behaviours associated with the last structure to make the disadvantages of the new one less of a problem. Gradually these reduce over time, and the problems of the new become apparent. By now there is a new set of managers who switch back to something very like the old, and the pendulum swings again.

So the new Edgelee managers may do better to resist any changes to structure for a good while; perhaps until they have really understood the way things are working at the moment. They could concentrate instead on cultures, on narratives, on gently helping people to weave new narratives where they are not victims but are in control. Then think about what structures would help them genuinely to be in control – so that the structure supports a spirit of care rather than hindering it.

The Edgelee management team will need to demonstrate progress towards government targets, including the introduction of the EIS, if they are to retain the support of the SHA and if they are to promote the 'can do' spirit that will be necessary for their ongoing success. However, they cannot determine priorities without discussing them with their key clinical staff, and without a good look at evidence and information. Where they have time they will benefit from using approaches from all the boxes of the Matrix in Chapter 5. Initially, they may need to enact certain activities quickly to meet externally imposed deadlines, and this may mean forgoing some of the middle and right-hand columns, but this should be seen as a temporary measure. They may get away with this early on, without increasing reactivity, if they make their reasoning clear, but unless they move quickly into real engagement, real opportunities for opinion formers to influence priorities and the direction of travel, the organization will soon be trapped in a vicious spiral of blame, helplessness and underperformance.

So far Edgelee managers have disbanded the IPS service as an efficiency saving. Of course, this has nothing whatever to do with efficiency: it is a straight cut. The presentation of the decision in this way is certain to increase the culture of 'victim-ness', of reactivity, of dependency, when the only way this organization will ever be successful is if its staff are proactive, taking true responsibility for their own effectiveness and for effective working relations with others. As soon as she can, Trisha and her colleagues need to learn about improvement (Chapter 4), so that when efficiency savings are needed they will be able to suggest the least worst option, and can be ahead of the game in introducing improvements that offer better services in the most efficient way. To do this she will need to generate information, information of the kind we explored in Chapter 4. Services of this kind tend to be awash with both data and information but do not bring it together in a way that enables decisions to be made. No-one likes collecting data when they can't see any reason for it, so it is often poor quality, but once Trisha starts to display the control charts and uses them as the basis for discussions at her management meetings her teams will soon start to make sure the data are sound.

The frustration of a real manager trying to transform the effectiveness and efficiency of these services will be very great. They will need to remind themselves, and frequently, that 'it is systems that fail, not people'; that these passionate clinicians have been badly let down by being undermanaged, by not being required to think clearly nor to work together productively and efficiently. As a result, they have been thwarted in their attempts to provide the kind of services they wish to. Real managers need to feel compassion rather than anger for the individuals concerned, while remaining strongly opposed to any obstructive behaviours, attitudes and practices they present. No, this is not easy, it's hard. Simple but hard. That is just what *real* management is.

Combining practice with management

'Well we know the missing £2 million is your fault, Mark', joked Karen, Mark's sister-in-law, as the family gossip gave way to conversation about work. 'You and your PEC colleagues. The PCT has always bailed St Swithin's out before so you must have told them their consultants weren't worth paying for!' Karen was joking at Simon's expense, and the group had been friends for so long that this was all taken with good humour.

Mark, Sarah, Simon and Guy had all been at medical school together and had remained friends. Mark and Sarah were married and both worked in general practice. Simon had specialized in paediatrics and worked at St Swithin's, a major teaching hospital, and Guy was a consultant in cardiology at the local hospital Borough General, where his wife Karen was the head of OT services. Simon's wife Ruth had been a nurse when they first met her, had become a nurse practitioner in general practice and more recently had been working on – well, what had she been doing? All sorts of roles within the local PCT. She and Mark bumped into each other quite a bit as he was a member of the PCT's professional executive committee, or PEC.

'Yes, I said they should only go ahead after they'd had a good look at the paediatrics budget', laughed Mark, but he didn't take the joke any further. St Swithin's had just announced that it would have a £2 million deficit this financial year and the press had been covering this enthusiastically. Mark's was one of the PCTs that was refusing to find additional funding.

'Mark's rethinking whether he wants to be on the PEC', Sarah filled the gap. 'He's seeing the PEC chair in a few days to talk it through so he's not seeing the funny side just now. I can see why he wants to give it up, the pressures are immense.'

'Oh but he's such an important asset to the PEC', Ruth said quickly. 'Mark,

I do understand the pressures but it's so important that good people like you are involved, is there anything in particular you are finding frustrating?'

'Oh, frustrating? Where do I start?' Mark replied. 'How about being asked to make impossible decisions, like this one: do we spend money on a small number of very sick children in a plush new building? Or on a large number of adults with mental health problems who receive a lousy understaffed service in wards that are old, decrepit and thoroughly depressing? How about spending huge amounts of time and energy on talking about money when what I care about is clinical services? How about other GPs constantly whining that we're not being fair, or managers expecting us to do all the dirty work when it comes to giving bad news to other doctors. That's just for starters! Want any more?'

They all laughed. 'Apart from that, Mrs Lincoln, how did you enjoy the show?' one of them said.

'I sympathize about the time and energy wasted on things that don't matter', said Karen. 'There is now an hour-long meeting every day about breeches in the A&E targets, that involves everyone analysing yesterday's figures, saying where things went wrong and giving an action plan about how this will not happen in the future. I wouldn't mind so much, although it is a lot of time out of the day, but I made almost all of these suggestions two years ago when I did that work on delayed discharges. We could have implemented them all by now, in a properly planned manner involving all the clinical staff, and got them well embedded. But instead, people receive edicts to say that they must do x, y or z, with apologies that there isn't time to consult them because of the pressure to reach targets. Most of these changes don't need extra money either, there was no reason not to get on with them much earlier, people just didn't care before.'

'Yes, we can grumble about politicians and their targets,' said Guy, 'but they have put some energy into the system, they are getting things sorted out.'

'Hrmph,' said Sarah, 'only on the surface. Things are just as bad as they were underneath. I still have patients getting lost between St Swithin's, Borough and us, letters getting lost so I don't know that changes have been made to medication and I prescribe the wrong thing.'

'But that's not to do with politicians', said Guy.

'No, of course it isn't, it isn't even to do with money, or not a lot', said Sarah. 'It's about people caring about making these things happen so that they set up the systems that deliver it. Think of your example of the cardiology one-stop shop at St Swithin's. That was a great idea, the specialist cardiology outpatients clinic near A&E, so there was good cover, near the medical secretaries, so the tests could be done, the report written up and given to the patient to take away with them. Fantastic, that would have made life easier for us, for you, for the A&E staff, for patients, for everyone. It only needed a small amount of space to be freed up for a few staff to be moved, and it was all promised, remember, and then suddenly it has gone. A victim of another diktat to meet another target.'

'Yes, where is all the new money going?' asked Simon. 'It doesn't seem to be coming to any of us and between us we represent primary, secondary and tertiary care, so where is it going?'

'There are lots of new managers, of course', Guy remarked. 'Every time you turn round there's another post been created, and their salaries have gone through the roof.'

'But not enough to account for all the money, even if we count in the fact that all of your salaries have gone up too', noted Ruth. 'The new building at Borough must be part of it, the new premises for practices and health centres, the new clinics for smoking cessation, some of the stuff I'm doing on involving patients . . . There's a lot going on.'

'Just not as much as we keep promising people', said Mark. 'We keep raising people's expectations and then they get so demanding and litigious we have to practise so defensively, just when we're all under pressure to make sure we don't make any inappropriate referrals.'

'Oh Mark, you know that isn't true really', Ruth said exasperatedly. 'I think you're just passing on the views of some of the GPs at your last forum meeting. I heard it was a grumble from beginning to end. I know from the work I'm doing with patients that they truly understand that everyone has a budget and that choices have to be made, and they aren't at all unreasonable. Added to which, they're able and willing to take much more responsibility for their own conditions once they have been on one of the Expert Patient programmes – but can I get GPs to refer them on to those? No, they say patients will just be taught to be even more bolshie, to know how to be even more demanding, but the reverse is true. I can show you evidence of that.'

'So you're having problems with whingeing GPs, are you Mark?' asked Simon. 'Not surprising of course, that's all you all do all day!'

'Yes, yes, very funny,' said Mark, 'and you don't, I suppose. What about that orthopaedic team where the consultants can't agree among themselves on a protocol and are all doing their own thing? It's a nightmare to refer to, they all have different processes for accepting referrals, for keeping in touch with us, for discharging patients, we just don't know where we are.'

'Well that's up to you now, isn't it?' said Simon. 'You're in charge, the PCT, you call the shots. Wasn't that what they were all about? Bringing primary, secondary and tertiary care under the same roof, providing some, commissioning others and with the clinicians closest to the patients in the engine room? You say what you'll commission and we'll have to fall into line. We could do with you getting tougher actually. The problem is a few consultants who have been around a long time, who are used to being autonomous, who see protocols and agreed processes as a loss of clinical judgement. Most of us are fine about it, it's a generation thing, the more pressure you bring to bear the more likely we are to bring them into line.'

'But why does exerting this pressure always come down to me?' asked Mark. 'Not you, the PCT', Simon replied.

'But who at the PCT?' asked Mark. 'Whenever people want a bust-up with difficult doctors it's the GPs on the PEC who are called in to do it. You've just described issues that you and your managers should have sorted out years ago. Who's now asked to deal with it? I am. The PEC GPs are going to a meeting next week with one of the teams you've described, and we'll be the ones expected to say the hard stuff that no one else has had the courage to say. It's the same with GPs who aren't performing, making too many inappropriate referrals to Guy, for example. The PCT will want us to go and talk about it with them. Why should it be us? Our referrals patterns are fine (mostly), Borough consultants have decided which referrals are appropriate or not, the PCT managers have done the analysis practice by practice, why should it be *us* doing the dirty work? Why not Guy? Why not our local managers? I can't work magic. I'm a clinician who can give views about things that affect me personally, but this doesn't. If I do say what they want me to say I make life more difficult for myself, my fellow GPs feel got at and are resentful, and I'll have a hell of a job getting a patient admitted to that Swithin's team next time I need to. This is a job that is no fun at all.'

'When you started you thought you could really make changes,' said Karen, 'you had a whole list of things you wanted to implement, what happened to all of those? Surely you can see it has been worthwhile?'

'That's just it', replied Mark. 'I can't see any of the changes I wanted. I said that to the chief executive the other day, that I didn't feel any of my ideas had been taken up, and she was surprised, said she thought they had worked really hard with us and that if we weren't here they would have done things very differently. And I can see that's true, they do ask us what we think about things and they do listen and design their agenda accordingly. It's just that the things they ask us about aren't the things I care about. For example, when we discussed relations with Borough recently (and how to spend less money with you, Guy), we had great ideas about outpatient clinics and reducing the length of stay, but actually all they wanted was ideas about how to reduce admission rates. Of course we came up with some and they seemed pleased, but it wasn't our priority though, and they still haven't done anything about outpatients, which is what would make our lives so much easier.'

'So you've been colonized by the managers, is that it?' Guy asked. 'I know I've tried very hard to avoid being a tame clinician. It's hard though. Unless you work with them you can't get anything done at all.'

'Not colonized exactly, tame perhaps, but actually I just think I'm pretty invisible to them. They speak a language I don't understand, and seem to have to do all sorts of technical things I can't get my head round. Take practice-based commissioning, for example, or better still, developing local priorities. Both exciting opportunities to make a difference, right? Wrong, they just involve filling in lots of forms in particular ways and submitting them to people I never meet who seem to speak another language. I do sometimes wonder whether I should try and get on top of that, but it seems a waste of my skills, I'm a good GP, why should I try to become a mediocre manager? I don't seem to chair the forum meetings well (you're right Ruth, they do just turn into a complaining session) but that doesn't seem to matter to them, they don't ever comment on it. I could do with some help frankly. Whenever I introduce one of our new initiatives (which I do support) the GPs all say "So what do you want us to give up then?" How can I answer that? I know they are busy but I also think they could work a lot smarter and less hard if they just invested some time in some of these new approaches. Yes, the Expert Patient programme, Ruth, referring carers to the carers' forum too. A lot of time saved further down the track, but they won't give them a chance, these ideas. I hear that in my sleep: "What do you want me to give up then?" And blow me if the managers didn't say exactly the same thing to me the other day. I was asking why we couldn't define some local priorities to meet real local needs (carers is what I was thinking of at the time) and the response was: "So which of the national targets do you want us to miss then?" It's like dealing with sulky children, the lot of them.

'And so often I'm just caught in the middle. Take the Queenstown practice. There is a trio of truly committed GPs, doing far more than many of their colleagues, dealing with much more complex cases because the community mental health teams and the social workers know they can refer to them when no one else will take them, and they are becoming swamped. They've asked for extra resources and the PCT have offered something ridiculous like a session a month or something. I've tried to speak up for them, but now that the GPs are behaving emotionally in the way they are interacting with the PCT they seem to have been written off, no one believes they will really go ahead and close down. They will though. It's a mini-tragedy, actually. They are good doctors who need support. There are lots of ways they could organize themselves better and not feel so pressured, but while they feel this way they can't see that. If the PCT would only help them through this crisis we could keep them on the rails. But no, you see, caught in the middle.'

'Yes they are keen on "emotional intelligence" ', said Ruth. 'They don't seem to realize that there is a lot of commitment and talent out there in people who do respond emotionally to things. Somehow we have to find ways of supporting them and harnessing that emotion rather than blaming and judging. It's a kind of political correctness almost. A bit like their mantra about openness and honesty. They seem to go overboard sometimes and start to blame people for being obstructive when they are just presenting a counter view. Remember that time I challenged them over the reports that needed to go to the coroner's office, Simon? When we had a half-finished report in the files and the director concerned insisted it should go as part of the documentation and I knew it gave completely the wrong impression? Well I was told off in no uncertain terms for being defensive and obstructive. They had to back down in the end because one of the LA services named in it threatened to sue for defamation if it went in its unfinished form, but it was a kind of political correctness that overrides judgement sometimes.'

'Yes, getting directors to listen is a real problem', said Mark. 'I just can't get anyone to listen to me about Jill, the modernization manager. I know she talks a good business but she never delivers on anything, I've lost track of the times she's let me down, and I know I'm not alone, but whenever I try to talk with her line manager I get the feeling I'm being seen as the problem – not her.'

'Yes, I've noticed that', said Ruth. 'I've done the same and had the same response.'

'Just as well there are other good modernization people around then', said Guy. 'I never thought I would say this but I found the pathways work we've done in cardiology hugely useful – enlightening almost. It's prompted us to think sensibly about things I used to take for granted, and helped me to see why GPs were finding our service so difficult to engage with. Of course the GPSIs[5] help, now that we know some of the primary care folk personally we have more confidence in them, and I notice that's rubbed off on our nurse specialists and admin staff as well. They used to talk disparagingly of primary care and they are now much more positive. We still have some difficulties when we refer to the specialists at your place, Simon, but it's getting better. Even they were surprised, I think, when they came to the pathway meetings, to find that they were making life quite so difficult for patients and for the rest of us. That clinic they are setting up a week before surgery to make sure that all the test results are up to date and so on has cut down the number of cancelled ops considerably.'

'Yes, we've found that too,' said Sarah, 'that's all working much better. It's still a pain knowing who to refer to if we have an elderly patient who falls and we think it may be cardiac in origin. Do we refer to care of the elderly or CHD? The PCT won't pay for internal referrals, so if we get it wrong the patient bounces out again to us rather than being referred on to the right one automatically. That's so stupid, can't someone do something about that?'

'Well', said Simon, 'if we changed the model so that a hospital like St Swithin's ran all the services for the local population we wouldn't dream of that happening.'

'Yes, take over the world, why don't you?' asked Sarah.

'Well, I don't see why it's any worse that PCTs running everything, just different', replied Simon. 'Karen, you've always said you don't want your services being sucked out into the community, that it would be much more inefficient and you'd be dealing with much more trivia instead of people who really need you. Haven't you said that?'

'Yes, I have said that and I think it's true. I do think both perspectives are needed though, the acute and the primary care.'

'Not least to meet the needs of carers', said Mark. 'It's bad enough now. It would surely be worse if we were all managed by the hospital.'

'That's the second time you've mentioned carers, Mark', said Karen. 'Any particular reason?'

'Yes, I've been dealing with one of our patients who is going under, so unnecessarily, I just hate to see it happening.' Mark frowned. 'Eleanor Brown has been such a lovely patient of mine, ever since I started at the practice. Sarah, you know her. She's 80 now and her husband has MS. She's caring for him at home, has done for years, but he's becoming more and more dependent and she's finding it increasingly difficult to cope. The district nursing team visits, and the home care team, and the physio (the OT and dietitian have been involved too). But the burden on Mrs Brown is immense. Especially now that Suzi, one of our district nurses, is carrying an extra caseload, to cover someone on maternity leave. (Honestly, maternity leave! Why is pregnancy such a surprise to NHS managers, a workforce with large numbers of women of child-bearing age and no money set aside for maternity? Other staff just have to cover. At the moment there are three district nurse teams without leaders, so they are all hugely stretched.) Anyway, where was I? Yes, Suzi has had to reduce the nursing input to the Browns, so Mrs Brown is having to get her husband into and out of bed herself, at 80. She asked the home care team to help her the other day and they said they couldn't because they hadn't had the right training. Mrs Brown was furious, pointed out that she hadn't either, and what did they suggest, leaving him in the chair all night? She was nearly in tears when I visited last week. Said she just didn't understand how a care plan could be agreed with her, and then reneged on just because of staff shortages. She wants to be thought of as part of the team herself, and have her hours respected too. She asked why decisions about which staff to deploy don't take into account her needs.'

'Aren't they supposed to now?' asked Sarah. 'Aren't they supposed to have their own assessment by social services, and isn't there a Carers' Forum, I remember a strategy for carers, don't I? Last year some time?'

'Yes, yes and yes,' said Mark, impatiently, 'the Carers' Forum is a good thing, it helps carers to access the social services assessment and gives other support too, and yes that was all described in a strategy paper, and the Forum coordinator was appointed as a result. But GPs don't refer to the Forum, the coordinator is having a hard time getting in to see them in their practices, gets fobbed off with the manager and just isn't getting the results she hoped for. GPs do very little for the carers, they are so focused on the person being cared for. That was what I was agitating about making a local priority. There are a few

QOF[6] points relating to carers – three, I think – but just not enough to make anyone take it seriously. I was hoping we could find some local resources to encourage them to do so, that's when I was asked which of the national targets I wanted them taken away from. Honestly, these people are being so badly let down and I can't get anyone to take it seriously. What's the point of being on the PEC if I can't influence something so important and so basic? I really feel I could achieve more, spend my time more effectively going to see the Browns.'

'Oh Mark, this is obviously a real dilemma for you, whether being on the PEC is worthwhile enough to justify all the work and aggro. If it would help at all to discuss it, as I know most of the people involved, do give me a ring', Ruth offered.

'But let's drop it for now,' said Sarah, 'I've had enough of work, I want to hear what you all think about the new Tarantino film.'

Questions

1 If you were Ruth, how could you support Mark?
2 Can the friends influence this health economy for the better?
3 What difference would generosity and discipline make?

Discussion

How can Ruth support Mark?

Ruth is a friend of Mark's and knows him to be an excellent GP and also committed to thinking beyond his practice to the health of the community. She can also see that he needs support in his corporate role on the PEC, and could encourage him to seek it, but just what kind of support?

Mark is having difficulty in:

- encouraging fellow GPs to consider proposals he believes will be beneficial for them and their patients;
- having his concerns, enthusiasms and ideas taken seriously by managers;
- discussing issues with managers in a way that makes sense to them both.

He himself points out that he could easily become a mediocre manager instead of an excellent GP, yet he finds that he cannot influence events as a GP.

People with dual skills, both clinical and managerial, can be highly influential. If they can speak both languages and understand the enthusiasms and the legitimate concerns of both groups then they can be a major factor in ensuring that energy and commitment are exploited and not wasted. They do this by encouraging both groups to consider the views of the other, and by challenging their peers, in whichever group, to think constructively about their reactions and responses. But Mark's worry that he could become a mediocre manager instead of a good GP is a perceptive one. It would be all too easy for him to become bogged down in jargon and deadlines, and lose sight of the distinctive contribution he could make. If he does so it will be because he has got caught up in the complicated easy, rather than the simple hard.

In the wealth of detail surrounding such activities as the local development programme, or the preparation for practice-based commissioning (or whatever is the current newest policy initiative), it will be easy to feel it is necessary to understand every term and debate every point, or to give up and leave the 'technicalities' to managers. Working on the simple hard would involve concentrating instead on developing real management skills (of the kind described in this book), and on seeing patterns rather than details. Patterns? For any new initiative, you need to understand its background (what is driving it) and its significance in terms of outcomes (what it may achieve), of inputs (resources that it will require) and of risk (what may go wrong and what impact that may have).

For Mark to be able to do this he is going to need support in keeping the simple hard in mind when faced with yet another set of policy initiatives and deadlines, and, perhaps even more immediately, he needs to learn how to challenge his colleagues effectively. At the moment he is presenting ideas he believes in, and meeting, as he himself notes, "sulky child" behaviour from both GPs and managers. Without realizing it, they are inviting him into a complementary ego state, either to join them in "sulky child", with the government or a particular policy as the nasty parent, or to become the critical, blaming parent himself. He needs to be shown some simple ways of staying calm, and of dealing with *what* is said, rather than how it is said. All those involved are intelligent people dealing with things they care about, so they will be able to devise solutions if they can stay focused and in a positive frame of mind. Using 'I' language will be important here: 'Actually I found when I tried it that it worked fine, a few problems with . . . but on the whole it was much better than the way I'd been doing it before', or, if necessary, 'Well it may not be the best way forward, but we don't have a choice and I do think that it will have benefits, so let's get on with it with a will and not waste our energy fighting it.'

Behaviours like these can be infectious (as we saw in Chapter 6, they are invitations to others to behave well too), and while the initial effort to adopt them may be great, it could be thought of as an investment worth making. Mark has an opportunity to practise these just waiting for him: the regular meeting, that he chairs, with other GPs. Ruth could usefully discuss this with him, or recommend some training or reading that will help. This alone will make the role seem much more 'doable'.

What about the decisions Mark finds so hard: whether to spend money on this service or another? He hates having to make these when he knows that both services are needed, and is almost angry (certainly frustrated) at being required to. His natural reaction will be to blame the lack of resources that makes such a decision necessary, but he can be much more constructive than that, he can encourage much more effective use of resources in all services (Chapter 4) so that care improves across the board. Before he can do so he may need to consider the way he responds to these situations (in the terminology of Chapter 6, activating events). Is he bringing to them an irrational set of beliefs that are leading him to some unhelpful conclusions? If so, it is worth challenging those beliefs. For example, he may believe that it is simply not right that such choices need to be made and that if they do he can't stand it (see Chapter 6), and this belief may lead him to feel anxiety, depression and unhealthy anger. If he can examine those beliefs and see that there is always a need to make choices and that he is as well placed as anyone to contribute to those decisions, then he can move into the much more empowered position of concern, sadness and healthy anger.[7]

Can the friends introduce this health economy for the better?

The friends are finding lot of different people in the health economy to blame. Are they justified in doing so? Or is there any responsibility they could take for helping things to work better?

Clearly, where people have responsibilities to fulfil and do not do so, then we have some justification for blaming them. For example, Karen and Guy both note that '*they* didn't do anything about' the recommendations Karen had made in her report about the causes of delayed discharges, Sarah blames targets for the sudden removal of an agreed pot of money to implement the one-stop specialist cardiology shop, they almost all suggest that someone is to blame for not enough of the new money coming into their part of the service, patients are blamed for being litigious, governments for raising expectations. Do they really think that managers, politicians and patients are all at fault? Perhaps, although it isn't usually articulated in quite that way: the people usually blamed are 'them'. 'They should have implemented those changes two years ago', 'they didn't do anything about . . .', 'they don't care about . . .'

Let us look at who 'they' are in these cases. Karen investigated the cases of delayed discharges and presented her findings and recommendations, then 'they' didn't act on them. Whose responsibility was it to act? Well, Karen will have been asked to investigate, so the person who commissioned the work is certainly one of 'them'. His or her manager too will probably know of the work, and be in a position to hold both Karen and her manager to account, so he or she could be included. But we saw in Chapter 7 that responsibility goes hand-in-hand with information, so we ought really to include anyone who knew of these recommendations and did nothing about them. What about

Karen herself? The members of the board or committee she presented them to? Members of the professional groups she had consulted and who had received a copy of the report? Now that they all knew that better outcomes could be achieved if things were done differently, then they all had a responsibility to try to make that happen. Waiting for 'them' to do something about it is, we said in Chapter 7, irresponsible. That is a strong statement, and many of the people involved will hold little power to influence the behaviour of others, but they can all change their own behaviours, and if everyone did that – well, in many situations that is all that is needed. Some of those people *will* be in a position to influence others, because of either their organizational authority or their professional status. They carry a greater responsibility. Whoever they are, now that they know something needs to be done they must think through carefully and realistically (not naively, but not being defeatist about it either), what they personally can do to support it, and then do it. If we all truly believed that there is no 'them', only 'us', we would have to do this. We would have to think about our responsibilities in relation to every decision made by the committees we sit on, and to every idea we come across in conversation that will enable the system to work better.

So Sarah, Mark, Guy and Simon can all help to ensure that the very next pot of money that becomes available is spent on the one-stop shop develop-ment; they may even be able to help people to think of a way of doing it without needing that money. They may find, when they try, that the next free money is immediately earmarked for something else, and they may find that they agree that this 'something' is a higher priority. Now they needn't feel disgruntled about the lack of the one-stop shop, because they see why it isn't happening. Or they may find that the money is being diverted to a quick fix to meet a government target. They would be right to be angry at this if it doesn't secure any long-term improvements in the system, but they can dispel that anger too if they resist the temptation to rail against politicians, and try instead to see the world from their point of view (Chapter 5), accepting that targets can have their uses. In that frame of mind they can lobby managers with alternative means of meeting the targets with integrity.

Mark, in the case, reported another interesting kind of blame. He observed that the PCT managers were reacting against a team of GPs who were excellent clinicians but were behaving emotionally in their interactions with the PCT. While this level of emotion is not helping the team to devise solutions to their problems there is no point in castigating them or punishing them for this; they need help. People in the greatest need of our help along the maturity continuum are also the most aggressive and 'difficult'. Choosing to see the need rather than the behaviour is hard work, but whenever we respond in anger, whinge to others, take an easy way out by agreeing with someone that the world is against them, then we are part of the problem rather than its solution. The PCT needs to help in practical terms (if necessary on a temporary basis) so that they can find space to think, and help in behavioural terms too. The danger of an understanding of concepts like proactivity or emotional intelligence is that we use them to judge other people rather than to help them (and ourselves) to respond more effectively.

What about the big question – where is all the money going – and its unspoken corollary, that 'they' must be spending it? Who should be keeping track of where it is going? Whose responsibility is it to do so? Anyone who cares about the way the system is working. So Simon, Guy, Sarah, Karen, Ruth and Mark all need to be taking an active interest in this. If high-status influential people like them don't make it their business to know, then they are not taking responsibility for the system and they don't have any right to complain when it prevents them from being as effective as they would like to be. Ruth needs to help Mark to see that it isn't enough to be a clinician advising managers based on your own clinical experience, nor is it appropriate to see working with managers as colonization or tameness. If you care about the way you work, you will have to take an interest in the system around you and if you don't you can't blame "them", you can blame only one person, yourself.

What difference would generosity and discipline make?
One of the themes of this book has been the importance of generosity and discipline. Is this theme relevant here? Let's have a look.

The consultants of the St Swithin's orthopaedic team need to agree on their approach. It may be that all of them are refusing to discuss a common approach, or that one is much more resistant to it than are the others. Until now managers and other clinicians at St Swithin's have ignored this and are hoping that the job plan associated with the new consultant contract will sort it out or, failing that, then pressure from the PCT. But this is a problem that St Swithin's itself needs to address. If they try to hide behind any other kind of bogey man, they will be much less effective and no better able to solve the problem (of consultants with unrealistic expectations) the next time it arises. Managers and clinicians there are not choosing to care, they are not prepared to engage in acts of work or courage in order to nurture the growth of the consultants involved (and more indirectly of their patients).

The board of the PCT have approved a carers' strategy but, now that they have appointed a coordinator, they are not ensuring that this work is proceeding satisfactorily. Again, they are not choosing to care, to put in the ongoing work to find out how things are going. This kind of continuing awareness, and judicious choice of when to act and how, is fundamental to real management. Real managers don't decide a policy, or even a value (for example, managers deciding they will be as open and transparent as possible), and then implement it on autopilot. They are constantly interpreting situations and choosing how and to what extent their policies or values can be translated into action in this instance.

Similarly, real managers are alert to all sorts of information and, if they hear something that doesn't fit, they check it out. They are dedicated to reality. In the case, Mark and Ruth have both noticed that a particular individual is just not doing the job they need her to be doing, and are finding it impossible to persuade her manager to take their concerns seriously. We can all end up with a misleading impression of a situation or of someone's performance for a number of reasons, which is why we need to respond with a mind at least partly open to any contrary views we encounter. While most of the people we deal with will be trying to do their best, albeit in different ways, and the methods of interacting with them that are described in Chapters 1 and 2 will help us to make the most of them, there are a very small number of people who spend so much of their time persuading a few key individuals that they are doing a wonderful job that they never get around to doing so.[8] They can have glittering CVs, having held good positions in prestigious places, often for fairly short stints but nevertheless on an impressive trajectory, and they may come armed with glowing references, although not from the people most closely involved with their work. But what you always need to remember is that it is their work for you now that is important, not an impressive track record, and you need to employ all the tools of Chapter 1 to ensure you know just how they are doing. You must find out from other people and not only from them. Again, failure to do this is a lack of discipline.

Guy reports that now he has got to know the GPSIs in cardiology he finds he is more confident in discharging patients, not only to their care but to their colleagues in primary care generally. The admin staff and nurse specialists have also stopped using dismissive language when talking of primary care. Is this a sign of increasing generosity? The GPSIs were interested in cardiology before, and their colleagues' clinical acumen has not changed. The only difference is Guy's knowledge of them as people. So he is still as ungenerous as before, he is just including more people within his circle of regard. Because health care involves patients crossing so many boundaries, it is highly important that HCPs of all kinds can respond generously to their colleagues in other parts of the system, without necessarily knowing them. Understanding the breadth of the system and the impact we can all have on the other parts of it helps us to do this, as both Simon and Guy have found in their experiences of thinking about patient pathways.

Sarah and Simon are both convinced that systems will work better if their organization is in the driving seat, as if all the problems will be resolved with the 'right' attitude at the top. Since the problems are inherent in the clinical task this won't make any difference; it is in the quality of relationships on the ground that good performance lies.

Carers are being let down, uncared for. Who is it who is not caring? Mark is doing his best for Mrs Brown, and the PCT has appointed someone to coordinate work with carers. GPs see carers regularly when they see the person they care for, and there is a requirement that social services assess their needs, yet they are not being cared for. So some or all of these people must be failing to care. Can we really say that? We saw in Chapter 2 that care isn't a feeling, it is a set of actions, acts of work and/or courage. Is Mark engaging in acts of work or courage on behalf of carers? Yes he is, he is working hard with Mrs Brown, and lobbying the PCT for attention on behalf of carers more generally. He could be more effective if he invested time in thinking about who best to lobby, what their interests are, how he can persuade them of the needs of this group, if he could think through with them who else they need to convince and so on. In other words, if he used Chapters 1 and 2. Instead he has met a hurdle and is thinking of giving up. No matter how much help he provides to Mrs Brown, he will achieve more for carers if he stays in his role and fights *effectively* on their behalf.

What about the PCT board? They have approved the carers strategy, but that is all they have done. They aren't looking to see what is happening now, keeping an eye on what else needs to happen for results to be achieved. Management decisions are not one-off affairs, they require constant tweaking over time. A strategy is never the end, it is always a beginning.

GPs probably feel very concerned about the carers they meet, but they are not doing enough for them, they are resisting the attempts of the forum coordinator to see them and they are not referring people to the carers' forum, or ensuing they receive their social services assessment. Similarly, social services have an assessment process but are not doing enough to ensure it is being used. Neither can be said to care except in that mushy sentimental way that isn't much use to anyone. As for the managers of the home care service, in protecting their staff (and themselves from liability for health and safety claims) they are leaving carers completely at a loss. This cannot be an isolated incident; if they have a policy about it, it must occur regularly. The policymakers, when drawing up their policies, need to include the needs of carers and not just of their own staff; they need to include contingency plans for this kind of situation, if necessary drawn up with other organizations too.

Perhaps it is because there are often so many different people and agencies involved that no one cares, and everyone can comfortably blame someone else. But this is a very aggressive form of lack of care – because it is not just failing to enable potentials, it is actively destroying them, and is an example of where a focus on illness rather than health can lead to appalling results.

The other case of lack of generosity and discipline is again on the part of the GPs, those who won't engage with the work Ruth is doing to empower patients and enable them to make better use of health services and take better care of themselves. If they chose to care they could consider undertaking an act of work, putting in the time to meet Ruth, or even taking the time to read letters and leaflets, to find out what support for patients is available. This would also be an act of courage, in taking, as they see it, the risk that the patients might become more demanding. If they were to behave with discipline and be 'dedicated to reality', they would first check out the evidence, and discover that this risk is minimal.

If there is one, disciplined, thing Mark could do for himself to help him lose his feelings of frustration it is to think about and then write down what it is he would like to achieve in his PEC role. An excellent way of doing so is described in Chapter 6. To do this he would list the different roles he plays as a member of the PEC, and these might include: colleague, chairman of the locality group of GPs, provider of a general practice perspective, champion for excellent primary care and contributor to the setting of PCT priorities. Then he would write down for each one of them what it is he wants to achieve. If he also completes the weekly schedule, he will find he has a clear sense of purpose and a diary of commitments, each of which he knows is important, and he will be able to reflect daily on what he has learned, and on what he has contributed. He will also be able to prepare for the day ahead. The sense of satisfaction he gains from the progress he observes will more than compensate for the time that this takes.

What difference would generosity and discipline make?

Notes

1   Early intervention aims to promote an individual's recovery from psychosis by prevention, early detection and more effective treatment at the beginning of illness.
2   When he talks of 'the centre' Chris is referring to a rather amorphous amalgam of people in the Department of Health and policy makers in government.
3   Individual placement and support, a scheme to enable people with mental health problems to get back into the workforce.
4   The new consultant contract requires consultants to agree a job plan with their employer organisation. The plan captures in writing a number of units of activity (P.A.s) which the consultants are deemed to be undertaking, and in many cases this would be the subject of dispute. PAs specify, among other things, the amount of direct clinical care (DCC) and supporting professional activities (SPAs).
5   GPs with special interests, i.e. GPs taking on a more specialist role.
6   Quality and outcomes framework, a means of incentivizing GPs to focus on particular aspects of care.
7   He will also be able to avoid the trap of wasting his time on decisions that are essentially about financing rather than management. Think of this private sector comparison. A company will have to talk with its bank and other financial advisors about overdraft facilities, equity release schemes and so on in order to finance its activities, its cash flow, its capital expenditure plans. It's operational managers will be involved in decisions about what money is

needed but not at all in the conversations about how the money will be raised. In health care, too, lengthy discussions between boards about financial brokerage should not waste the time of people like Mark.

8   These have been described in the literature as organizational sociopaths. We could think of them as organizational conmen (and women), with you, their manager, as the victim.

9   Concluding thoughts

Real management is about what you *do*

This book has been about how to become a real manager, someone who really manages health care. It has been about how to *behave* in such a way that you become a master of the 'art of getting things done'. It hasn't focused on attributes or qualities, or even competences; in the main it has described ways of approaching situations that you can start to use straight away. And this is an important point: real management is essentially about action, about *you, acting*. Often, when I ask people what they are going to do in a particular set of circumstances they describe information they will gather, analyses they will undertake, papers they will write and presentations they will make – and sometimes some or all of these may be necessary. Just as often, however, they are a means of delaying, or of trying to avoid, the one conversation that could resolve the issue without the need for any of them. The complicated easy is so much more tempting than the simple hard.

As you begin to act as a real manager, you will inevitably become more skilful in what you are doing. Take the three rules described in Chapter 1, for example. When you start to use them you will do so in the ways described there. As you acquire more experience, you will become more accomplished in the skills of active listening, giving developmental feedback, perceptive questioning, active reflection and creative, collaborative problem-solving. And when you have more experience still, you will often feel very relaxed about allowing goals and solutions to emerge without any preformed ideas on your part.

It is this increasing skill, and the change in attitude that is likely to accompany it, that is reflected in the thought that management is as much about what we become as what we achieve.[1]

You start to be a real manager by doing things, the kind of things described in this book; and as you do them, you may become someone slightly different, you may acquire attributes and skills, but it is that way round.

Real management is fundamentally different

I want to emphasize the point that real management in an organization is not about doing existing management roles better. It is about seeing the management role in a different way. Just imagine if real management became established throughout an organization: clinicians of all kinds would be taking responsibility for their own behaviours, for improving systems, for delivering care as good as they want it to be within constraints they can see as reasonable. Managers would be supporting this activity and attitude by providing information, prompting strategic thinking, encouraging these constructive behaviours and discouraging any that weren't; above all by making sure that the three rules were implemented throughout the organization and by behaving with generosity and discipline themselves. Here, there is a completely different set of dynamics: proactive HCPs being prompted, supported and challenged by organizational managers, as co-owners of the organization and of its problems and potential. Really managing health care *means* everyone focusing on health care. Apart from anything else, this avoids the charge that clinicians and managers have two different sets of values. Everyone will be concerned with service performance (activity, outcomes, expenditure) and the organization becomes the means of doing this, rather than the HCPs focusing on service activity and outcomes, and managers on expenditure and the needs of the organization.

Responsibilities, too, will be held in rather different places from where they currently sit. Take rationing, for instance. At the moment, if two patients need to be admitted to a mental health ward and there is only one bed, the responsibility for deciding who receives the treatment they need, and who doesn't, rests with the clinician. But the clinical decision is that they both need treating. If only one can receive that treatment, then that is not a clinical but a rationing decision. Which is the profession that deals with reconciling different interests? Politics. But politicians will not accept responsibility for decisions they deem to be unnecessary because the shortage of capacity arises because resources are being wasted. So we need clinicians and organizational managers with real management skills to work together to ensure that resources are being used to their very best effect, and to demonstrate that this is the case. Then any rationing decisions that are necessary can go back to where they properly belong.

Similarly, the responsibility for drawing up an organizational structure will shift. Instead of being the prerogative of the chief executive alone (with much restructuring inevitably accompanying any change of incumbency), this will be jointly held by all those focusing on how the organization can support the effective delivery of good health care.

It can be difficult to perceive the radical change that real management would lead to because we are so trapped in the existing paradigm. Think, for example, of the term 'clinical engagement', much in vogue as I write. It sounds as though it shares many sentiments with real management. In practice, though, it has come to mean that 'lead clinicians' are sought for cross-boundary strategy groups, e.g. *older people* or *sexual health*, and a space is held on every organizational committee from locality groups to IM&T[2] committees. So it turns out to be an exercise in finding clinicians who will engage in an organizational perspective and not the other way round. It didn't have to turn out this way, but the existing mindset has taken a good concept and turned it into a degenerate form.

You may be irritated at my description of a really managed organization and accuse me of wanting to wave a magic wand. You may also want to ask me how I propose to get from where we are to that utopian ideal. But that is to operate again from within that paradigm. It isn't up to me or anyone else to impose it, it is up to us to describe it and try to live it, and leave it to others to decide whether to do the same. If we want to see it happening on more than a local scale, then we need to devise systems[3] that enable and reward real management behaviours, and discourage and penalize the kind of behaviours that managers have learned, by being rewarded for them, over many years.[4] And then we need to get out of the way. We need to adopt the same kind of non-doing that I described on a personal level in Chapter 6. This is important. At the moment I am constantly struck by how, in the UK, at every level of the organizational hierarchy, managers complain bitterly: often about the way people in positions more senior to their own are 'imposing' strategies, processes and targets upon them. It becomes quickly apparent, however, that the freedom they seek is the freedom to impose their own strategies, processes and targets on those they in turn 'manage'. At every level, people need to see their role, instead, as challenging and supporting people nearer the front line to make their own decisions, build their own strategies and become co-owners of the organization. The way to do this is to ensure that the three rules are enacted at every level, and in a spirit of generosity and discipline.[5] Anything else will inevitably lead to degeneration of ideas and approaches that are sound in themselves but not in the application.

Perhaps the most persuasive action we can take is to help people to reflect on the fact that the management models we have at the moment just aren't working. We are pouring more and more money into health care and seeing very little extra return for it. And because this is happening in so many places, in so many countries too, we can see that it isn't the people who are incompetent, it is the model.

Real management engages with the wider system

There are discussions about the nature of health care policy taking place in many countries and we need to find inventive solutions to the many dilemmas we currently face. Can we find ways to:

- improve health care for all and not just for the wealthy, while at the same time allowing people who are prepared to pay more for their care to do so;
- offer people choices[6] in areas where they want them, while not eroding those values and principles of the public sector that are worth cherishing;
- make essential services (like health care) accountable to the public?

If so, then we need HCPs to take an informed, proactive, outward-looking interest and to come up with ideas about health and social policy that they are happy then to debate, defend, amend and eventually champion.

In doing so, we will almost certainly need to shoot some sacred cows. Hatred of markets, for instance, and support for central planning. In the UK, we have for years set a few clever people the task of deciding for us how many doctors, nurses, physiotherapists, and so on we will need in 10–20 years' time. As a result, we consistently have a problem of capacity not matching demand and we go and recruit qualified staff from other countries, some of which can ill afford to lose them. We could go on doing this, or we could leave it to enterprising 18-year-olds to vote with their feet and decide for themselves what they think the market for different roles and skills will be by the time they qualify and beyond. From what we know about the 'wisdom of crowds',[7] we can be fairly sure that the 18-year-olds collectively will come up with much better answers than the experts. Here, introducing a market may allow us to behave *more* ethically rather than less. There will be many other examples where thinking afresh could lead to the diversity of ideas we need.

More than this, though, if we care about the health of all (and not just health care) we need HCPs to take an interest in macro issues: the nature of society, of our economy, of the global economy. We need them (you, us) to take an intelligent interest in policy debates about, for example:

- how to introduce checks on corporate power without stifling the ability of corporations to continue to contribute to society the massive benefits they have done;
- the pros and cons of globalizing professions;
- WTO debates and the nature of a governance at a global level.

We need able and committed people (you, us) to take an intelligent interest rather than indulge in knee-jerk reactions to misleading and undemanding arguments presented under the lazy headings of 'right' or 'left-wing'. These are complicated issues that need attention and care, and we mustn't leave this debate to others. Our care for our patients and populations surely needs to extend to some of these wider issues.

Really managing – anywhere, any time

When we looked at the three rules in Chapter 1 we saw that you can implement them whether or not you have any formal authority. You can use them if you are a member of a team, or when interacting with someone who is formally managing *you*. The same applies to nearly everything in this book. I know that there is a terrible disempowering force within large, particularly public sector, organizations. Indeed, many of the current performance and risk management processes actively enhance this disempowerment. There is a prevailing spirit of 'they haven't done this', 'they won't let me do that', 'nobody's told me to do X, only Y', and a reliance on having formal authority given to you before you can start taking responsibility. But real management isn't like that. You start with just yourself and your immediate working relationships. No one has to sanction it, no one can stop you doing it, you just start. You don't have to announce it, or tell anyone at all; there's no need to get any egg on your face, and you don't even need to find a lot of extra time because it will quickly save you so much.

Of course, as we are talking about the simple hard a lot of it won't work immediately (that is why it is termed hard). And in your efforts to change your behaviour in one direction you will often stray too far and need to shift direction again when you realize it. Susan Jeffers[8] refers to aeroplanes and autopilots when she says that at any given moment while in the air a plane is never on the right course – it is moving too much in one direction and will have to be corrected back to another. So even the best real managers will constantly be getting some things wrong and there is no need to berate ourselves for doing the same. So we can not only start at any time, we can start again when we need to.

You may have noticed that nowhere in this book have I advocated emotional intelligence, and there is a reason for that: emotional intelligence is just so difficult. Many of the approaches described here are what might be considered part of an 'emotional intelligence toolkit', and will help us to behave in a more mature fashion. However, if you do find you are becoming angry or hostile or moving into the negative ego states described in Chapter 6, then I suggest you don't beat yourself up for your lack of emotional intelligence and instead use that negative energy to achieve something productive.[9]

For clinicians, perhaps the greatest incentive of all for starting to behave as a real manager is that the quality of your clinical care is likely to increase. (I illustrate how this might happen in Appendix 2.) But, for *all* of us, real management is important, and it doesn't require heroism, just quiet determination, and the preparedness to apply gradually some of the tools described here. Real management is important – to patients, to communities, to HCPs alike. If you are in a service or department that doesn't seem to have any, if you are surrounded by people who are concentrating on the complicated easy, or who are not generous and disciplined, then it will have to be introduced by someone. If no one else is prepared to do it, I guess it will be up to you. And as you don't need any special attributes or competences you could start right away, now, with your next decision.

Notes

1 Expressed by an interesting management development centre called Waverley, whose work is informed by a spiritual dimension. You can find them on www.waverley.uk.com
2 Information management and technology.
3 Eventually we might even be able to let them evolve.
4 Regrettably, some competent people are so trapped in the existing model that, although they appear to be superior performers within this system, they would probably need to make way for others if real management was to take hold system-wide.
5 One manifestation of fury at imposition is the huge resentment at the time of writing (May 2005) about the targets imposed by central government in England. I believe the fury is misplaced and that the problem lies not with the target but with the ways in which the 3 rules have been applied. As far as rule number 1 is concerned, it would be better if performance targets could be agreed rather than imposed, but in this I believe the government is much closer to what the public expects than are the HCPs. So it has a right to insist. The government then also needs to observe Rule 2, by ensuring that resources are adequate, and that there are skills within the system to achieve the targets. Overall here it has done this. It then needs to stand back and confine its role to giving feedback, rather than insisting on prescribing particular ways in which the targets should be reached. Most importantly, it also needs to ensure that civil servants are not being prescriptive either.
6 One of the things I have noticed in every organizational aspect of my life (work, community, voluntary, family) is that whenever decisions are taken on behalf of someone else they are almost never the same as they would have taken for themselves.
7 Surowiecki, J. (2005) *The Wisdom of Crowds* (London: Abacus). The author

argues, with some supporting evidence, that the average of the individual decisions taken by members of a crowd is, subject to certain attributes of the crowd, always were accurate than that of even the most expert individual.

8   In *Feel the Fear and Do It Anyway*; see Chapter 6, note 4.

9   As John Hunt, Professor of Organisational Behaviour at the London Business School, wrote in a review in the *Financial Times* (March 2001) of Daniel Goleman's (1998) book *Working with Emotional Intelligence* (New York: Bantam Doubleday): 'Maturity is admirable but organisations also demand innovation and creativity. Neither innovation nor creativity flourishes when emotions become sanitised.' He described emotional intelligence as a 'process for social control; an emotional form of bureaucracy; a clinic for consenting adults'.

Appendix 1
How not to be 'nice'

Here are some common situations in which you may feel tempted to be 'nice' rather than effective, and some alternative ways of responding.

Asking someone to alter their behaviour

Someone keeps doing or saying something you don't like. Don't be 'nice' and put up with it. Instead, try the XYZ formula:

When you say/do X
    I feel Y
        I'd rather you did Z.

For example:

When we are in team meetings and you start to raise your voice and become annoyed with other members of the team (X)
    I feel anxious and embarrassed (Y)
        and I would rather you dealt with their points rather more calmly. (Z)

Making a request

You want to ask someone to do something, someone you formally manage or to whom you have no managerial responsibility. Don't be so 'nice' that you fail to convey what it is you want. Try the following.

1   *Ask* them to do it. Don't hint that it needs to be done, wait for them to offer or grumble that it isn't being done. Ask outright, pleasantly but firmly:
    'Will you please . . .?'

2   If you think there may be some reluctance, you can still be pleasant and firm but you may need to offer more explanation. Don't give more than is needed (you will sound apologetic and easy to refuse). Try this three-part approach in which the action required is clear and the benefits to both parties are spelt out:
   (a)   An 'I' statement, e.g. 'I need these figures by tomorrow in order to . . .'
   (b)   A 'Will you please?' request
   (c)   An indication of how doing the action will benefit the other person.
3   If they refuse, do not take it personally. Remember that they are rejecting the request and not you as a person.

Responding to a request

Someone tries to delegate a task to you and you are unsure about whether or how to refuse it. Don't simply agree in order to be 'nice'. Try the following.

*   Be aware of your emotional reaction to the request.
*   Give yourself time to make a decision, e.g. 'I will need to think about that', 'I need more information before I can decide', 'I will let you know by Tuesday'.
*   If you decide to say no, say no *before* you say anything else.
*   Only explain if they will benefit from an explanation.
*   Expect to feel uncomfortable if they express anger, disappointment or dismay.
*   Remember that you are rejecting the request and not the person.

Refusing to take back responsibility you have already delegated

This example was devised with a group of Area Deans of the Church of England but the principles are generic.

Someone's great aunt's cat's illness prevents them reading on Sunday, and they 'phone to tell you, expecting you to find someone else to do it. Instead of being 'nice', try being gracious with the person but ruthless with time . . .

'Thank you very much for letting me know, I appreciate your doing so, especially as there's really no need. If you will just let the person who is taking over from you know what the reading is then I don't need to be involved any further. I'll look forward to seeing you as soon as this crisis has passed. Thank you again'.

If they persist in asking you to find a replacement – how about: being graciously clear that this is their responsibility, and that you will help them think through how to do it, but you won't take it over.

'I'm so sorry that I just don't have time to do that for you. If I were you I would try Mrs X or Mr Y. If you find they can't then perhaps Miss Z would 'phone around for you – I always find her very helpful, I'm sure you will too.'

If they persist further, then you may need to inform them of what you agreed with them (in rule number 1):

I'm so sorry, if I do it for you, I'll have to do it for everybody and that simply isn't possible. If you remember, we did agree that you would take responsibility for finding a replacement if you aren't able to do it. Unless you'd like me to ask for a volunteer, on your behalf, at the beginning of the service, I'm happy to do that.'

Being gracious but firm is much more effective than being nice.

Appendix 2
Clinical practice and real management

The simple hard aspects of good clinical care and those of real management are very similar; it is in the complicated easy that they differ. The comparisons in Table A2.1 illustrate this.

Table A2.1   Simple hard aspects of clinical practice and real management

Clinical practice	Real management
• The interaction is seen by both parties as a meeting between experts. One expert has a detailed knowledge of the relevant abnormality and of prognosis, treatments and risks. The other has expert knowledge of his or her lifestyle, personal priorities, hopes and fears. These two kinds of expertise must be brought together; this requires an openness to the other and to what he or she is saying that is unencumbered by any stereotyping and prejudgement.	• Real managers engage similarly with their 'clients', who are their staff. We saw in Chapter 7 that *real* managers do not solve problems, they sell them; so they deal openly with their staff, recognizing that unless the two kinds of expert knowledge (strategic and operational) are brought together, no satisfactory solution will be devised. They listen to their HCPs unhindered by stereotyping in their judgements.
• The transparency standard[a] requires that a clinician's reasoning is made transparent to the patient. Such transparency requires clinicians to engage in ongoing consideration of their own reasoning. They need to note and challenge any 'leaps of abstraction'.[b] They must also be aware of their own feelings, conscious of the causes of unpleasant emotions and the ensuing behaviours.	• Real managers also make their reasoning transparent to their staff. They too reflect upon any leaps of abstraction and try to be aware of the impact their feelings have on their behaviour.

Continued

Table A2.1   Continued

• Where bad news must be given, in this ideal interaction it is given with genuine care; the clinician empathizes (brackets themselves)[c] with the patient and does not allow his or her own feelings of discomfort to impede effectiveness or empathy.	• When bad news must be given they do not delegate its telling to a minion or send it in writing: they give it personally, in full understanding of its implications for the receiver.
• When asked to make a difficult decision, the good clinician agonizes but retains the ability to act. Similarly, when supporting a patient who is making a difficult decision, the clinician supports them in that difficulty with information and empathy, without trying to take the decision for them.	• When asked to make a difficult decision, real managers act decisively, but they are also fully and passionately aware of the negative consequences of each option. When they have delegated a difficult decision they also support the decision-maker but leave the decision with them.
• The course of action recommended (or agreed with the patient) may differ for different patients with the same clinical condition since their circumstances and personalities differ.	• Real managers select different approaches with different staff according to their perception of personalities and preferences.
• Good clinicians gracefully accept challenges to their way of seeing, or thinking, from patients, carers, colleagues and members of other professions. They incorporate such new information into a review of the evidence on which decisions about diagnosis and treatment are based.	• Real managers similarly encourage challenges to their thinking and actively seek dissidents and devil's advocates.

[a] Quoted in Seedhouse (1991); see Chapter 2, note 11. The 'transparency standard' is advocated by American ethicist Howard Brody. According to this standard, adequate informed consent is obtained when a reasonably informed patient is allowed to participate in the medical decision to the extent that the patient wishes. In turn, 'reasonably informed' consists of two features: (a) the physician discloses the basis on which the proposed treatment or alternative possible treatments, have been chosen; and (b) the patient is allowed to ask questions suggested by the disclosure of the physician's reasoning and those questions are answered to the patient's satisfaction. According to the transparency model, disclosure 'is adequate when a physician's basic thinking has been rendered transparent to the patient'.

[b] 'Leaps of abstraction' is the term used by Senge (1990; see Chapter 6, note 14) for the unsound conclusions we make from limited evidence, which then form a dangerously faulty platform for further reasoning. He suggests noting them but also voicing them to allow the subject of the abstraction (usually the person we are talking to or about) to comment on their validity.

[c] See Peck (1979; see Chapter 2, note 12) and the description of empathetic listening in Chapter 2 of the present book.

Thus real managers and good clinicians alike spend time and energy on the simple hard, and HCPs who develop their real management skills become better clinicians too. They recognize that the ways in which they work with others require attention, time and energy in their own right. They adopt behaviours that are generous and disciplined, and gently but firmly challenge behaviours that are not.

Appendix 3
Further reading

In this appendix I mention a few books and other resources that I think you may enjoy. These are in addition to those referenced in the chapters, and are by no means a comprehensive list, but a set of interesting tasters.

Chapter 1

For practical work on managing teams in health and social care, John Øvretveit's book *Coordinating Community Care* (Buckingham: Open University Press, 1993) is excellent. All John's books are highly practical, developed with real people reflecting on real situations.

Motivation can be approached from a number of different angles, and it is well worth finding a copy of the classic 1966 paper in the *Harvard Business Review* (Jan./Feb., pp. 109–20) by Frederick Hertzberg, 'One more time: how do you motivate employees?', in which he distinguishes between intrinsic and extrinsic motivating factors. Many managers in the public sector find it a particularly empowering concept, because so many of the factors that are centrally controlled (such as pay) turn out to be extrinsic (or 'hygiene') factors rather than intrinsic motivators.

If you would like to see some vignettes and examples of how to use this chapter, you can also try my website www.reallylearning.com.

Chapter 2

Some of the most interesting work on professionalism is being done by educationalists, such as the Association for the Study of Medical Education, whose website can be found on www.asme.org.uk.

For an excellent guide on how to negotiate with others, try *'Getting to Yes': The Secret to Successful Negotiation*, by Roger Fisher, William Ury and Bruce Patten (London: Arrow, 2003).

The really learning website again gives examples of how to work with others. Try www.reallylearning.com/Briefing_and_debate/Conundrum/conundrum.html.

Chapter 3

To examine further some of the reasons you feel why you do about where you are working, you may find this helpful. It includes a succinct introduction to the work of W. Bion, influential observer of group dynamics. *The Unconscious at Work: Individual and Organisational Stress in the Human Services*, by Anton Obholzer *et al.* (London: Routledge, 1994).

To see the public services from the perspective of the politicians introducing policy, try *1 out of 10. From Downing Street Vision to Classroom Reality*, by Peter Hyman (London: Vintage, 2005).

Chapter 4

If you are going to read only one book about improving quality then make it *Curing Health Care: New Strategies for Quality Improvement*, by Donald Berwick, A. Blanton Godfrey and Jane Roessner (San Francisco: Jossey Bass, 1990). If you can find time for another, more technical tome, then it is worth looking at Donald J. Wheeler's *Understanding Variation, the Key to Managing Chaos* (London: SPC Press, 2000). Of course, the classics by Deming (*Out of the Crisis* etc.) and are worth a look, but I think the man must have been more inspiring than his writing. *The Goal* by Eliyahu M. Goldratt and Jeff Cox (London: Gower, 3rd edn 2004) is also well worth a look. It has spawned an industry of its own called the Theory of Constraints and you can explore that in later books, but the 1989 original is the most fun.

You will also find a case study illustrating the use of many of these concepts in V. Iles and S. Cranfield, *Developing Change Management Skills* (London: SDO, 2004). Available free from www.sdo.lshtm.ac.uk/publications.htm.

The website to watch is that of the Institute for Healthcare Improvement at www.ihi.org.

Chapter 5

These concepts are explored much more fully in *Developing Change Management Skills* (see above for Chapter 4), where their uses and limitations are explored in the context of five case studies. At the risk of sounding egoistic, that is undoubtedly the best place to start.

To find out more about the three schools of thinking about strategy, the classic text for the 'classical' or deliberate school is the Harvard text *Business Policy: Text and Cases*, by J. Bower, C. Bartlett, H. Uyterhoeven and R. Walton (New York: McGraw-Hill, 1997). For a UK text, try *Exploring Corporate Strategy*, by Gerry Johnson and Kevan Scholes (London: Prentice Hall, 2003).

The leading exponent of the emergent school is Henry Mintzberg. *The Rise and Fall of Strategic Planning* (New York: The Free Press, 1994) sets out these ideas. Perhaps the most useful if you are seriously interested in both the classical and emergent schools is *The Strategy Process*, by Henry Mintzberg, James Brian Quinn and Sumantra Ghoshal (New York: Prentice Hall, 1998).

To follow up on complexity theory, it is worth first gaining a good grounding in systems thinking and for this you can't beat *Systems and Decision Making: A Management Science Approach*, by Hans Daellenbach (New York: John Wiley and Sons, 1994). If you then pick up on chaos theory by reading the highly accessible *Chaos: Making a New Science*, by James Gleick (London: Minerva, 1994), you are then ready for some of the more serious complexity books (just try typing that in on Amazon), but actually you already have what you need to understand the management books that rely upon it. Ralph Stacey has written prolifically, Margaret Wheatley, in *Leadership and the New Science: Discovering Order in a Chaotic World* (San Francisco: Berrett-Koelher, 1999), inspirationally; but I prefer *The Soul at Work: Unleashing the Power of Complexity Science for Business Success*, by Roger Lewin and Birute Regine (London: Orion Business Books, 1999), which isn't nearly as cheesy as it sounds. The difference between the approaches has to do with whether the authors take complexity in human organizations as fact or metaphor; the last of these three takes it as a deep metaphor, which suits me fine.

Chapter 6

If you can bear the 'self-help' section of a good bookshop there will be plenty of useful books (as well as loads that are not very useful). The ones I have found people enjoy most are all referenced in the chapter: M. S. Peck, *The Road Less Travelled* (first two-thirds) (London: Arrow, 1990); S. Jeffers, *Feel the Fear and Do It Anyway* (New York: Random House, 2001); S. Covey, *The Seven Habits of Highly Effective People* (New York: Free Press, 2004).

The chapter refers to two psychological therapies: transactional analysis and rational emotional behavioural therapy. For an introduction to the theoretical assumptions, the historical context, and development and the therapeutic strategies of a wide range of therapies, try Windy Dryden's *Handbook of Individual Therapy* (London: Sage, 4th edn 2002).

To gain an insight into the Alexander Technique, don't be put off by the title but try *Indirect Procedures: A Musician's Guide to the Alexander Technique*, by Pedro de Alcantara (Oxford: Clarendon Paperbacks, 1997).

Chapter 7

If you have read this chapter without throwing the book out of the window and haven't read the following, I think you would enjoy them: Peter Jay, *The Road to Riches, or The Wealth of Man* (London: Phoenix, 2001); John Kay, *The Truth about Markets: Why Some Countries Are Rich and Others Remain Poor* (London: Penguin, 2004); Matt Ridley, *The Origins of Virtue* (London: Penguin, 1997); Paul Ormerod, *The Death of Economics* (London: Faber and Faber, 1995); John Gray, *The Delusions of Global Capitalism* (London: Granta, 2002).

Conclusions

Daniel Goleman's book on emotional intelligence has spawned an industry (about which, as you will have seen, I have reservations), but the original book is well worth a read: *Emotional Intelligence: Why It Can Matter More than IQ* (London: Bloomsbury, 1996).

Index

Page numbers in *italics* refer to boxes, figures and tables; *a* = appendix; *n* = note.